Richard Clark's

Greek Islands Anthology

A compilation of Richard Clark's Greek Island Notebooks

BY THE SAME AUTHOR

The Greek Islands – A Notebook

ISBN: 9781466285316

ASIN: B005O044PS

Crete – A Notebook

ISBN: 9781475188943

ASIN: B008N9ES1M

Rhodes – A Notebook

ISBN: 9781483971285

ASIN: B00DJI8TDU

Corfu – A Notebook

ISBN –9781492877097

ASIN – B00J22FOTY

First published in America and Great Britain 2014
Copyright © 2014 by Richard Clark
Book design and layout © 2014 by Cheryl Perez
Cover design © 2014 by David Richardson

ISBN – 13:9781497578777
ISBN – 10:1497578779

www.richardclarkbooks.co.uk
www.facebook.com/richardclarkbooks

Praise for The Greek Islands – A Notebook

'Clark is particularly good on the colours, flavours and scents of Greece. He has got under the skin of the place in a way few outsiders have been able to.'
Mark Hudson – *winner Somerset Maugham Award, Thomas Cook Travel Book Award, Samuel Johnson Prize*

'This is a beautifully written book, not just a travel companion but a journey in itself through Greek history, its culture and the countryside. Reading this book is an education in itself and I found myself so much the richer in having read it.'
E.J. Russell – Bestselling author of *Return to the Aegean* and *Aegean Abduction*

'What I liked most about the book was that it was personal and with that came an honesty, no wrappings, no embellishments other than descriptions of Greece itself. I would recommend this book both to people who have never been to Greece as well as to seasoned travellers. It was a joy.'
Sarah Alexi – Bestselling author of *The Greek Village Series*

'My library contains almost all of the noteworthy books about Greece and her islands and this will be a welcomed addition. I will place it next to my collection of books by the late and great Patrick Leigh Fermor, because I think Richard Clark's writing is as close to Fermor as we will ever come again.'
Aurelia Smeltz – Author of *Labyrinthine Ways, A Lone Red A*pple

Praise for Crete – A Notebook

'I was really surprised and delighted by the book. I read every word. The author is a fine writer and describes the island vividly. It's not a guidebook although there's a lot of information here that should be in any good guidebook. He travels around the island in a clockwise direction, writing short essays as he goes, which are a mix of personal memoir, history, and an evocation of place. The last one he does very well, as it brought back memories to me of my own travels around the island. He really does capture places well.'

Mike Gerrard – Author of *AA Spiral Guide to Crete*

'I love the way Clark writes, it is personal, it is human and deceptively simple. A book crafted so carefully you almost believe that it's a notebook, were it not for the flow.'

Sarah Alexi

'Unsurprisingly, travel literature constitutes the vast majority of my reading these days, and I devour as much online and off as I can. In examining other writers' style and content, I have become accustomed to dipping in and out of work. The extent to which I have been unable to put Richard Clark's book down is a tribute to its compulsive readability.'

Travel journalist **Emma French** *www.phileasfrench.com*

Praise for Rhodes – A Notebook

'Richard Clark writes with great authority and a deep affection for his subject matter, which comes from his long association with Greece… This is an excellent read. I look forward to the next book in the series.'
Marjory McGinn – Journalist and bestselling author of *Things Can Only Get Feta*

'Well worth a read - and don't miss the Crete book too. Clark lived in Crete and has travelled all over the island, and the book made me long to see some of the places he describes so lovingly.'
Jen Barclay – Bestselling author of *Falling in Honey*

'This is a book that has been written with great care and love and it shows. An absolute pleasure.'
E. J. Russell

'Trying to describe Richard Clark's style of writing is like trying to describe dew on a spider's web, or the line between sky and sea, his use of words is so beautiful, subtle and soft it pulls you wholeheartedly into his world. Right from the intro, his laid back, gentle monologue just keeps the pages turning. There is poetry in his words and through his eyes. I recommend anyone missing Greece, visiting Greece or just wishing they could go to Greece to take a look!'
Sara Alexi

Praise for Corfu – A Notebook

'This is another delightful book in the Notebook series of guides to the Greek islands. Richard Clark has an easy, relaxed style and his journey around Corfu feels like spending a leisurely few days with an old friend in a favourite location, enjoying long meals in seaside tavernas or enjoying dramatic moments on a beachside terrace while a thunderstorm rolls in from the mainland.

Marjory McGinn

'Richard Clark's descriptive prose of Corfu and the other Ionian islands instantly transport the reader there to these mellow and beautiful places and this alone makes it worth buying.

E. J. Russell

For My Uncle Henry

Acknowledgements

My *Greek Islands Anthology* is a compilation of my previous four books: *The Greek Islands – A Notebook; Crete – A Notebook; Rhodes – A Notebook*; and *Corfu – A Notebook*. As such, for those readers who have read the previous books, most of the material contained in this volume will be familiar. Some updating has been done, although the content within remains largely the same.

For those new to my books, this is a memoir of places I have visited, people I have met and things I have experienced on visiting many magical Greek islands over the years. I am aware that there are many islands that do not feature here, for the very simple reason that I have not visited them. These omissions in no way reflect the worth of these islands, just that, as yet, I have not been lucky enough to have become acquainted with them.

I make written notes all the time when I am travelling, but some of the notes I take are mental and, as such, liable to misremembering or embellishment with time. If this has been the case in any instance let me apologize in advance. It would be negligent to write about Greece and not make reference to the wealth of myths and legends which lie at the heart of that extraordinary country, but by their very nature these are open to interpretation; I apologise in advance if my reading of them differs from any previously understood by the reader. To anyone who has bought any of my earlier books and to the critics who have been so generous with their kind words, let me say a massive thank you for helping make them so successful. Their popularity has exceeded my wildest expectations.

I have been overwhelmed by the support and encouragement I have received from fellow writers particularly Mark Hudson, Sara Alexi, E.J Russell, Marjory McGinn and Jen Barclay. A huge thank you is also due my editor Barnaby Harsent, cover designer David Richardson and interior designer and eBook formatter, Cheryl Perez and as always a huge thank you to my family, Denise, Rebecca and James.

Richard Clark's

Greek Islands Anthology

Crete

Crete – The Cradle of Civilization

Greece's largest island, Crete, is also the most southerly part of Europe. It stands at the gateway between that great continent and the diverse cultures of Africa to the south and Asia to the east. Its geographical position has made it strategically important to any number of invading armies throughout its long and turbulent history. Coupled with its exposure to some extreme forces of nature, these factors have created an endlessly contrasting and intriguing landscape and culture, which are unique even among the Greek Islands. More than any other place I have visited, Crete wears its heart on its sleeve, an unashamed product of its past and proud to be the 'cradle of civilization'.

Although embracing the culture of the rest of Greece, it has very much got its own individual identity. Isolation from the motherland for such long periods in its history has lead to its own distinctive customs, dialect, food and culture, of which Cretans are justifiably proud. Only the fifth largest island in the Mediterranean Sea, it was from this remote piece of land, no more than 160 miles long and at its widest 38 miles across, that the beginnings of modern European civilization emanated.

Three different mountain ranges stride across the centre of the island running from east to west. Between their peaks nestle fertile plains and spectacular ravines hewn out of the limestone by mountain springs. There are long, sandy beaches fringed with palm trees, and deserted shingle coves snuggling under vertical cliffs – and all is bathed in the spectacular, ever-changing blues of the sea and the sky, their peerless fusion defying description.

Like the rest of Greece, Crete derives much of its income from tourism, but Crete is unusual among the islands as it has an agricultural base sufficient to support itself in the absence of foreign visitors. Fruit orchards, market gardening, stock rearing and fishing supplement the staple crops of olives and grapes. The indigenous population of some 600,000 is almost split half and half between those who live in the towns and those who live in rural areas, with the northern coastal cities being the most heavily populated. The climate in this part of the island is temperate, but on the south coast it can be more extreme with summer temperatures frequently reaching the mid 30s. In winter, snow covers the mountains and the high plateaux but the coastal regions usually remain mild. The variety of the landscape, climate and culture certainly appeals, but what makes so many people return time and again to this enchanted isle is surely the people.

Proud and open, they are generous and always welcoming to strangers, there is little crime and most of this is amongst Cretans themselves and likely to be based around family disputes.

Food is important yet unpretentious, the simple fare served up at most tables is fresh and unadorned and constitutes the healthiest diet in Europe. Eating is a valued social event where family and friends get together to discuss – often loudly – the issues of the day and meals can last for hours, particularly on a Sunday. It is this enthusiasm for their land and its people, essentially their love of life, which keeps drawing me back here. There is so much to discover that there is always something new to learn; always a new discovery around the corner in the alleys of a mountain village, a new view to glimpse between the peaks of a mountain pass. These are difficult times for the whole of Greece, but they have been through much worse and whatever the EU, foreign banks or their politicians subject them to they will, I suspect, always hold a welcome for those who respect their country and customs.

Arrivals – By Sea or Air

For most people their first experience of the tantalizing island of Crete will be Heraklion's Nikos Kazantzakis International Airport. And let me assure you that things can only get better. The only thing worse than arriving at this airport is departing from it. That Crete's greatest writer lends this airport his name is an undeserved aggrandizement – as is the moniker 'International'. This windswept patch of concrete perched on a cliff top several miles from the island's capital is international, only in the most literal sense that planes from other countries land here.

The airport is a victim of the island's own success as a tourist destination. It has been extended several times but has failed to keep up with the demand of the more than two million holidaymakers who land here every year. A new airport has been in the pipeline for some time, but in the current financial climate finding a commercial partner is proving difficult. With this in mind, the expected opening date of 2015 for the new airport, which is to be built to the south east of Heraklion in Kastelli, currently seems wildly optimistic.

Getting off the plane, however, does lend hints of the pleasures in store, as the two things that always hit me are the heat and the smell. Frequently windy, the air tumbling seawards off the mountains as the door to your aircraft is thrown open hits you with its warm infusion of wild herbs and arid dust.

On my first visit to Crete I was fortunate to arrive by sea and, if time and circumstances allow, I still believe that is the best way to approach any island, taking the time to savour its character as it unfolds. The view changing from the panoramic, slowly gaining focus as you get closer and can pinpoint your destination.

Back in 1982, as I approached the coast of Crete for the first time, I sensed its smell drifting in on the early-morning breeze long before landfall. Before I caught sight of the island slowly emerging from that misty dawn, a wild bouquet garni of sage, thyme, rosemary and parched earth made its first tentative introduction to my senses. A smell that is now redolent of one of my favourite places on earth.

It had not been my intention to catch a ferry from Piraeus to Heraklion in that late spring of 1982. I had flown into Athens hoping to transfer to a flight to Crete. But Greece was experiencing some, not unusual, industrial action at the time and, if I wanted to get to Crete that weekend, I would have to go by sea.

Landing in Athens the day before, I had met up with friends who worked on yachts sailing out of Glyfada Marina, in a suburb to the south of the city. As well as the strikes, Greece was in the grip of a heatwave and Athens was at a standstill. My taxi's meter ticked up into the thousands of drachma as we edged towards the coast through the honking hoards of vehicles and shouting drivers.

A yellow haze floated over the city. The pollutants emitted from the gridlocked vehicles hung in the lifeless air, unable to escape over the four mountains of Aegaleo, Parnitha, Penteli and Hymettus that barred its progress inland.

Pollution in the Eighties had reached a point where it was causing considerable damage to Athens's archaeological sites. Not to mention the health of its citizens. Since the Nineties, strict government measures have been in force and have made a significant difference. But, in 1982, as I sat in that taxi, I could almost feel the fetid air clasping me by the throat. Eventually the traffic thinned as we inched towards the coast road, and south to Glyfada.

As soon as the sea came into view my perceptions started to shift. The light reflecting off the deep blue of the Mediterranean began to work its soothing spell. Before experiencing this balm so eulogized by all who visit here, it is hard to appreciate the unique nature of the light, and how any attempt to describe it is doomed to failure.

Squinting at the pile of banknotes in my hand, it took some time to count out enough to pay my fare before lugging my bag through the marina gates. It was not long before I was sitting on my friends' yacht with a beer in hand. This was the stuff of dreams.

The next afternoon I caught a bus for Piraeus, the seaport of Athens, which lies about six miles from the city centre on the Saronic Gulf. In one of the numerous shipping agencies I bought a ticket to travel overnight to Crete.

My ferry was in port, engines thudding as cranes winched supplies into the hold. Sweating hard, I climbed the gangplank and, emerging on deck, made my way forward to the bow of the ship. Finding a suitable space, I was joined by an array of fellow passengers. Old women in black clutching baskets of clucking chickens, smart businessmen in suits, heavily-laden backpackers, men in traditional Cretan dress, all of life was represented. Ferries are lifelines for the islands, and in those days they were more popular than expensive air travel. I had little choice, but I never regret making my first visit to Crete by boat.

As the sun got lower the crew cast off their lines and the ship headed seawards. Leaving Athens astern it pushed forward into the slightest of swells, drawing a white wake across the azure water. The sun turned to a golden ball on the western horizon then sank, the lights of Athens leaving the only remaining mark of the capital on the already darkened sky.

That night was spent on deck. It was still gloriously hot and few people went below except to eat. I was too excited for real sleep but dozed in the warm air, made comfortable by the breeze created as the ship made headway south.

Walking down onto the jetty on arrival, I was met by a cacophony of sound. Friends and relatives loudly greeted passengers as they disembarked, car horns sounded to draw attention to their whereabouts, and tourists were opportuned to stay at any number of pensions, all at the best price in town! Wrestling my bag from enthusiastic room sellers, I made my way through the port gates. Blue and white painted fishing boats lay moored in the old harbour opposite the crumbling Venetian arsenals as I hailed a cab to take me to a rendezvous with my agent at the Mediterranean Hotel, from where I would go on to meet my new employer.

Heraklion – A Walk Around the Capital

All my most recent visits to Crete have been by air and by the time I get outside the terminal I am pleased to pick up my car and get away from the built up area around the airport. It is the same for any regular visitor, but it would be unwise to leave Heraklion behind without visiting the city itself or the Palace of Knossos just four miles to the south. These two places are fundamental to an understanding of the historical legacy of the island. To spend some time at each of these places helps the visitor gain a wider appreciation of Crete and its history and culture.

Driving into the city, I usually head for the port area where there is often space to park up and walk. I then head for the old harbour with its mix of fishing caiques and pleasure yachts all moored in the shadow of the Venetian Fort, which protects the old port from its position at the end of the sea wall. From here I turn inland to the one place etched on my mind as being at the heart of the city of Heraklion, Lion Square; officially named Plateia Eleftheriou Venizelou in honour of the prominent Greek statesman, Eleftherios Venizelos.

Born near Chania to the west, Venizelos was instrumental in securing Crete's independence and later unification with Greece. He then went on to become the country's Prime Minister. Despite this, locals and tourists alike know the square that bears his name as Lion Square. Still, the man does have Athens International Airport named after him, among many other tributes.

The aforementioned lions are those at the centre of the Morosini Fountain which stands near where the plateia joins Heraklion's main thoroughfare of 25th August Street. The square is never quiet, always buzzing with people going about their business by day, or revellers stopping for a pick-me-up late at night.

The lions stand at the top of the fountain supporting a dish, which at one time is believed to have held a marble statue of the god Poseidon. The beasts spout water from their mouths. This cascades into a sedate pool below that is circular in shape with eight petal-like lobes protruding from the circumference where at least forty people could have sat and filled up their water carriers at once. The side of the pool is decorated with dolphins, nymphs and an array of other mythological sea creatures.

The fountain was built during the early 17th Century under the guidance of the then Venetian Superintendent of the City, Francesco Morosini. It was the culmination of a brilliant, and practical, feat of engineering. It became a precious public source of water for the citizens of the region that was brought from high up in the mountains in Archanes via a 10-mile long aqueduct into the town centre, and then through underground pipes to the fountain itself.

The lions are a reminder of the Venetian Lion, the symbol of St Mark, the patron saint of Venice, and it was on this saint's day, the 25th April, in 1628 that the fountain was opened to the public.

Like most places around the world where water can be collected, it became a social, communal meeting place. During the Turkish occupation, however, its use was segregated, and in 1847 vertical marble columns were added and the sides enclosed so the fountain could be used for ritual cleansing before Muslims went to the nearby mosque to pray. An inscription at its apex declared it renamed as the Fountain of Abdulmecid, after the then Sultan of the Ottoman Empire. When Turkish rule came to an end, the columns were demolished and the fountain was later restored to its original condition in 1900.

Ongoing restoration work of the historical centre of the city has seen much of 25th August Street become pedestrianized, which does create a calmer, cleaner, and quieter environment around the Square. This street is the one that travellers have traditionally used to get to the centre of the city after having docked in the harbour. It holds a promise of so much as it is lined with incredible buildings.

At the bottom of the street are shipping agents competing to sell tickets to destinations around the world, car-rental showrooms, banks, souvenir shops and *gyros* sellers. The buildings that house these businesses look old, but are in fact neoclassical, built following a brutal event that took place on the 25 August 1898 after which the street is named.

Following uprisings of Christian Cretans in rural regions of the island, the Muslim Turks retreated to the relative safety of the fortified towns. The Turks were feeling increasingly threatened after their recent defeat in the war with Russia on the northern borders of the Ottoman Empire and pressure by the international community to find an equitable solution to the Cretan question.

The concessionary appointment of a Christian, Stylianos Michali Alexiou, as a director of the tax services was the last straw for many Muslims. Their anger manifested itself in a violent attack on some customs clerks as they travelled to work, escorted by British soldiers.

The rioting spread throughout the city. Christian homes were set on fire and many Cretans were murdered as well as 17 British soldiers and the British Vice-Consul, Lysimachos Kalokairinos.

It was this act more than any other that further hardened the attitude of the 'Great Powers' of Britain, France, Russia and Italy to the Turks' reluctance to cede further control to the Cretans. It led indirectly to the end of the Halepa Agreement that provided the island with a Christian Governor General, an elected assembly and police force.

After the burning down of many of the buildings, the street that had been known by the Turks as Vezir Tsarsi, was renamed after the day that changed history. Today, close to Lion Square are three of the most important historic buildings in the city, which fortunately survived the devastation.

Leaving the harbour behind as you walk uphill, on your left is St Titus' Church, named after an apostle of St Paul who became the first bishop of Crete. A place of worship has occupied this site since the 10th Century.

Housed in the original church was the skull of the saint, which was smuggled to Venice after the Turks drove the Venetians from the city in 1669 AD.

The original Byzantine church was then converted into a mosque, which it remained until it was destroyed by an earthquake in 1856. Following its destruction, the church was rebuilt again as a mosque. Set back from the main thoroughfare in its own square it has a sublime symmetry and is topped by a galleried dome.

The palms growing outside set off the cream stone. At night when the church is illuminated the grey dome shines blue, and the magnificent stained glass of the windows give of their best. A minaret that formerly stood on the site was taken down in 1925 when modifications were made and the church rededicated to Agios Titus. Inside hang paintings depicting famous acts of Cretan martyrdom and the life of the saint, whose skull was returned to the church from Venice in 1966 and is held here in a gold reliquary.

Just a few steps up the road from the serenity of Agios Titus is the magnificent Venetian Loggia which, along with the 'Lion' fountain, was also the brainchild of the prolific Francesco Morosini. Finished in 1628, this is the last and only surviving Loggia built in the city by the Venetians and is now the Town Hall.

In Venetian times the Loggia was like a gentlemen's club, where the great and the good, the movers and the shakers would meet to discuss affairs of state and relax with a glass of wine. It was the administrative capital of Heraklion, or Candia as it was then known.

The Loggia was built in the style of Renaissance architect Andrea Palladio, and is heavily influenced by his design for the Bassilica in Vincenza in Italy. As is befitting of a building based on the work of the man who is arguably the most influential architect in modern western civilization, this two-storey masterpiece based on ancient Greek Doric and Ionic styles, is held by many to be the finest building on the island.

Next door to the Loggia and opposite the Morosini Fountain is St Mark's Bassilica. This building now houses Heraklion's public art collection, but originally was built as a church to honour Venice's patron saint.

Nothing like as ornate as its namesake in Venice, the facade of this building features five classical Greek-style columned arches, the central one leading to the door of the gallery. Originally it had a bell tower in its south-west corner, a smaller reproduction of the clock tower in the Piazza San Marco in Venice. This was torn down and replaced with a minaret under Turkish rule. This in turn was demolished following Cretan independence.

With these inspirational buildings and squares lining 25th August Street it is hardly surprising, though a little unfair, that this thoroughfare was known as Odos Planis or the Road of Illusions. The name refers to how this vision of the great city flatters to deceive the visitor first arriving from the port. It is difficult to argue against the fact that architecturally the area does prove hard to live up to, but walk further on and you will encounter the vibrant permanent market where the past meets the present in a setting that has been the commercial hub of the city for centuries.

But it is in Lion Square that you have time to sit and let the city pass you by, meet friends, grab a snack or contemplate returning home to bed. For me it was a place to have a coffee on my way to work, somewhere to sit and read or mark papers in the afternoon, a place where people knew to meet up in the evening when none of us had phones, and a last stop for a night cap of Metaxa before heading home to my apartment just around the corner in Marco Avieri.

Just a short stroll away is a small park dedicated to Crete's most celebrated artist. The bust of El Greco (The Greek) looks over Theotokopoulou Square, otherwise known as El Greco Park. What used to be an unruffled oasis is now a more popular spot, with cafes spilling out onto the surrounding pavements, but it still remains a welcome patch of green away from the hubbub of 25 August Street.

Greece's most famous artist was born in Candia, now Heraklion, in 1541. But it was in Spain, in the city of Toledo that he created his best-known works. Something of a maverick, his style is hard to pin down, but his influence on numerous schools of modern painting, including cubism and expressionism is undeniable. His work is appreciated more now than when he was alive, at a time when many of his contemporaries found his unique style difficult to categorize.

El Greco's real name was Domenikos Theotokopoulos. The son of a wealthy trader, he began his training by painting icons. The Cretan School in Heraklion at the time was at the heart of post-Byzantine art and it is appropriate that, in his later career, El Greco was renowned for his blend of traditional Byzantine painting with a western European style. His art became an embodiment of the place of his birth, which stands astride the fault line between Byzantine and European cultures.

Just off Kalokerinou lies the 19th-century Cathedral of Agios Minas. A large, if unexceptional, building, it shares the same square as the much smaller 15th-century church of Agia Ekaterini, which is the home of the Museum of Religious Art. Inside can be found the most awe-inspiring examples of Cretan icon painting anywhere in the world. It is ironic that there are no works exhibited here by El Greco, the only two on the island are hung in the splendid Historical Museum on the coast road near the old harbour. At the heart of the Agia Ekaterini collection is the vibrant work of the late 16th-century artist Michaelis Dhamaskinos who was a contemporary of El Greco's and, some believe, his mentor. Six of his paintings are on exhibit here. Unlike El Greco, however, despite having also worked in Italy, Dhamaskinos throughout his life stayed pretty much true to the strict conventions of icon painting.

El Greco's style is reflective of his career painting in Crete, Italy and finally in Spain, where he created the work for which he is best known. Masterpieces such as *The Buriel of the Count of Orgaz* (Santo Tome, Toledo), and *The Holy Trinity* (Museum Del Prado, Madrid) are to be found in his adoptive country of Spain, but it is in Greece that he is revered as a national hero.

In Nikos Kazantzakis' semi-autobiographical masterpiece *Report to Greco* he writes of his fellow Cretan: 'Art is not submission and rules, but a demon that smashes the moulds', Greco's importance as one of the most influential figures in the world of art had not gone unnoticed in the island of his birth.

An illustration of the esteem in which he is held in his native country was the purchase by the National Art Gallery in Athens of his painting *Saint Peter* for $1.2million in 1995, much of the money being raised by donations given by ordinary Greek citizens. The renowned musician Vangelis Papathanassiou, perhaps most famous outside Greece for his soundtrack to the film *Chariots of Fire*, released a limited edition signed CD titled *El Greco* to contribute to the fund raising.

In his birthplace this small public garden is a fitting tribute to one of the world's greatest artists who, despite being appropriated by Spain, displayed a heart that is recognized as truly Cretan.

Heading back past Lion Square, walking south brings us to the enthralling street market which runs the length of 1866 Street from the Meidani crossroads up to Kornarou Square between Evans Street and 1821 Street. In front of the shops that line the road stand stalls selling all manner of produce; fruit and veg, meat, cheese, herbs and spices, oil, honey and wine. The shops that lurk behind these colourful stalls are darkened Aladdin's caves, stuffed with all the necessities required for everyday life. The shouts from the stallholders, mingled with the smells of their wares are a distillation of all that is best about Crete. To walk up this wonderful street is to experience the essence of the mountains, seas and villages that make up this ancient land.

The school where I used to work was in Evans Street, which runs parallel to the market. When I first started working there I used to weave my way through the early morning throng to prepare for my lesson at 8 o'clock as the stallholders made ready for their day's trading. After my first few days in the job, I realized I would have to take a detour.

Many of the stallholders and shopkeepers had children in my classes and, when they realized that the stranger walking through the market was their offspring's teacher, they would call out 'Hey professor, come in and have a drink'. It didn't matter that it was not long after sunrise!

Their hospitality was genuine and well meant, but consisted of small carafes of intoxicating raki. I could be stopped several times on my short journey, and by the time I got to school I could often be feeling somewhat heady.

Mantinades – A Very Cretan Custom

It was 10 o'clock on a Saturday evening when my friend Minos drew up alongside Alexanders, a local taverna of choice near El Greco Park. We were heading out of town towards Archanes, although where our exact destination was I never fully established. Minos was determined to show me something he felt he had been unable to put into words. A musician himself, a classical guitar teacher and musical director who spoke good English, he believed he had been unable to offer an adequate explanation of *mantinada*. So, we were heading to the mountains.

Some miles outside Heraklion we stopped outside a building, seemingly in the middle of nowhere. It was an undistinguished concrete structure with walls washed in white and a couple of token pottery urns with straggly flowers to soften the starkness of the structure in daylight hours. However, on entering it was apparent that this was a creature of the night. Going inside, the building seemed to double in size and was jam packed full of people, some in traditional Cretan dress, all the men smoking and talking at once in equal measure.

Minos seemed to know everyone in the room. After much hand shaking and back slapping we joined a small group of his friends at a table already laden with mezzes of vine leaves stuffed with rice, tiny cheese pies, deep fried squid, sea urchin, meatballs, olive paste, small grilled fish, salad and, of course, bread in abundance. A tumbler was upturned and filled with deep red wine with a bouquet that cut through the pungent smoke that hung in the air. On the small-raised stage three musicians took up their instruments, a lyra flanked by two lutes. The lyra struck up, its unique haunting tones flowing like waves over the conversation, quelling it until all that could be heard was the music.

Then the Cretan lutes took up the accompaniment as the lead lyra player stopped playing. Holding bow and instrument in his left hand out to one side, he started to talk into a microphone. The sound was lyrical and the words recognized by most of the people in the room. This was an example of the folk tradition of *mantinada*.

Mantinades are short poems recited with or without the accompaniment of music, as a performance or just as a conversation. They are rhyming couplets that must contain fifteen syllables. They originated during the fifteenth century when Crete was a Venetian protectorate, the word *mantinada* itself emanates from the Italian *mattinata*, meaning song of the morning.

Unlike other formalized short poems they are less pastoral than the Japanese haiku and less frivolous than the English limerick. They express in a stylized way how people feel about everyday life. Love, death, happiness and sorrow are the most usual subjects, but nothing is taboo. Mostly they have been passed down by word of mouth, but new ones are constantly being composed, the best of which are now being recorded for posterity.

A *mantinade* can be a single, self contained poem embracing the complete expression of an idea or be part of a succession of couplets that form a longer narrative or even a conversation where couplets are used as dialogue until the subject is exhausted. The use of *mantinades* in day-to-day conversation is unusual nowadays, but the tradition is kept alive at gatherings such as the one I was attending.

When the audience had been warmed up with a couple of solo narratives, the performer elucidated responses from the audience, an approach they warmed to with increasing enthusiasm as the night wore on.

My understanding was too slow and vocabulary too small to understand most of the couplets and it is difficult to translate examples retaining both the meaning and the strict form. However, since the advent of the internet, collections of *mantinades* are being submitted and recorded so I have been able to find a couple of translated examples which might make the tradition more clear. These come from the Cretan Folk Poetry Collection of Yannis Pavlakis:

> '*The everything of the world is zero, the life of the world is naught.*
> *It is from nothing to nothing that eternity is wrought.*'

> '*I want my darling filthy - it's the dirty girl I trust.*
> *To keep her to myself and make the rest flee in disgust.*'

What was clear from this evening was that the tradition of *mantinades* was alive and well and, like such traditions in other cultures, was not a minority interest. The art was embraced by everyone in the room that night. Some poems caused laughter, others were insightful; some were quickly improvised, others were studiously thought out; many would be forgotten, some remembered for posterity.

Kazantzakis' Tomb

On first sight, Heraklion is not beautiful. Modern concrete buildings erected following the devastation caused by relentless bombing in the Second World War stand cheek-by-jowl with more traditional-style Turkish and Venetian architecture. In summer the heat, dust and petrol fumes combine with the noise of motor horns and shouted conversations to assail the senses. But, in time, I have come to love the city for all its humanity and unexpected pleasures. Crete's capital is unpredictable and, beneath its rough exterior, extraordinarily welcoming.

When the noise and heat get too much, I sometimes take a walk inland, climbing the slight incline through the market on 1866 Street, dodging the cars round Kornarou Square before passing into the smaller streets up towards the old city walls.

Here bouzouki music mingles with Europop emanating from open windows. Elderly widows in black weeds sit stringing beans as boys and girls hold conversations on mobile phones from the back of their scooters.

And on to the mighty walls, built by the Venetians to protect the city and still impressive in stature. It is here, to the south of the town, looking down on the mosaic of buildings and maze of streets, that Nikos Kazantzakis is buried. The author, a modern Greek hero, did more to expound the Cretan spirit than any other writer.

Little known outside his native country, the film adaptation of his book *Zorba the Greek* is, for many people, their only touchstone to his work. The book itself is a good starting point for anyone seeking a deeper understanding of Cretan psyche and history. The Mikis Theodorakis composed soundtrack to the film is played everywhere and the name of Zorba which adorns bars and restaurants is pervasive on the island.

The grave is marked by a simple wooden cross and a plaque with the inscription, 'I hope for nothing. I fear nothing. I am free'. I have often visited this place when I needed time to reflect. On each such occasion I have found it profoundly calming.

Kazantzakis was buried here following his death in 1957. Although religion was fundamental to his beliefs, his probing of religious themes in search of philosophical truths were seen as threatening by the church and he was excommunicated two years before he died. So it is here that Crete's most famous son lies, atop the walls of his beloved city, in unconsecrated ground.

The legacy of Nikos Kazantzakis is difficult to avoid throughout Crete. Which is as it should be. For most of us, when arriving by air, we land at Heraklion's international airport that is named after the man who is arguably modern Greece's greatest writer.

His work, most notably the eponymous, larger-than-life Alexis Zorba, is unrivalled in characterizing what it really means to be Greek and, more specifically, Cretan. Born in Candia (Heraklion) in 1883 when Crete was still under Turkish rule, he went on to study law and later philosophy before becoming the most internationally acclaimed Greek writer of the 20th Century. He was nominated for the Nobel Prize for Literature in 1957, losing out by one vote to the French absurdist writer and philosopher Albert Camus who, by his own admission, generously declared Kazantzakis a hundred times more worthy of the honour than himself.

Not only did Kazantzakis upset the Greek Orthodox Church, his novel *The Last Temptation of Christ* was also listed in the Vatican's Index of Prohibited Books, a precursor of the furore Martin Scorsese's film adaptation of the work was to cause in 1988.

Those who claim that Kazantzakis was not a religious man misunderstand both him and his art. He did not adhere to the conservative prescribed version of Christianity as preached by the organized religions but, like most philosophers, was searching for truth. His semi-autobiographical work *Report to Greco*, published in 1961 three years after his death, gives a good insight into his life and philosophy.

The leading figures in his novels whether they be Jesus, Saint Francis, freedom fighters or, most famously, Alexis Zorba all struggle with the tensions inherent in what it is to be human. This is often expressed with his protagonists' sense of duty being put in conflict with the more basic needs of love and the enjoyment of living life to the full.

It was Kazantzakis' portrayal of Christ as a man struggling with these emotions that angered the religious zealots. His reply to those who excommunicated him was, 'You cursed me holy fathers, but I bless you, my conscience is clear, I hope that you may be as moral and religious as I am'.

Zorba the Greek remains, though, his most popular book. The story is narrated by a young intellectual who sets off to visit Crete to leave his bookish ways behind and experience the life of working people by reopening a disused lignite mine. While awaiting his ship in a taverna in Piraeus, he encounters the elderly Alexis Zorba. The pair strike up a friendship, and the narrator agrees to give the enigmatic Zorba a job as his works foreman. Zorba has the ability to totally absorb himself in the moment, whether it is working hard or seducing the elderly courtesan who is their landlady.

Through their conversations and Zorba's love of music and dancing, he teaches the young intellectual something he had been unable to learn from his books – what it means to be fully alive. Although their mining project ends in disaster, the narrator has gained something much more valuable.

'I felt again just how simple a thing happiness is – a glass of wine, a roast chestnut, a wretched little brazier, the sound of the sea. Nothing else. And that all that is needed to feel that happiness right now is a simple, frugal heart.'

It is easy to see why, for so many people, the work of Kazantzakis summarizes perfectly their feelings about Crete.

There is another discreet memorial to the writer in Heraklion, which is something of a hidden gem. I had heard that there was a room dedicated to Kazantzakis in the city's Historical Museum. Although small it is well worth a visit as it is well curated and reveals much about Cretan culture and history from the Byzantine to the present day. Its brilliance is that all the collections have a sense of continuity, which connects the past with the present.

The museum is situated on Venizelou Road, the coastal route that leaves the old harbour going west, and is housed in a modest neoclassical building, which has been extended to accommodate more artifacts. Inside is pleasingly sedate, which encourages the visitor to linger over the exhibits, allowing time to see them in the context of Crete's turbulent history. The first room you enter presents an overview of 'modern' Cretan history spanning the period following the Roman occupation in the 3rd Century AD to the present day. The centrepiece of the room is a huge model of Heraklion (or Chandax as it was then known) in the 17th Century when it was under Venetian control. The model is interactive and visitors can illuminate the most important historical landmarks by pushing switches.

Collections of pottery and sculpture, coins and jewellery chart the social and economic history of the island and fragments of frescoes and icons illustrate the fragile spiritual balance of a people subjected to frequent invasion by foreign powers. The jewels in the crown of the artistic exhibits are two paintings by the local artist El Greco – *The View of Mount Sinai and the Monastery of St Catherine* and *The Baptism of Christ* are the only two paintings by the master on exhibition in Crete.

Exhibits following the development of olive and grape growing and other types of farming, and a replica of the interior of a typical agricultural worker's house provide a useful insight into how island life had been through the ages and proves a valuable benchmark with which to compare contemporary life as you travel through the island.

More collections inform about life under Ottoman rule, the struggle for independence and *enosis* (union with Greece), the dark days of the Second World War, and the life of Nikos Kazantzakis. The great writer is remembered by a replica of his study and the library from his home in Antibes in France. The walls are lined with first editions of his works and his life and achievements are documented to provide the visitor with a clear insight into the man and his legacy.

Although less celebrated than the town's Archaeological Museum, the breadth of the collections here gives a wider perspective on Crete in the past. As you emerge from the shadowy, cool building to the brilliant sunshine refracting off the sea opposite, there is plenty to reflect on which will embellish travels further afield.

Homer: The Father of Western Literature?

It is hard to move anywhere in Crete without encountering mythical characters. This is where Homer comes in. The epic poet goes a long way towards explaining the legends. But even Homer's interpretations of events cannot be definitive and are constantly disputed by academics. But for the layman, they relate as reliable an account as any other.

When you consider that there is still disagreement about whether Homer existed at all – or indeed if works attributed to the poet are an anthology of those by other writers that have been homogenized through rewriting into a coherent Homeric style – you'll begin to appreciate how slippery the subject matter is.

There is even controversy among the classicists who do believe in Homer's existence as to when he actually lived. Given that the stories the poet wrote about had been passed down orally for many centuries, the room for different theories is legion.

There is, however, some consensus on these issues which, not being an expert, I intend to accept. And the Homeric rendering of events is as likely to be as correct as any other version of the truth on offer.

It is broadly accepted that Homer lived around the 8th Century BC. It is also widely held that the poet was the founding father of the tradition of western literature. The two major works most frequently attributed to him are *The Iliad* and *The Odyssey*.

Both epics are written interpretations of stories previously passed down verbally and relate the tales of mythical gods and goddesses and legendary heroes of the Trojan Wars, believed to have taken place in about 1200 BC, and the years that followed.

The Iliad was the first of the two works to be written and predates *The Odyssey* by a couple of decades. *The Iliad* starts when the wars between the Trojans and Achaeans (Greeks) had been on the go for almost a decade. The actual conflict in question is understood to have happened some 450 years prior to Homer's writings.

Following one battle, the leader of the Achaeans, Agamemnon, and his bravest warrior, Achilles, take a pair of Trojan women hostage, claiming them as prizes of war. Angered, the god Apollo sends a plague to devastate their people.

Seeing the havoc wrought upon his forces by the plague, Agamemnon agrees to give his woman, Chryseis, back to the Trojans; but demands that Achilles then surrenders his prize, Briseis, to him. Achilles, insulted by the demands of his leader, takes to his tent and refuses to enter combat. From his self-imposed retreat he asks his mother, a sea nymph, to request of Zeus, the king of all gods, that he bring down Agamemnon.

Now the odds are stacked against the Achaeans, with Zeus on the side of the Trojans and Achilles refusing to enter battle. Heroic fights take place between the great soldiers on either side, Hector against Ajax and Paris against Menelaus, but the Greeks cannot stem the Trojan tide and are pushed back to behind their defences on the coast.

Under siege, all looks lost for the Achaeans until a guilty but proud Achilles hatches a plan whereby his great friend Patroclus will enter the fray disguised in his armour. Buoyed up by the belief that their great warrior has relented, the rejuvenated Achaeans drive the enemy back inland, away from their ships. But, with one last effort, the retreating army counter attacks and Apollo causes Patroclus to shed his armour. With his true identity exposed, Hector kills Patroclus.

Enraged that his friend has been murdered, Achilles persuades the gods to forge him a new suit of armour and rides out in his chariot at the head of the Achaean warriors and enters the battle seeking revenge. Finally, Achilles kills Hector and ties his body to the back of his chariot and drags it back to camp.

Hector's father, the ruler of Troy, King Priam, is distraught that his son has not had the burial that befits such a brave warrior. Zeus agrees and sends the god Hermes with Priam to plead with Achilles for the return of Hector's corpse. Putting his feelings of vengeance aside, Achilles relents. He releases the body to the Trojans and calls a truce so that Hector can get the burial his bravery and status deserve. The Trojans finally defeated, Homer's second masterpiece, *The Odyssey*, is set a decade after the end of the war.

In Ithaka the people still await the return of their king, Odysseus, not knowing whether he is alive or dead. After ten years without leadership, his restless subjects have seized Odysseus' lands and infiltrated the palace where his wife, Penelope, remains faithful to her husband. Her son, Telemachus, is all that stands between the mob and his absent father's kingdom and he lacks the support to expel the rebels. A plot is hatched by one of the insurgents, Antinous, to kill Prince Telemachus and take over the kingdom.

Odysseus is very much alive and desperate to return home to his family and country. But he has been kidnapped by the nymph Calypso who is in love with him, and has kept him imprisoned on her island Ogygia. Zeus dispatches his messenger Hermes to Calypso to plead for Odysseus' release.

Moved by Hermes' testimony, Calypso allows Odysseus to build a ship and flee the island, but the god of the sea, Poseidon, whose son Odysseus previously blinded, creates a storm to wreck the vessel. Blown off course, Odysseus is only saved by the intervention of the goddess Athena. The king finds landfall at Scheria, thought by some to be modern-day Corfu, where he is shown hospitality by the king of the Phaeacians. Here he recounts to them the tales of his long journey and how he ended up a captive of Calypso.

He tells, among other stories, of the land of the Lotus Eaters, a place so idyllic it is almost impossible to escape; of his blinding of Poseidon's son, the giant cyclops Polyphemus, to escape his murderous clutches; and his journey to the underworld for an audience with the prophet Tiresias. Following a long night of recounting his adventures, the Phaeacians grant him safe passage to Ithaka on a magic ship and, disguised as a beggar, he lands back on his homeland, determined to regain control of his kingdom.

When Penelope encounters the beggar at the palace she has a sense that he may be her missing husband and stages an archery competition promising to marry the winner. Odysseus wins and with the help of his loyal son, kills his adversaries and eventually reclaims his wife and kingdom.

For anyone wishing to gain an understanding of ancient myths and legends, Homer's interpretations are as accessible as any. For the contemporary reader they make a connection with Greece's ancient past, conjuring up images of the gods, goddesses and mighty warriors, which contribute to its timeless spirit.

In the Court of the King

Knossos lies just four miles south east of Heraklion. It is a place that has inspired much conjecture since its rediscovery in 1878. The site's controversial excavation and partial reconstruction by English aristocrat archaeologist Sir Arthur Evans in the early 20th Century has given it the dubious accolade of a must-see destination. Its reputation as the most important archaeological site on Crete, and arguably in Greece, can contribute to its ability to disappoint.

At peak times, in high summer, a visit there can be a claustrophobic experience as crowds of visitors are borne back and forth from their resorts by a procession of squealing coaches. But viewed with the luxury of time and space, Knossos is captivating. Like most of the island's more popular archaeological sites, it is wise to go early in the day or, if at all possible, out of season.

Getting up at dawn, the whole of that late summer Sunday stretched out before me. Following Evans Street through the city walls to meet the dusty Leoforos Knosou, I climbed away from the clamour of Sunday bells waking the metropolis and into the hills. By 8 o'clock the sun was already finding its strength. The heat and the dust thrown up by the occasional vehicle made slow and steady progress the only option.

Four miles might not be far, but an hour into my walk, as temperatures nudged into the thirties, my progress slowed to a halt outside a taverna. Apart from an elderly man savouring an early morning coffee, the place was deserted.

The man glanced up from his newspaper and welcomed me with a staccato '*ella*' (come in). I needed little encouragement. By then the prospect of refreshment was most welcome.

As I sat down the man bellowed a command. From the shadows inside the taverna emerged an elderly woman who I took to be his wife. She approached my table and I gave her my order for a lemonade in halting phrasebook Greek, at which she smiled and uttered a surprised '*poli kala*' (very good).

Although little less than a mile from Knossos, I suspect this taverna was not a haunt for tourists. By and large they would drive past en route to the palace, and my few words of Greek singled me out as an object for my hosts' hospitality. The man came and sat at my table as his wife produced, not only the bottle of lemonade I had ordered, but some small cheese pies and stuffed vine leaves.

Over the cold drink and mezzes, the owner was keen to talk and find out where I came from and what I did for a living. I could just about explain that I was English and that I was a schoolteacher.

On hearing where I worked, he exclaimed that his grandson was a pupil there. This was cause for raki to be called for and toasts of '*yamas*' and '*eleftheria*', (cheers and freedom) to be drunk.

Early in the morning on a sweltering day, the spirit began to take effect with undue haste. If I were to get to Knossos I would have to take my leave. Asking for the bill, my request was waved away. Any further attempt to insist on paying would have been futile. Indeed, to my truly hospitable Cretan hosts, it would have been offensive. Not for the first, or last, time I was experiencing Cretan hospitality or *philoxenia*. What little they have, they will share with a stranger. I have found their generosity of spirit to be unmatched.

I resumed my journey towards the palace. The sun, now much higher in the sky was beginning to show signs of real ferocity. But my prompt start had paid off and I was still early enough for there not to be too many other visitors about.

Stepping onto the site it is immediately apparent that Evans' reconstructions do endow the palace with a sense of place. The columns and highly-coloured frescoes act as a context within which the visitor can better imagine how Minoan civilization might have been. A process that would be more difficult if the site consisted of little more than just a pile of rocks, however authentic they might be. But how sympathetic these reconstructions are is controversial.

Although often believed to have been discovered by Evans in 1900, the site was first investigated by the appropriately named Cretan merchant, Minos Kalokairinos. It was Minos who began the first digs there 22 years earlier. However, it was the vast private wealth of the English archaeologist that allowed him to purchase the whole site and enabled him to conduct an extensive excavation.

Employing a large staff, it was not many months before he had revealed much of what we now know as the Palace of Minos. Evans will go down in history as the man who named the palace, and the civilization that built it, as Minoan.

It is impossible not to be drawn to the familiar three red pillars framing a fresco of a bull. This abiding image, reproduced so many times, is a classic example of the controversial work done by Evans and his team. The bull painting is an enhanced copy of the original that resides in the Archaeological Museum on Eleftherias Square in Heraklion. It is the extent of such enhancements and Evans' vision that has provoked much of the debate about the reconstructions. If the Palace itself gives a context to the Minoan civilization, it is the museum that gives it authenticity and is well worth a visit; particularly while your experience of the site itself is still fresh in the mind.

Turning my back on the bull fresco, the whole expanse of the palace was laid out before me, the remains of more than a thousand interconnecting rooms surrounding a square. This was the 'new palace' that dates between 1700 and 1450 BC. The original old palace which occupied the same site is understood to have been destroyed by an earthquake and been built some 200 years previously and there is evidence of settlements in the area going back a further 700 years to 2600 BC.

The civilization Evans labelled as Minoan was named after the mythical King Minos of Crete. The son of Zeus, he was recalled every nine years to his father's birthplace, the Diktean Cave, to have a refresher course in kingship. The cave, high in the hills that surround Lassithi Plateau, near the village of Psychro some 30 miles to the south east, is now a popular tourist destination. Hundreds flock there daily to see an impressive display of stalactites and stalagmites and even bigger displays of souvenirs.

Failing to heed his father's lessons, Minos tried to trick the god of the sea, Poseidon, who had presented him with a bull as a gift, in the expectation it would be sacrificed in his honour. Instead Minos made sacrifice of another animal. Enraged, Poseidon caused Minos' wife to fall in love with the bull, and the result of their subsequent union was the half-man, half-beast Minotaur.

Minos had the monster thrown into a labyrinth. There it was kept at bay by being fed a diet of young men and virgins shipped to the island from Athens. Unhappy at the youth of their nation being served up as dinner to the Minotaur, the son of the King of Athens, Theseus, volunteered as a sacrifice, and with the help of Minos' daughter, Ariadne, managed to kill the beast.

The presence of bulls in the wall paintings, carvings and other artifacts discovered at Knossos has led to the legend of the Minotaur and the Minoan civilization being inextricably linked. A popular myth recalls that the labyrinth where the Minotaur roamed lay beneath the Palace of Knossos itself, and was constructed by the master builder Daedalus.

After killing the Minotaur, Theseus eloped with Princess Ariadne, but the relationship didn't last. After spending one night together on Naxos, Theseus abandoned his lover. King Minos, ashamed of his wife's infidelity, imprisoned Daedalus and his son, Icarus, inside Knossos so that the secrets of the labyrinth wouldn't be discovered. All land and sea routes were heavily guarded making escape from the island seemingly impossible. Undaunted, the master craftsman invented wings made of feathers held together with twine and wax. Strapping these to their backs, Deadalus and his son escaped Minos by flying away.

Daedalus warned his son not to soar too high, as the sun would melt the wax, or swoop too low as the spray from the sea would saturate the feathers. Unheeding and with the folly of youth, Icarus flew too close to the sun and his wings fell apart, plunging him to a watery grave.

A distraught Daedalus washed up in Sicily with an angry Minos hot in pursuit. But the King's revenge is ultimately foiled. He meets his end when the daughters of King Cocalus, who had taken it upon himself to protect Daedalus, poured boiling water into Minos' bathtub.

Such myths and legends largely derive from the works of Homer and, more recently, the Roman writer Ovid who died in 17 AD. These writers were, in turn, giving their own interpretations of ancient legends that had been passed down through many generations, mostly by word of mouth. As such, there are many variations of the stories based around these classical characters. It is as well to remember that any one interpretation is probably as valid as another. The 20th-century English writer Mary Renault gave her own voice to the legend of the Minotaur in her popular 1962 historical novel *The Bull from the Sea*.

Whatever the legitimacy of the myths, there is much to be learned about actual Minoan civilization from hard evidence unearthed by Evans and his successors. There is no doubt that these legends originated in this ancient culture. It is thought that Stone Age man arrived on Crete sometime during the 7th millennium BC and established a settlement on the site of Knossos.

By around 3000 BC other settlers had brought with them skills such as making pottery and working copper, which gave rise to what we now know as the Minoan civilization some 400 years later.

By 2000 BC the Minoans had begun to build highly-sophisticated settlements. These include those at Faistos, Zakros and Malia, but the grandest of them all was Knossos. These towns had two-storey buildings, drainage and sanitation, but around 1700 BC they were all flattened by a massive earthquake. It is after this period that the palace was rebuilt. It was even more sophisticated and advanced than its predecessor and the heyday of the Minoan dynasty was to flourish for a further 250 years.

Latter day Minoan society was highly structured. Its wealth was built on trade. Minoan merchants would travel to mainland Greece, North Africa and even as far as Spain to sell copper and tin, pottery, gold, silver and saffron. Although a class system operated in society, it is clear from the construction of houses, even in the poorer areas of Minoan settlements, that the wealth created by such trade was distributed among all the citizens. In the newly-rebuilt Knossos, streets connected the buildings, and water and sewage services were delivered through clay pipes. Remarkable when you consider that more recent cities, such as London, did not benefit from an effective sewerage infrastructure until the mid 19th Century AD.

Internal and external staircases connected the different levels of the tiled-roofed buildings and paintings of goddesses and gods adorned the walls. Frescoes, again indicating a link between the mythical Minotaur and Minoan society, depict the sport of bull jumping, where an athlete is pictured leaping over the back of a charging beast. The presence of bull imagery and statues suggest that these were sacred animals and that the rulers were feted as gods. Statues and frescoes of priestesses draped in snakes also have a religious significance.

The palace was the hub of the cultural, religious and economic life of society. In its prime the whole settlement is estimated to have had a population of 100,000 people. Archaeologists and historians have learned much by the painstaking excavation of Knossos and other Minoan sites on the island. Houses had under-floor heating and the earliest known flushing toilet was discovered at Knossos. By 1450 BC, however, this highly-advanced society had all-but disappeared.

A number of theories have been put forward as to the cause of this demise and the destruction of the palaces. At first it was thought that they might have fallen victim to the same massive earthquake that struck the island of Santorini 60 miles to the north, with the resulting giant tsunami overwhelming Crete.

This episode is now thought, however, to have occurred almost a century before the destruction of the Minoan settlements. Evidence of volcanic ash settling on the island has revealed only the thinnest of layers, and these lie beneath the level of some more recent Minoan building.

The most commonly accepted theory is that invaders overran the Minoans, and indeed many of the palaces and towns show evidence of fire damage. What is certain is that, following this period, society went into a steep decline and fell under the rule of invading Myceneans from the north.

Whatever the truth about the end of Minoan civilization, its legacy remains the most powerful influence on modern Cretan society. It is impossible to spend any time on the island without it being referenced either in the names of shops and restaurants or in souvenirs, pottery and postcards. Despite the controversy about Evans' restoration of the Palace, the importance of its discovery and subsequent excavation is undisputed in its significance.

Treasures of the Past – The Archaeological Museum

In the north-east corner of Heraklion's Plateia Eleftherias is home to the most impressive collection of Minoan artifacts in the world, as befits the birthplace of western civilization. The current museum was opened in 1952 and its 20 exhibition rooms house finds from across the island spanning the 5,500 odd years between the Neolithic and Roman periods. The bulk of the exhibits are Minoan and come from the palaces of Knossos, Malia and Phaistos and numerous other sites around the island. These finds include sculptures, paintings, mosaics, jewellery and coins, all exhibited with explanatory notes to contextualize them.

A walk around the museum will augment any visit to Knossos or any of the other archaeological sites across the island. The exhibits are so extraordinary and numerous that it is difficult to do more than pick out a few highlights. The figures of the bull leaper and snake goddess from Knossos come to mind, as does the Phaistos Disc.

Taking pride of place in Room III, this clay disc about the size of a tea plate came from the Old Palace at Phaistos near Agia Triada on the south coast of the island, and is stamped with pictures of characters and objects including fish, flowers, ships, arrows and axes as well as human figures all spiralling in towards the centre. In all there are 45 different symbols making up the 241 characters on the disc. It is thought that this is one of the very first examples of moveable type, the hieroglyphics having been stamped into soft clay using different seals. The story that these pictoral representations tells still remains a mystery, but that it is an early form of written language is not in doubt. The characters formed on both sides of the disc are examples of Cretan Hieroglyphs, further examples of which can be found on the Arkalochori Axe which was discovered in a sacred Minoan cave to the west of the Lassithi Plateau and which is also on display in the museum.

Moving on into room V there are examples of the other two scripts emanating from Minoan times, known as Linear A and Linear B. These appear similar and related and are both found on stone tablets. As yet Linear A remains a mystery unlike Linear B of which significant steps have been taken in deciphering the language, which is now held to be an antecedent of early Ancient Greek.

If the miracle of these scripts lies in their significance in the history of written communication, more immediately uplifting spectacles are to be found in rooms XIV, XV and XVI. These are the marvellous halls of the frescoes, which contain restored wall paintings mostly from Knossos and Agia Triada. My favourite is the brilliantly fresh and uplifting Dolphin Fresco taken from the walls of the Queen's Apartment at Knossos. The vibrant blue and yellow representations of these extraordinary mammals were painted onto the wet plaster of the walls using mineral and vegetable dyes. These dolphins are so miraculous because they are timeless, and these masters of the sea still have a special symbolic importance on Crete today. Other notable paintings include the *Bull Leaper* and the famous *La Parisienne*, part of the *Campstool Fresco* from Knossos depicting a striking raven-haired priestess, bejeweled and wide-eyed, taking part in a traditional banquet. Also known as the *Minoan Lady*, it is clear looking at her red lips and dark eyes that such women of the time used some kind of make up and had a quite sophisticated beauty regime.

The wealth of exhibits and the history to which they relate can prove overwhelming, but a visit to the museum does provide a taste of the cultural heritage of the island and helps imbue the places still to be visited with a sense of their own past.

Crete's Musical Soul

In winter Heraklion changes faces, and its society moves indoors. Restaurants and music venues situated off the main tourist tracks throw open their doors to local trade. It is now that the *boites* open up. Dark and intimate, lit by candlelight and often below street level, they play host to the *rebetika* music of Greece.

It is hard to find an equivalent to *rebetika* in western music; although it does have the shared sentiment of much Blues. It is sad, soulful and fiercely individualistic. It encapsulates the story of Greece and the Greek spirit, and is inevitably a product of both these things.

The individualism it expresses and its evocation of freedom has made *rebetika* controversial over the years. The music has even been banned by a number of ruling administrations who saw it as a threat to their authority. In the form it is recognized today, *rebetika* emerged in the early 1920s. It grew indirectly as a result of Greece's disastrous incursion into Asia Minor to try to seize Smyrna, and the other Greek inhabited regions of what is now western Turkey, from the Ottomans.

In 1922, after some initial success, the Greek forces were driven back out of Smyrna by the Turkish troops of Kemal Ataturk. Following brutal reprisals by the Turks on Smyrna's predominantly Greek population, it was agreed that all Christians would leave Ottoman territory for Greece and, likewise, Muslims living on Greek territory were to be displaced to Turkey. This mass migration created a huge refugee problem. Millions of people of both races and religions were exiled from the countries of their birth.

Up to 1.5 million people of Greek origin took the long trek to Greece. Some settled in Thessaloniki but most in Athens, from where many were helped to emigrate, often to America or Australia. Out of the refugee camps small bands of musicians emerged, playing songs in the style of their old homeland in Smyrna.

Rebetika is believed to have derived from the term *rebetis* that means 'petty criminal'. This was probably how many of the indigenous Greek population viewed the refugees. But the music struck a chord, and the musicians were first hired in the clubs of Athens. As the refugees dispersed throughout Greece, the popularity of the music also spread. The songs are usually accompanied by bouzoukis, which had been used by the Greek population of Asia Minor before being brought into Greece by the musicians on the 'long walk'.

The early forms of these mandolin-like instruments had three pairs of strings, but these days instruments are made with four, which are played with a plectrum. The music is frequently melancholic, dealing with themes such as loss, exile and fighting for freedom.

As mentioned, numerous authoritarian rulers saw these songs as subversive and *rebetika* was banned by successive dictatorships. Yannis Metaxas in 1936; the occupying Germans during the Second World War; and the dictatorship of the colonels between 1967 and 1974, all tried to suppress the music. They felt threatened by the individualism expressed and thought it evoked a refusal to be ruled by anyone.

My first introduction to *rebetika* was through the music of the popular female singer Charis Alexiou. Her album of traditional *rebetika* songs called *Ta Tsilika* was released in 1983. Prior to that her music had ridden the wave of *rebetika's* explosion in popularity following the fall of the Colonels in the Seventies.

As a young woman Charis collaborated with one of the most famous of all *rebetika* musicians, George Dalaras, on his definitive album *Mikra Asia* released in 1972.

The music is unlike that of the traditional dances played when people come together to celebrate weddings, name days or other social occasions. *Rebetika's* style is more introspective and personal. There are certain songs where people will get up to dance alone. Their right to personal time with the music is respected, the spell going unbroken by unwanted applause. No one else will take the floor until the dancer has finished and returned to their table in silence.

It's OK to Rustle Sweet Wrappers

Midnight Express, is a 1978 Alan Parker film adaptation of a book by Billy Hayes about the prison horrors of an American arrested for drug smuggling in Turkey. I had seen the film when it came out in England but went again to see it in Heraklion's Astoria Cinema on Eleftherias Square.

The film is a tense drama, usually played out to a silent audience. Cinema going in Greece is seldom such a sedate affair with audience participation being the order of the day. And in the case of this particular movie it was extreme. The film was in English with Greek subtitles, but throughout it was impossible to hear any on-screen dialogue.

The loudest cheer of the day was reserved for the particularly brutal murder by the American prisoner of a Turkish guard that leads to him escaping in the uniform of his victim. What would, in other countries, have been met by a stunned silence or at most a shocked gasp was heralded with cheering, clapping and whistling as the Turk met his gruesome end.

This attitude highlights perfectly the strained relations between the Greeks and Turks, which shows little sign of abating. As the historical victims of Ottoman imperialist ambitions, more recently the mutual disrespect has manifested itself over the issue of Cyprus. Although this has been rumbling on since the Turkish invasion of the island in 1974, the Turkish government is still unyielding over the issue; even to the extent of allowing it to become a major stumbling block over their ambitions to become members of European Community.

Since 1925 Cyprus had been a British Crown Colony, which, by the 1950s, was pressurizing for union with Greece. In 1960 Cyprus gained its independence but unrest between the minority Turkish population and the Greek Cypriots was never far from breaking out into violence. In 1974 the military dictatorship in Greece, in an attempt to curry political favour in their own country, engineered a coup against the ruling government of President Archbishop Makarios.

The ensuing military intervention by Turkish forces to stop the rebel government annexing the island with Greece saw the country split into two, it still remains divided by a United Nations buffer zone known as the Green Line.

In 1983 Turkish Cypriots declared Northern Cyprus a Turkish republic, a state not recognized by anyone except the Turkish government. The Greeks on the other hand still hanker after *enosis*, with Cyprus becoming part of Greece. The wound is still very much open and, it seems, getting no closer to healing. If the whole incident in 1974 did have a positive side, it was that it led to the fall of the military junta in Greece, paving the way for the establishment of the new republic.

A Welcome Shower

The first rain of early autumn came when I was in Heraklion's Eleftherias Square. Waiting for a bus outside the Archaeological Museum, the first drops came like a forgotten memory after so many months of drought and searing temperatures. For the locals it was welcome, and they stood relishing the shower as it cleaned the air of the terracotta dust that for several days had been blowing in on the wind from North Africa.

It is true what the locals say, that this 'long tongue' of the *sorokos* blowing up from Libya can make you feel cranky at best. People complain of feeling on edge and of having headaches as the wind whips up sand and blows it into eyes, impregnating clothes with desert dust. These winds happen several times a year and when they blow themselves out the sense of relief is tangible.

The winds can bring nothing good, stirring the seas around the island to a frenzy as fishing boats run for the safety of harbour. Legend has it that such a wind heralded the destruction of Knossos and the Minoan civilization.

That day we were just pleased the wind had abated and, with that, the added bonus that the long summer drought had come to an end. The air was still warm as the heavens opened, drenching us to the skin, but nobody ran for shelter. They just stood soaking up the rejuvenating rain as it fell, purifying the sky of the detritus of summer.

The weeks that followed were some of the most perfect. Warm and fresh with clear blue autumn skies, the evenings cool and peaceful. The tourist season was coming to an end and most Cretans' minds were turning towards the olive harvest and time with their families following the long, hard days working in the towns and resorts.

Early Morning Loukoumades

The real essence of Crete is embodied in simple food and drink and good conversation in a relaxed atmosphere. Regularly, in experiencing all three, long nights would seamlessly turn into early mornings. Although until recently tavernas and bars were supposed to shut at 2.00am, this was rarely observed.

Frequently on winter nights I've found myself, in the early hours, heading towards Heraklion's fish market on Karterou Street to a small ouzerie where, behind the steamed up windows, traders discussed the price of the catch over warming shots of raki or ouzo.

Wrapped up against the night's cold, we would divest ourselves of scarves, gloves and jackets then order plates of steaming *loukoumades* straight from the stove. These golden dough balls, deep fried and flavoured with sugar or honey and cinnamon accompanied by a hot chocolate often proved the perfect antidote to the excesses of the night.

There are few tastes that can bring back memories of winters in Crete in such a way: memories of a time when life moved more slowly and was more serendipitous, it is a dish so simple, but rich in reminiscences. The batter is just flour, yeast, salt and warm water left to prove for an hour before being deep fried, coated in a honey syrup, then sprinkled with cinnamon. Delicious!

Crab on the Menu

Shellfish in Greece is not as cheap as one would suppose. Despite the 'Europeanisation' of restaurants over the last 25 years, I have not seen crab on the menu for a very long time. The last time I experienced eating it in Greece was in a dilapidated old ouzerie near the Olympic Airways office in Heraklion.

Even by the standards of the day this place was basic. Candles and the glowing of an indoor barbeque provided the only light. Seating was on a muddle of stools and benches around old barrels and packing cases that served as tables.

The place was packed with workers, fishermen and market traders weathering the Saturday night storm in the cozy, warm, embrace of this unadorned drinking joint. The tiny windows ran with condensation, and the noise of animated discussion made more reserved conversation almost impossible.

On one table the men squeezed along their benches to make room for us. As if out of nowhere, clear, cold raki was brought in *carafachis*, the small vessels gleaming with condensation in the candlelight.

Then came the crabs, plates of small crustaceans each the size of a large coin, in their shells, straight off the barbecue. The trick was to crack the shells on the table and pick out the meat with your teeth before discarding the husk.

Looking down, the floor was littered with the shells of dead crabs and I noticed the occasional live one walking among the debris. On passing the cooking area I could see why. The crabs were delivered by the sackfull and just thrown onto the barbecue live. Many of them escaped the hessian bags before meeting their demise and scuttled away to hide in corners of the smoke-darkened room.

If dubious about the primitive nature of our meal, a few shots of raki soon erased any squeamishness on our part and the whole experience brought welcome warmth to the winter's night. Many years later I searched for the ouzerie but could not find it. I suspect it has been lost in the property development that has taken place since, or maybe I just can't remember its exact location. The former is more likely, but either is possible.

Greece's Day of Pride

If any colours can be said to represent Greece they are blue and white. Brightly painted blue shutters and doors are features on the faces of the brilliant white buildings that glisten in the sun across the whole of the nation. Blue eyes stare out of the white hulls of the fishing caiques that bob up and down at anchor in a thousand harbours and bays around its coasts. Most days in spring, summer and autumn the bluest of blue seas meets a white sky bleached by the fierce midday sun.

On one day in particular, the blue and white is even more in evidence than usual. On October 28th each year, the blue and white flag of Greece flutters from every available pole, mast or makeshift halyard across Heraklion, Crete and the whole of Greece. It flutters in remembrance of a noble nation's clear act of defiance, standing up against the Axis powers in World War Two, despite the devastating consequences.

The day is a national holiday and is celebrated with parades, feasting and dancing to mark one of modern Greece's finest hours. More than any other moment in Greek history this day epitomizes their belief in the battle cry from the War of Independence against the Ottoman Turks in the 1820s, *elefteria i thanatos* – freedom or death. Ochi Day quite literally means 'No Day', and marks the succinct reply given by Greek Prime Minister Ioannis Metaxas in response to an ultimatum from the Italian fascist dictator Benito Mussolini in 1940.

Following a party at the German Embassy in Athens, the Italian Ambassador to Greece, Emanuele Grazzi, approached Metaxas with Mussolini's demand that Greece should permit Axis forces to enter the country and take up whatever strategic positions they saw fit or face war.

The Prime Minister answered with the one word, '*ochi*' and that moment is now celebrated on October 28th each year. This was the start of Greece's bloody involvement in the Second World War. Within one-and-a-half hours of this refusal to cooperate, Italian troops were streaming over the border into Greece from bases in Italian occupied Albania.

The Italians, although vastly outnumbering the Greeks and having much superior firepower, were pushed back across the border in a humiliating defeat that many believe proved decisive in the final outcome of the war. Hitler was forced to commit large numbers of German forces to assist the Italians, and in so doing critically delayed his invasion of Russia, resulting in his troops having to fight on that front during the Soviet winter.

Although Greece succumbed to the military might of Germany, there was fierce resistance to the invaders that kept vast enemy resources occupied until mainland Greece was finally liberated in 1944.

Whether it is apocryphal or not, I would like to believe that it is true, as is claimed by many Greeks, that the nine blue and white stripes on the Greek flag symbolize the number of syllables in those three words, *elefteria i thanatos*, which so embodies the spirit of its people. How appropriate it is that this proud country is awash with blue and white flags on this special day.

A Dance on Zeus' Grave

'If snow falls in Heraklion, Zeus will die' my friend Vasilis had once mentioned in passing. I should have known better than to believe him because, although one of the most charming people you could meet, he was born without the reliability gene.

January was getting colder and colder. It became increasingly difficult to keep warm, particularly with my slightly naïve Cretan wardrobe of clothes. Coupled with this was the fact that, although I paid for heating in my apartment, it only came on in the mornings and evenings when I was at work – the times agreed by the other residents of my block.

I went to the market and invested in a heavy woollen jumper and a primitive heater that looked like a zinc satellite dish with a single exposed element in the centre. It would glow, lethally, before blowing the mains fuse in the flat. The biting wind blew through my louvred shutters and around the balcony door, creating an inescapable, bitter draught. I have only ever been as cold once since, and that was standing in a blizzard beside a geyser in Iceland. But this was Crete, less than a month earlier I had been swimming in the sea!

After days with the freezing gale showing no sign of abating I succumbed. I awoke one morning shivering and with an excruciating pain in my ear and the thickest of headaches. I had no phone in the flat so I dragged myself to work. My boss, Manolis, took the situation in hand the instant I walked into school. He whisked me off a few doors down the street to a room packed with coughing, wheezing people that I quickly identified as a doctor's waiting room.

'We may be some time', I thought as Manolis went to talk to the receptionist. Almost immediately the consulting room door opened and the doctor called my name. Manolis accompanied me into the surgery. After the routine checks, I was provided with antibiotics and painkillers the size of Frisbees right there and then. We left through the still-full waiting room. Back at the receptionist's desk, I noticed Manolis pass her some red plastic counters. This was the first time I had seen this practice in operation, which I later understood to be some sort of currency used between local businessmen. It was a sort of informal bartering system which, as well as being convenient and exclusive, may also have had some accounting advantages.

I felt a bit guilty about jumping the queue and wondered whether my privileged treatment was also part of this local business coalition. When I asked Manolis about this he said of course not, it was because I was a guest in their country and, more importantly, a teacher.

I was to experience this time and again, teachers in Greece are held in the highest esteem. In tavernas, carafes of wine were frequently brought to my table as gifts from other customers whose son, daughter, nephew or niece may at one time have been a pupil of mine. Sometimes I would go to pay my bill, only to be told it already had been settled.

After three days on the pills my condition improved, unlike the cold weather. As on most Saturdays, following morning school, a group of us would meet up at Terpsis, a taverna just off Plateia Daskalogianni. It was customary for us to kick off our weekend with a cheap meal, some wine and football on TV. The nights were drawing in, with dusk settling not long after 5 o'clock. Not much keeps the Greeks away from their football but through the large plate glass windows of the restaurant big, white flakes of snow began to fall. Within seconds conditions outside were almost blizzard.

Closely followed by us, all the customers in the taverna had rushed outside. Holding out their arms with palms upwards, bending down to touch the snow, laughing like children they instantly knew how to make snowballs as the blanket of white got thick enough to scoop off parked cars. The whole square became one massive snowball fight with children and adults revelling in, what for most, was a unique experience.

One of my friends lay down and started making snow angels, and their example was followed by most of the children in the square. Then we set about making a snowman, everyone joining in. After an hour or so we needed to get inside to warm up, but many of the locals played on until it was time for the children to go to bed and the grown ups to go home for dinner. We were going dancing.

We headed down from Elefterias Square towards the harbour along the strangely silent, snow-covered, Doukos Bofor to a traditional Cretan music club called Kastro. Nowadays this street is home to many different entertainment venues and clubs, but back then Kastro stood alone. We entered through the small front door into a dark cavernous hall already starting to fill up with locals.

We were with a number of Cretan friends who gave our orders to the waiters. They would then scribble them on the paper tablecloths crossing out the orders after they were delivered. The lighting in the room was low and the air was full with the smoke of hundreds of Karelia cigarettes being drawn on simultaneously.

Crackling with excitement, everybody seemed to be talking at once. The musicians appeared on the small, slightly-raised platform and began tuning their instruments. The band was led by a lyra player backed by bouzoukis.

The lyra is the embodiment of the sound of Crete. A three-stringed instrument with a pear-shaped body, it is played upright resting on the musician's knee. As the bow is drawn across the strings its melody haunts, rising and falling, increasing in intensity and pace until it reaches its climax.

As the lyra starts to weave its magic it delves into the soul of every Cretan. Men and women, young and old all fall under its spell.

A young man was the first to get to his feet and moved to the floor in front of the musicians. Another, then several more in quick succession joined him. Arms around each other's shoulders they formed a line slowly stepping left and right, flicking out their feet in unison.

The musicians began to wind up the tempo and, as they did, the dancers keep pace. At the leading end of the line the man who first took to the floor held up a red scarf and acrobatically leapt into the air, slapping the heal of his boot with his free hand.

As the music gained pace his jumps got higher, always at one with the music. The audience was drawn in to the performance, clapping and shouting encouragement. The music got faster and faster, all the time increasing in volume until it seemed impossible that the dancer could keep up. But he was drawn along by the power of the lyra. Glistening with sweat he never fell behind the rhythm, his jumps becoming more spectacular until the music reached its crescendo. And stopped.

The dancers left the floor to applause. A group of women, some in traditional costume of long, white embroidered pinafore dresses, others wearing more day-to-day clothes, took their place for a similar, if less acrobatic, dance. The night continued in this vein. Endless carafes of wine arrived on tables along with a myriad of mezzes. Conversation was in snatched shouts across the table.

Everybody danced, whatever their age or ability, and all were greeted with enthusiasm and encouragement. I was pulled onto the floor by my friends and joined the line sandwiched between two of them. All inhibitions quickly vanished as I followed their lead and the bewitching spell of the music took over. Cries of 'bravo', and 'opa' bolstered my confidence as the pace quickened, pulling us relentlessly towards the end of the dance.

Exhausted yet invigorated I collapsed into my seat for a welcome drink and a rest. It was not long before I was cajoled onto the floor again, protesting less each time. And so the night went on, when we finally fell out onto the street it was 3 o'clock in the morning. The snow had vanished.

Ross Daly – The Music Master

With his long hair blowing behind him as he sat astride an ancient motorbike with attendant sidecar, Ross Daly cut a remarkable figure in Heraklion when I lived there. But if his appearance was exceptional and distinguished, in no way could it reflect the talent that lies within this enigmatic musician. His story is extraordinary and I have been lucky enough to meet him on several occasions.

Ross speaks perfect Greek with a strong Cretan accent and is considered to be one of the finest lyra players and composers in Greece. To hear him play, it is easy to see why. I have listened to him playing music at impromptu gatherings in people's homes and in large concert venues, but wherever and whenever he plays, he achieves an extraordinary alchemy between himself, the music and the audience.

Born in England of Irish decent, he spent his childhood and formative years travelling the world with his family. First taught piano by his mother, he started learning the cello in America at the age of eight before taking up classical guitar when he was 11 years old and living in Japan. His prolific virtuosity has continued throughout his life, during which he has concentrated his musical sights mainly on the Eastern modal musical traditions. Travels in India, central Asia and the Middle East provided different musical influences, which radically changed his life, and the music he creates.

Determined to become an accomplished lyra player, in 1975 he came to Crete, which he had previously visited in 1970 and 1972. For six months he wandered from village to village listening to, and learning from, local musicians. Eventually he settled down in Chania under the tutelage of the master lyra player and composer Kostas Mountakis with whom he studied for many years.

The Cretans have taken Ross to their hearts and similarly he has greatly contributed to the musical landscape of the island. He has developed the lyra itself adding 22 sympathetic strings to the conventional instrument that resonate when the traditional three playing strings are bowed. He is also artistic director of the Musical Workshop Labyrinth which he established in 1982 and is now based in the small village of Hoedetsi, some 13 miles up into the hills to the south of Heraklion. Housed in a restored traditional manor house, the building is home to Ross' eclectic collection of approximately 250 musical instruments from around the world. Importantly the workshop seeks to introduce musicians to the musical idioms expressed through traditional music from across the globe.

Musicians come from far and wide to learn in traditional music masterclasses taught by the finest exponents of these various forms. Ross himself is fluent in his mastery of a wide range of stringed instruments both bowed and plucked. As well as the aforementioned lyra, he also plays another traditional Greek instrument, the boulgari, as well as the ud and saz, both of Turkish origin, the Afghan rubab and the rabab from Egypt.

His musical collaborations have seen him play with some of the greatest artists in the world and he has performed at major venues on all continents including UK locations as diverse as the Isle of Wight Festival and London's Queen Elizabeth Hall. In 2004 he was artistic director of the cultural programme for the Olympic Games taking place in Heraklion, which consisted of 15 concerts in which more than 300 musicians from all corners of the world performed.

To date he has released upwards of 35 albums of his own compositions and arrangements of traditional works he has stumbled across during a lifetime travelling. To Ross music is almost a religion, the way that he connects with himself and his audiences on a spiritual level, he believes it to be his essence and it is the strength of this connection which makes listening to him play such an all-embracing experience: it is not just entertainment, it is his whole world.

In most countries of the world he would be considered a superstar, but that is not Ross' way. Although held in the highest esteem, he is humble and self-effacing, insisting that it is the music that is important. It is for this reason that Crete suits him and he suits Crete, he respects and embraces the spirit of the place and sees his work as part of that whole big picture, whether it be creative improvisation or interpretations of traditional music.

I had not seen Ross for many years so decided to contact him to see whether he would mind me writing about him and the Musical Workshop Labyrinth. As usual, his response displays a modesty that is the mark of the man, 'I would be honoured to be mentioned in your new book'. Thanks Ross, the honour is all mine.

A Traditional Existence

My back felt as though it would go into spasm as we hit yet another pothole on the road which led out of Heraklion to Archanes. Perched with my bum just inches from the rear mudguard of the oldest, single-cylinder 250cc BMW motorbike I had ever seen, I wondered how it had managed to survive so many years. It was made of sturdier stuff than I was.

It was only a short journey I had been assured by Vasilis, the proud owner of the redoubtable machine on which we were bouncing uphill at an alarming rate. Ten miles might not seem far but, back then, this particular Cretan road was something of a challenge. To top that off, the late-autumn wind cut to the bone, making the short trip appear to last an eternity.

Vasilis had asked me to accompany him back to his village, as he had to return to vote in an election. He was a friend who worked as a waiter in my local taverna and I had been teaching him English. He said his mother would welcome the chance to show me some *philoxenia*, the traditional kindness of welcoming strangers.

When we arrived, despite the cold, she was outside sweeping the step up to her doorway. Vasilis was about my age, in his early twenties, but his mother was already a widow, dressed in the traditional black weeds. If I'd been asked her age I would have said around 70 years old, but common sense told me she was a lot younger, maybe by as much as 30 years.

Life was tough for the majority of Cretans who made their living from the land or at sea, this could be seen in the lines etched deep on Maria's face, which lit up at the sight of her son and me arriving on his battered motorbike. '*Ella, ella*', she called, 'come here, come here', as she ushered us through the front door, its green paint bleached by years of summer sun and peeling with age.

I had never been inside one of the traditional Greek cottages before and, like others, had been seduced by dreams of the simple life living in such a house. In the summer, with the sun reflecting off the peeling, faded stucco, and the residents sitting outside around a front door surrounded by pots of flaming orange begonias, the life appeared idyllic.

Stepping over the threshold into Vasilis' family house brought home the reality of how hard life for many people living in paradise could be. The room we entered served as both the main living and sleeping area, with a couple of wooden single beds pushed against two of the walls, a small table covered with an embroidered cloth and four upright chairs with rushwork seats. In one corner stood a wood-burning stove, with a single upholstered chair in front of it.

The floor was bare concrete covered by two woven woolen rugs. Off this living area, through an arched opening, was a tiny room, which housed a sink and a simple hob, more resembling a camping stove, and fuelled by bottled gas. There were shelves containing a few kitchen essentials and a tiny fridge. A door led from here to a back yard and outside toilet.

Maria disappeared into the adjoining room and fussed over filling the long-handled *kafebriko*, or coffee pot, with coffee grains, sugar and water before heating it on the hob making us a warming cup of Greek coffee, *metrio*, or medium. This was served in small white cups with a glass of water and a piece of baklava each. Maria had not bought one of the delicious nut, cinnamon and honey pastries for herself. As I thanked her she nodded, smiling all the time, then removed herself to her chair in front of the fire.

Vasilis had arranged for us to meet some friends of his at a local taverna that evening, then to spend the night at his family home before the election the following day, after which we would return to the city. One thing was playing on my mind. There were only two beds in the house. He assured me this would not be a problem.

Returning after our meal, I noticed a foldaway camp bed had been made up in the room. When it was time for bed I made to get into the put-you-up but I was told in no uncertain terms that I was to sleep in the bed made up with extra blankets and that Vasilis would have the other bed. Maria was adamant that that was the way it was to be.

Throughout the night I was grateful for the extra bedding as the wind rattled through the poorly fitted window frames and under the door, reaching even through the layers of blankets. I thought about how tough life was for the majority of everyday Greek people without the home comforts we take for granted. Vasilis waited tables to support his mother and try to secure some money to make the foundation for a better life. He still farmed his family's few olive trees in the autumn and hoped to buy some more. But his real dream was to open a jewellery shop to serve the burgeoning tourist industry.

Whenever I hear myself harking back to the halcyon days of a Greece before tourism had taken such a hold, I think of that night and the hospitality and welcome I was shown by people who had so little, but were willing to share what they had.

Hats off for Freedom

To the uninitiated, driving in Crete can seem intimidating. The first time I ventured out from Heraklion, it was nerve wracking. Grasping the wheel tightly, on the edge of my seat, I asked for complete silence in the car.

Wrong! This is not the way to approach the adventure of driving on Cretan roads.

The only way to survive is to relax and not be panicked by other drivers. Sit back, wind down the window hang out an arm and go at whatever speed you are comfortable with. The whole experience is more like cruising along a waterway, where avoidance of oncoming vehicles or those overtaking is the only priority.

Realizing that the white lines on your right do not delineate a hard shoulder is crucial. This is more of an intermittent crawler lane that it is perfectly acceptable to drive in. It is often the only place to find some road space if the oncoming traffic is overtaking three deep or you are being hooted at from behind by an impatient driver.

At the roadside all over Crete stand little shrines. Miniature churches which bear testament to one of the country's least enviable records. Each year, almost without fail, Greece tops the European Community chart for road deaths.

That they notch up almost three times the number of fatalities per 100,000 people per year as the UK is quite some achievement. Particularly considering the much lower volume of traffic.

To visitors' eyes, some of the driving is reckless at best and often appears downright suicidal. On roads that are littered with blind bends, unprotected sheer drops and indifferent surfaces, the relaxed attitude to any Highway Code accounts largely for the abundance of shrines.

This, coupled with the knowledge that, in Crete, around a third of all drivers do not possess a valid driving license and have never taken a lesson, let alone a driving test, means the incentives for going into the shrine-building business must be high! Indeed off-the-peg shrines can be bought alongside concrete barbecues in hardware stores and some garden centres.

The news is not all bad. The shrines are offerings to God not only in remembrance of those who lost their lives, but also by those thanking God that they survived. In terms of votive offerings its a win, win situation for the

Good Lord. Inside the shrines are usually a bottle of holy oil, an icon, a lighted candle and sometimes a picture of the victim. These are lovingly maintained by the families of the deceased, or people giving thanks that they have survived a crash.

It is illegal to ride a motorbike, moped or scooter in Crete without a crash helmet. I suppose that slightly more people do wear them now than did in the early Eighties when I first enquired as to whether or not they were compulsory. The answer was 'of course' as though my question was a stupid one. But the evidence of my eyes belied what I was being told. Some people did have helmets, but they wore them like bracelets over their wrists or strapped to the back of the saddle, never on their heads – except in the case of rain.

In the last couple of years there has been a clampdown on all aspects of road safety and, if stopped by the police, a rider may be asked to put one on and, if terribly unlucky, be fined if the policeman is late for his siesta. But it is interesting that the main reason for not wearing crash helmets is not the heat or even a casual disregard for road safety, although these might be contributory factors. The real reason is that it is compulsory to wear one.

Freedom and Death (*Captain Michalis* in Greek) is an epic Nikos Kazantzakis masterpiece about the Cretans' revolt against their Turkish overlords in 1889. Its hero, Michalis, is the embodiment of the Cretan spirit that cherishes freedom more dearly than anything else. Crete has spent so much of its history subjugated to foreign powers that freedom is not taken lightly.

It is a matter of pride that people cannot be told what to do, even if that is to wear a crash helmet! There is no malice intended in breaking the law, hence the compromise illustrated by carrying the helmets instead of wearing them. Most Cretans are natural existentialists and their love of freedom at all costs can be illustrated by the many ways they routinely reject any kind of state-imposed authority.

Amnissos – Knossos' Port

Just along the old coast road from the airport is Amnissos. Believed to have at one time been the site of the port for Knossos, today it heralds the start of a strip of tourist development, which stretches, almost uninterrupted, east to the other side of Malia. The beach lies just below the site of the airport runway and is a great place to watch the aircraft precariously descending and touching down right on the edge of the cliff above.

It is one of the nearest stretches of beach to Heraklion. As such, it is a favoured spot for locals just popping out for a few hours. Often a group of us would visit during siesta time and have a barbecue before returning to teach evening lessons. In high season, with regular flights taking off and landing, the beach is far from peaceful and I suspect it is only its proximity to the capital that accounts for its popularity.

The current settlement consists of hotels, apartments, tavernas and tourist shops and seems reluctant to reveal anything of its historic past. But the site is notable for two reasons. Firstly it was mention of Amnissos in several of the Linear B tablets, represented as 'a-mi-ni-so', found at Knossos that helped British classicists Michael Ventris and John Chadwick decipher the early Greek language. Secondly, in 1932 the archaeologist Spyridon Marinaos discovered the remains of a burned out villa dating back to the Minoan period. The villa is now named the 'House of the Lilies' after a remarkable fresco which has since been pieced back together which has as its subject pots of white and red lilies along with irises and other flowers. This still life is the subject of a six-foot tall frieze, which can be seen in the Archaeological Museum in Heraklion.

The remains of the house itself are unspectacular without the application of some imagination and a little background knowledge to fill in the pictures in the mind's eye. The excavations lie at the bottom of Palaiochora Hill and illustrate the footprint of a significant villa that had ten rooms over its two storeys. Nearby are the remains of a smaller building thought to have been the home of the port authorities and, further to the west, the site of an open-air temple dedicated to the god Zeus.

The sunken remains of the harbour walls and jetty now lie beneath sea level, which has risen some 10 ft since the Cretan Bronze Age. The port is thought to have been the departure point for the Cretan fleet, which fought in the Trojan Wars and, in Homer's *The Odyssey*, the harbour of Amnissos is a stop off point for Odysseus on his protracted journey home following that same conflict.

The harbour was not linked at the time to the capital of Knossos by any waterway. Goods would have been transported to and from the port along a track running through the hills to the south. Alongside the route is a cave dedicated to the Cretan goddess of childbirth, Eileithyia, mention of which has also been discovered, elucidated as 'e-re-u-ti-ja', in Linear B script and is also mentioned in both Homer's *The Iliad* and *The Odyssey*. Votive offerings to the Goddess of midwifery going back to Neolithic times have been discovered in the cave, which is no longer accessible. Also inside the cave, so I am told, is a giant stalagmite, which was thought to resemble the baby bump of a pregnant woman. Legend has it that up until 500 BC pregnant women would travel to touch their stomachs on this speleothem to auger them well for the birth.

The port of Amnissos is thought to have been destroyed by the same disaster that befell Knossos, although evidence of pumice found amongst the remains of the port authority offices led Marinatos to believe that the town and the other settlements on Crete were destroyed by the catastrophic explosion of the volcano of Santorini.

Gournes – Desolation Row

The Cretaquarium is in Gournes, 10 miles east of Heraklion. It is a modern tourist attraction, which has breathed some new life into a desolate area that used to be the site of a US airbase. The Americans moved out in

1994, handing the keys back to the Greek government and leaving the whole area to fall into disrepair.

Overgrown with weeds, buildings were occupied by squatters and their contents looted; prior to the building of the Aquarium the whole area was a shadow of its former self. Since the 1950s the base had been a little piece of America on Cretan soil. At the height of the Cold War it was used by the US Air Force's surveillance services.

The local population had mixed feelings about the base. It brought many much-needed jobs to the area and local people were employed in the industries that serviced what was, in fact, a small town.

However, the Americans were perceived to have propped up the earlier military dictatorship, and their failure to intervene in the 1974 partition of Cyprus by the Turks also contributed to the wider population's muted enthusiasm towards the base's presence.

In 1981, Andreas Papandreou's Pan Hellenic Socialist Party (PASOK) had been elected to government on a platform of withdrawal from both NATO and the European Economic Community, although Greece's first socialist government pragmatically reversed these policies on their subsequent election. But among the people there remained strong opposition to NATO. Many Cretans, in particular, had sympathies that didn't lie on the side of the Americans during the Cold War.

Despite their political objections to the air base, as far as I know, the Americans who worked there were never treated with anything but respect, sometimes even when their insensitivity to the feelings of the local people didn't deserve it.

I once witnessed a US airman walking through the market in Heraklion wearing a flying jacket. Emblazoned on the back was 'I Bombed Saigon in 1968', a reference to America's scorched earth carpet-bombing of South Vietnam which claimed more than 10,000 victims.

I visited the base on several occasions, and it was just like a chip off the American block. Going there was to step into a different world. It had shops, a bank, in which a friend of mine worked, a bowling alley, cinema, church, hospital and numerous bars among a host of other modern facilities. Food and drink was scrupulously American and it was rare for its inhabitants to attempt to try and cross the cultural bridge between their way of life and that of the locals.

In stark contrast to the Americans, Greek service personnel were subject to far less luxurious conditions. On returning to Crete in 1984, a former pupil of mine, my ex boss' son, Yanis, insisted on taking us out to a bar. He was doing his three years of National Service, as all Greek men had to.

He bought a round of drinks for my wife and I and himself, the cost of which came to more than his government allowance for the month. He was lucky that he was the child of a reasonably wealthy family. For many at the time, supporting their sons through a protracted period of military conscription could be a considerable financial burden. Nowadays, the period of service has been reduced to nine months for most people and private wealth has increased, but the privations imposed still make the system a tough rite of passage.

If the base used to resemble a little piece of America, it still has a distinctly American feel to it, but now more a depression era desert scene, with tumbleweed blowing through deserted buildings. Turning off the national highway and driving through the area that used to be inhabited by the airbase, the irony for any of those who have visited the largely unsympathetic wholesale tourist development that has taken place just along the coast in Hersonnisos and Malia is clear. Here lies a vast area of land, right beside the sea, which can only be improved by being built on. The Cretaquarium and the nearby exhibition centre stand alone in acres of deserted wasteland.

The aquarium itself is worth a visit if you have a spare couple of hours. Inside are tanks displaying all sorts of sea life indigenous to the region; from tiny sublime seahorses to the loggerhead turtle, a species conservationists are desperately trying to preserve in island waters, particularly on beaches around Chania and Rethymnon in the north west of the island, Messara Bay in the south and Almyros Beach in the north east near Agios Nikolaos.

These loggerhead turtles have swum in the waters around the island since the time of the dinosaurs, but the massive increase in tourism over recent years has put their future in severe jeopardy. The loggerheads return to the same beaches every year between June and September to lay their eggs. Of course, these months coincide with the summer high season where sandy beaches are at a premium. Building and beach erosion and the paraphernalia of sunbeds and umbrellas all threaten the fragile environment of the nesting areas. After laying her eggs in the sand a mother loggerhead will return to the sea leaving the eggs, which will hatch after about 55 days when the young make their perilous journey across the beach to the sea. Only one in a thousand of these baby turtles will make it through to adulthood, and many adult loggerheads are killed or injured by being caught in fishing nets or hit by pleasure craft, so the odds are desperately stacked against them. A recent scientific survey has suggested that loggerheads do not reach maturity until they are 45 years old, which contributes to the species' vulnerability due to the time-scale required to reverse any fall in the population. As the turtles do not breed until so late in life they have a high chance of being killed before they can reproduce and the species can replace itself. This makes the conservation of these treasured creatures in the face of man-made pressures an expensive and lengthy job.

Other popular species among the 250 or so kept at the aquarium are the sharks, which patrol the largest of the tanks, exuding a predatory menace from behind the comforting barrier of a glass wall. Unlike the loggerhead turtle, any sharks that do inhabit the Mediterranean stay well away from the shore and there has never to my knowledge been a shark attack in Crete. Other nasties that can cause some discomfort, however, if encountered in the wild are on exhibit.

Top of the list are jellyfish that can drift inshore and lurk, barely visible, just beneath the surface in readiness for the unsuspecting swimmer. I have been stung on three occasions and it is not pleasant. Although I have not tried it, urine is said to take away the sting, although vinegar is as effective and anti-histamine tablets or a cream can also ease the inflammation.

Black spiky sea urchins also linger, clinging to underwater rocks. Stepping on them can prove agonizing, although unlikely to do lasting damage apart from that to your pride from the subsequent – and inevitable – embarrassing hop up the beach.

Removing the broken-off spikes with tweezers is the uncomfortable solution to this one. If you want to get your own back, there are some tavernas that serve up the roe of the little blighters with olive oil and lemon juice as a mezze. For those who adhere to the adage that revenge is best served cold, believe me – in this instance – this is not the case. To be fair, there are many Greeks who would disagree with my culinary assessment of this all-too-plentiful ingredient.

Other prickly, and potentially more dangerous, hazards that lie beneath the waves are not as likely to bother you, but their stings can be extremely painful and it is advisable to seek medical attention, although locals will tell you the aforementioned pee or vinegar will ease the symptoms. These pests are the red-coloured scorpion fish that swim among the rocks and the less flamboyant grey weaver fish that inhabit the sandy bottom of the seabed. Both species can frequently be seen when snorkelling and, if disturbed, will quickly swim away. The danger is in the unlikely event of stepping on one or, if fishing, taking your catch off the hook. Scorpion fish or *scorpidi* can also be seen on the menu in many a restaurant and once devoid of their poisonous spikes are delicious either grilled or in a fish stew.

The 'Party Towns'

Reemerging from the dark of the aquarium heading away from the sea across the deserted weed-strewn concrete and back onto the old national road, one can find the big resorts that inhabit the next few miles of coastline going east. These are the places that the new national highway to the south allows the discerning traveller to bypass.

I feel daunted to return to the coastal strip towns of Hersonissos and Stalis. Perhaps this is because they merge into Malia. These two resorts sit on the old coast road and can easily be bypassed by taking the new national highway, unfortunately until recently the same could not be said for Malia, which was difficult to avoid. Now the new road bypasses Malia as well, coming out about three miles to the east of the town.

Many people might consider my dismissal of these 'party towns' as unfair. I am aware that hundreds of thousands of tourists flock to these resorts every year and have a great time. There is no doubt that this stretch of coastline is beautiful, as are the beaches. The natural splendour of these places highlights the destructive influence of the incursion of generic US burger joints, fried chicken stores, faux Irish pubs and cafes selling poor imitations of north European cuisine.

Hersonissos sits at the gateway to this man-made hell. Out of season it shows glimpses of its former charms. Strictly speaking this is actually Limin Hersonissos, meaning the port of Hersonissos; Hersonissos itself being a small village inland. The original town was the port for Lyttos, a significant city during the Ancient Greek period. Mentioned in the Homeric canon, it is thought to be near the Psychoro cave, the legendary birthplace of Zeus, on the fringes of the Lassithi Plateau.

For those who choose to stop and walk down to the seafront, there is evidence of the former Roman settlement that inhabited this site. Most notably this takes the form of a pyramid-shaped fountain decorated with a mosaic depicting fishing scenes. There is little else to remind the visitor of the port's former glories, although there is an interesting living open-air folk museum called Lychnostatis, which has been built next to the sea to the east of the town. The irony of this won't escape the interested visitor, the exhibits depicting life as lived in a traditional Cretan village, which can be observed elsewhere in any number of real villages. The museum has been built amidst this concrete jungle to remember a way of life that is disappearing.

If visitors get fed up eating fast food and drinking lager, there is horse riding, a golf course and a couple of water parks nearby. However, for those who enjoy their thrills fast and wet there is a much better water park called Water City to the south, high up in the mountains in Anopoli.

I have never worked out whether the development of the 'party town' of Malia is a disaster or an ingenious plot by the Cretan authorities to confine the worst aspects of tourism to one area. A dangerous cocktail of the relentless pursuit of profit by Greek businessmen and the unceasing hedonism of holidaymakers has created a living hell out of what was once a Garden of Eden.

Putting the genie back in the bottle is proving difficult. The authorities are fighting an ongoing battle to try and balance the need for locals to make a living and the integrity of the island as a tourist destination. The police are increasingly coming down hard on drunken, violent behaviour in the resort, but as yet their strong-arm tactics have had little effect.

It was not always like this. Malia was a small town, stretching south into the hills from the old national highway. A single road, flanked with tavernas, the odd car-hire company and shops ran north, down to an expansive, golden beach. This road cut through plantations of fruit trees that flourished on the land between the coast and the main thoroughfare.

In 1985 my wife and I stayed in some apartments on that main road. From our balcony we could reach out and pick oranges off the trees. A stroll out from behind the pension would lead to the beach, maybe half a mile away, a walk uninterrupted by any buildings. Over the following 10 years, it seemed like every square yard had been built upon. The fruit trees were long gone, and in their place blossomed acres of concrete apartment blocks.

A pre-dawn drive from Heraklion airport to Agios Nikolaos some years later bore witness to the decline. Fights broke out along the main street and drunken bodies sprawled on the pavements. The crime rate in the town is staggering for Crete, which prides itself on how law-abiding it is. Murders are not unknown in Malia! Outside the town, such conduct is a topic of conversation returned to again and again by Cretans. They are in turn both shocked at the behaviour and grateful it is not in their back yard. Perhaps, occasionally, there may be just a hint of envy at the living to be made there!

It is interesting that the 2011 hit British movie *The Inbetweeners* was set in Malia, but in reality was shot on the Spanish Balearic island of Mallorca. I cannot comment on why such a decision was made by the producers of the film!

Malia – The Palace on the Plain

Going east out of Malia town, navigating the weaving quad bikes and coaches dropping off and picking up visitors, about two miles from the centre on the coastal side of the road is Malia's redeeming feature. Strangely, considering its location, it is often deserted.

The Palace of Malia is unlike most other Minoan palaces in that it is built on the windswept coastal plain rather than inland on higher ground. As well as the palace, remains of a town and a graveyard have also been discovered. If the site itself is not as instantly gratifying as Knossos, this is perhaps because it has not been reconstructed.

The lack of visitors and remote location allows space for the imagination to build the pillars and walls that transport me back in time. Although, in comparison to Knossos, the Malia Palace might hide its light under an archaeological bushel, this should not diminish its importance as a site, which many archaeologists believe has been more sympathetically excavated than its brasher and more popular compatriot.

The excavations found here reveal the second palace, which was destroyed in around 1450 BC, along with many other Minoan settlements on the island. Whether it was the same volcanic eruption that hit Santorini and the likely tsunami that ensued, or whether it was attacked and raised to the ground by Mycenean invaders is still cause for debate. But one thing is known, that the palace at Malia, unlike Knossos, was not inhabited again after this disaster.

Whatever the truth, we do know that this was the second palace to be built here following the destruction of the first incarnation, which was constructed in 1900 BC and was destroyed 200 years later by a suspected earthquake. Built of limestone and mud bricks around a huge central courtyard, the site was discovered by Joseph Hadzidakis in 1915 and in 1922 was put under the aegis of the French School, an archaeological institute in Athens, to proceed with more comprehensive excavations. Their work since has been painstaking and sympathetic and is still continuing.

As the hot breath of the August wind blows down the mountains it whips up the dust on this arid shelf of land perched within earshot of the crashing waves on the north coast. I wander around some of the ruins and take the aerial walkways spanning the more sensitive areas. Staircases ascend to where second storey rooms once stood but now lead nowhere but to the dazzling sapphire sky. They serve as a reminder of the fragile nature of even the most sophisticated man-made conceits. A place to look down on the imprint of a lost society – the altar where sacrifices were made to the gods, circular foundations of rooms built for the storage of grain and giant earthenware pots long since empty of oil and wine.

The place where the palace stood has changed not one jot since the time it was built, and is a perfect spot to contemplate the transience of man. What is left of the palace blends into these stark surroundings according it a timeless allure that the busier historical sites find difficult to match. This place has surrendered many artifacts; to my mind the most magical is the sublime golden ornament representing two bees holding a drop of honey that is now on display in the Archaeological Museum in Heraklion.

A walk to the sea then west will take you back towards Malia, turn east and Crete offers something of its real natural grandeur as the coastline begins to get more rugged. To progress at any sort of pace you will need to return to the old national highway and make sorties coastwards on the numerous turnings that head through the hills to the sea beyond.

Krasi's Claim to Fame

Returning from a trip to Lassithi Plateau for a lunch of mezzes and *souvlaki* grilled on an outside barbecue, washed down with marvellous local red wine leaves us snoozing in the car. As the road winds its way down from the Diktean Mountains that skirt the plateau, we descend Mount Selena and make a stop at a small village called Krasi.

Whether it is named after wine or not I am unsure but our friend Stelios, who is driving, tells us that any association with the Greek word for wine (*krasi*) is purely coincidental. The name is more likely to derive from the ancient Greek kras, meaning top, possibly due to its mountainside location looking down over Malia.

This pretty village, however, is renowned for its association with another drink, as some locals claim it to be the home of raki. In Crete, raki is distilled from all the leftovers of the winemaking process and its strength is variable, but always to be respected as it frequently reaches 70 per cent alcohol.

This can be dangerous stuff if drunk in large quantities and is best taken with mezzes and frequent glasses of water between *carafachis*, the small, glass vessels in which it is usually served. We settle to try some of the local brew in a taverna, sitting under the most extraordinary tree I have ever seen. This is Krasi's other claim to fame.

A plane tree, it stands at the heart of the village and is the largest in Europe. And, at over 1,000 years old, is believed to be the oldest tree on the island. Its trunk has a circumference of approximately 80 ft! Just across the road from where we sit is an ancient laundry where clear mountain water still gurgles out of a spring, cold and refreshing to drink or splash on your face to relieve the heat of the strident mid-afternoon sun.

We take to the car again and continue our descent towards the coastal plain just east of Malia. As the road flattens out, we pass through fields with huge polythene-covered greenhouses in varying states of repair. Through rips in the sides of some of them bananas can be seen ripening on the palms.

Stelios points out to us the holes in the road signs on these country tracks; these, so he says, are made by locals using them for target practice. Gun ownership in Crete is believed to be one of the highest in the world, although gun crime is virtually non-existent. The law is that gun owners should be licensed and over the age of 18, but a permit is not required to openly carry a firearm. It is likely that these laws, like many others, are not universally adhered to, and considering Crete's turbulent history, that is hardly surprising. To a Cretan it is his birthright to defend his family and his country against the forces of oppression.

Nowadays one suspects shooting at road signs just allows the men to keep their eye in, which is probably just as well as it is tradition for guns to be fired off at celebrations like weddings where, on occasion, people have been shot accidentally!

Phaistos – The Unsung Palace

The Minoan Palace of Phaistos is less heralded than its counterpart Knossos. This is due to the archaeological emphasis having been on conservation rather than restoration. Excavated by a team led by the Italian archaeologist Federico Halbherr, the founder and first director of the Italian Archaeological School of Athens, who was also responsible for significant work on the nearby sites of Gortys and Phaistos' summer palace at Agia Triada. His first digs were carried out around the same time Evans was excavating Knossos.

If the site is more remote than its famous counterpart, it is no less spectacular. It reclines, looking down on the Messara Plateau surrounded by the mountains with the island's highest peak Psiloritis to the north and the Asterousia range to the south. It is little more than a stone's throw from the coastal villages of Matala and Agia Galini. If Phaistos sometimes falls under the shadow of Knossos' celebrity status, it could be argued that here it was that one of the greatest archaeological mysteries of all time was discovered – the Phaistos Disc. The Italian Luigi Pernier, one of Halbherr's team, discovered the disc on this site in 1908. I have described it in more detail in the piece concerning the Heraklion Museum.

Like many ancient sites on Crete, the provenance of Phaistos is shrouded in mystery. Some legends have it that its first ruler was Rhadamanthys, the brother of King Minos who ruled Knossos, both of them sons of Zeus and Europa. What is certain is this palace lived a parallel existence to Knossos and was built on the site of a major settlement dating back to as early as 4000 BC; the first palace being constructed around 2000 BC.

The remains here do not tower above me, as they do in spectacular fashion in places at Knossos. But what is here is enough to fire the imagination as to what the palace might have been like. What I am looking at is the remains of the second palace. This was built around 1700 BC following the destruction of the first incarnation of the building, which was destroyed by an earthquake. Fortunately the new palace was built using much of what was left of the older buildings as its foundations. This has left an archaeological heritage, which has presented modern-day scientists with evidence of the oldest palatial buildings on Crete. These remains of the old palace can clearly be seen in some areas of the site, particularly in the north-east and south-west corners. Access to much of the original footprint is restricted as excavations are still taking place, and other vulnerable areas need to be protected from the ravages of mass tourism.

Sometime in the 14th Century BC, the New Palace was destroyed at around the same time as Knossos, probably by Myceneans who took control of most of the island.

Gortys – The Ancient Capital

Not the most popular archaeological location in Crete when set against Knossos and Phaistos, Gortys can still lay claim to a similar billing in terms of its historical significance. The site is extensive, and much is in the process of being excavated. It was the capital of Crete between 67 BC when the Romans conquered the island until 828 AD when it was sacked by Saracen invaders. Prior to this it is believed that here, on the plain of Messara, was the site of the first human habitation of the island. Although later, during the Minoan dynasty, it was subjugate to Knossos and nearby Phaistos.

In myth the settlement was named after Gortys the son of Radamanthys, the ruler of Phaistos who was the brother of the great king Minos of Knossos. Legend has it that it was here that the god Zeus, disguised as a bull, made love under a plane tree to Europa, a princess he had abducted from the Lebanon. The affair resulted in the birth of three children, Minos, Rhadamanthys and Sarpedon, who grew up to rule Lycia on the south coast of Turkey and was killed by Patrocolus in the Trojan War.

Gortys is well spread out and is not all accessible, but it is slowly revealing its secrets and the immense influence the town has had on the island's history. By the 1st Century BC, Gortys had already established itself as the premier influence in the Messara region, having succeeded nearby Phaistos, whose power was in terminal decline. Its position was further boosted by pragmatic support of the Roman invaders in 67 BC who, in return, declared the city capital of Crete, deposing Knossos. This prestigious title was then supplemented by becoming capital of Crete and Cyrenaica. From Gortys a Roman governor now ruled not only the island but also a significant amount of North Africa, including Egypt.

The mighty city held this position of influence until the earthquake of 796 AD did it significant damage. It clung onto its power until Saracens from Iberia invaded it 32 years later under the command of Abu Hafs. The raiders sacked the city, murdering thousands, including Archbishop Cyril of Gortys, selling any captured survivors into slavery. This marked the end of the

Byzantine chapter in the island's history. The capital was moved north to the new town of Candia, modern day Heraklion, which was built by the Muslims as a centre for piratical activities as they sought to control the eastern Mediterranean.

Prior to this, Gortys had been the largest Christian basilica on Crete with a cathedral dedicated to Saint Titus, the first Christian bishop who had been sent on a mission by St Paul to bring religion to the people of the island. The skull of the bishop now lives in the cathedral named after him in Heraklion. He died in 107 AD at the ripe old age of 95.

If it was from Gortys that Bishop Titus established Christianity, it has another extraordinary claim to fame. Following the rediscovery of the site by the celebrated Cretan archaeologists Stefanos Xanthoudides and Iosif Hatzidakis and their Italian counterpart Federico Halbherr, what is now known as the Gortys Code was uncovered.

Entering the enclosed site, having paid the small entry fee, I pass the remains of the magnificent Byzantine cathedral dedicated to Bishop Titus in the 6th Century. Although derelict, the impressive apse remains intact and the surrounding fallen masonry attests to the grandeur of the building, which during Gortys' period as capital of Crete would have been the most important church on the island. However, it is beyond these towering yellow, white and grey-stained walls that lies the current home of what many consider to be Classical Greece's most important legacy to the world, the Great Code.

This is the Odeon, the ancient covered theatre from Roman times, built during the reign of Emperor Trajan in the early 1st Century BC. From the remains were excavated the stones of a former structure which dates back some 400 years earlier. These contain the oldest and most comprehensive example of Ancient Greek law. Carved by hand, it is the work of a single stonemason and is now part of the walls of a modern structure built directly behind the four-stepped seating gallery of the theatre.

The laws are written in a Cretan dialect from Dorian times and read in two directions. The first line from left to right, the second right to left and so on as the reader snakes their way down the twelve columns of five foot high inscription which amounts to some 600 lines, which cover the laws that governed the hierarchical Ancient Greek society. Translations give a unique insight into a society, which although didn't see all people as equal under the law was, in some ways, surprisingly enlightened.

The code deals with civil law and gives us an insight into the society of the day and how it was structured. There was a clearly defined hierarchy of citizens, labourers and slaves. Among other things, the laws deal with inheritance, property rights, divorce, adultery, rape and adoption and the relevant fines for transgression. The code also enshrines the right of an accused individual to their freedom before they come before the court. Various fines were levied against any who didn't respect this right, depending on the social status of the parties involved.

The code seems most enlightened in the detail and equanimity it gives to property rights. If a wife dies, her property has to be put in trust and managed by her husband until the children come of age, if the husband remarries, the children would immediately inherit the property. Vice versa is true if a husband were to die. Adoption was commonplace and all adoptive children would hold exactly the same rights as the birth children of their parents.

It is extraordinary to think this code is the written manifestation of a sophisticated system of law, which up until the point it was inscribed on these stone tablets had been passed down by word of mouth. Here I am staring at the foundations that make modern governance possible. Behind the wall bearing the laws is a massive plane tree. Legend has it that this is the very same tree beneath which Zeus and Europa conceived the future King Minos. Young couples still visit the spot to pick a leaf from the tree as a good luck charm for their future fertility.

Leaving the fenced in part of the site, I walk back across the road, which crosses the river Mitropolitanos. Whether this is named after the tiny settlement of Mitropolis through which it flows or the reverse I am not sure, but I strike out in the opposite direction past a disused water mill and the remains of another theatre and start climbing the hills through which the river has carved its valley.

I am heading for the ancient acropolis which is the hill looking over the city. What looked an easy climb from below becomes a mammoth trek in the heat of the sun. I should have guessed, as *acropolis* means 'high city' in Greek. When I reach the top and plonk myself down for a rest I realize that I am the only person up here, others were rewarded by not aching and being able to breathe easily, but I had gained an unforgettable moment. Atop the acropolis are the still consequential walls of the Roman fortifications and also a few less substantial remains of a Greek temple. Even more impressive is the view across the Messara Plain with the whole extent of Gortys visible below. Running in from the mountains to the site of the Odeon and cathedral, the line along which the mighty aqueducts ran, delivering water to the city, can clearly be seen. Scanning to the south east, I make out the amphitheatre and stadium. The scale of the site is just mind boggling and alone, looking down, if I block out the cars in the car park, it is easy to be transported back in time. The landscape has changed little in thousands of years and the laws recorded in Gortys have also endowed us with a great lasting legacy.

The Ancient Health Spa of Lendas

It is hard to pinpoint what makes me return to Lendas. It is unassuming and less self confident than nearby Matala and Agia Galini. Looking slightly crumpled, it shuffles along the edge of a small, none-too-sheltered bay to the south of Gortys, which held it as a satellite port during the Hellenistic and later Roman period. It must have had some attraction, as the trek along steep and twisting tracks to Gortys would have been tortuous.

Out on a limb, it has the good fortune to remain a peaceful spot, and its other claim to fame is that in the 4th Century BC it was a health spa. Just before entering the village from inland, on the left are the remains of the old healing centre, which is open to the public until mid afternoon. This is the only existing imprint of the ancient town of Levin.

It is a sizeable site and, in its prime, must have been popular. Its attraction was the therapeutic waters that bubble up from the hillside springs, which were diverted into a system of tunnels and baths. The warriors of Gortys were the first to make use of its restorative qualities, lounging in the baths and letting the waters work their alchemy on bodies exhausted from their piratical adventures.

The fame of this relaxing spa spread throughout Crete and even abroad to mainland Greece, other islands and the north of Africa. When the Romans arrived in Crete and established Gortys as their capital, it did not take them long to discover the pleasures of the springs and they did significant restorations. Those who were cured of ailments would bring presents to the god of healing, which were hidden deep in a seven-foot square pit in a corner of the old temple. This was covered by a stone, which could only be accessed by the use of an early sort of key. However, when Italian archaeologists first rediscovered the site in 1900, the stone had been shattered and all the contents looted.

The scant remains of a large temple to the god of healing, Asklepios, gives an indication of the importance of this site in those days. A spectacular multicoloured mosaic of a frolicking seahorse fashioned in red, white and black pebbles remains remarkably vibrant after two-and-a-half thousand years in situ. A more modern 11th-century Christian chapel still stands near the site, but the healing qualities of the waters seem to have been consigned to history, and few people visit here now.

The beach, like the rest of the village is modest and the small plateia in its centre accommodates the tavernas, bars and basic shops providing for the simple needs of the traveller. Lendas has something of a faded past about it – although hippies no longer walk the streets, you can feel their ghosts walking the cobbled paths or lying smoking on the grey pebbles of the beach. From above, the bay is said to resemble the head of a lion, but I have yet to see any real resemblance, and indeed the name Lendas is a derivation of leonidas meaning son of a lion. The prevailing atmosphere is less of a roar and more of a whisper as locals sit watching the world go by in the shade of vibrant pink and purple bougainvillea plants cascading from the balconies above, and the cobalt sea gently ingratiates itself with the rocky shore.

Matala – At Last

My journey to Matala had been a long one, spanning some 27 years. Back in the early Eighties it still held a mystique unique on the island. This stemmed from its reputation as a destination for hippies of all nationalities on the trail eastwards towards Turkey and on to India in the Sixties and early Seventies. The irony of the heyday of these seekers of an alternative society almost exactly coinciding with the fascist dictatorship in Greece was clear to many of the locals at the time even if it had passed most of the temporary residents by, a large number of whom were Americans escaping a homeland deeply embroiled in an unwinnable war in Vietnam.

The appeal of this Shangri La was obvious. It is a small, idyllic bay with a part sand, part pebble beach fringed by tamarisk trees and cliffs tilted by earthquake and burnished by tsunami sliding down into the tepid waters of the Libyan Sea. Out of these extraordinary rock formations, some earlier Neolithic settlers had hewed around 50 caves out of the sandstone. Throughout Minoan times the village served as the port for Phaistos, which lies several miles inland and the caves were inhabited by fishermen and port workers. In 220 BC the Gortynians assimilated the small village and following the Roman invasion in 67 BC, the city of Gortys became the capital city of the island and Matala served as its main port. The Romans used the caves as burial sites. Legend has it that the Roman general Brutus visited the caves during this period (around 44 BC) and one of the caves is known as Brutospeliana in recollection of his visit, just after his involvement in the assassination of Julius Caesar.

Following the demise of the Romans, Matala reverted to a sleepy fishing village which, apart from a period as a leper colony during the Middle Ages, it remained, until discovered by the hippies in the early 1960s. The caves, despite their undoubted archaeological interest, had lain unprotected for all the intervening centuries. They became the ideal free habitations for the young travellers searching for a cheap alternative society.

An article about the hippies living in the caves was featured in the American magazine *Life* in 1968. Written by the celebrated investigative journalist Thomas Thompson it added to the attraction of the village as a destination for young people who sought to drop out of conventional society.

When I first visited Crete, Matala still maintained a reputation built on those earlier heady days and latter-day peace-seekers would still visit to pay homage long after the caves had been shut off to casual access. It was a long old journey from Heraklion by bus and with time off being in short supply I just never quite got around to visiting. However, the fascination lingered and I finally made the trip in the summer of 2011.

The reputation of Matala was further given credence by the fact that the iconic Canadian folk superstar Joni Mitchell visited for several weeks in 1970 and wrote the evocative and lyrical song *Carey* – a track off what is considered by many to be her greatest album, *Blue*, and makes reference to this small village in the lines; 'The night is a starry dome, And they're playin' that scratchy rock and roll, beneath the Matala moon.' The Carey of the title is believed to be a fiery red-haired American cook who lived in the cave community whom Joni hooked up with on her visit there. That the singer visited is in no doubt but other stories about Bob Dylan and Cat Stevens dropping by appear to be more apocryphal. Another myth is that Zeus brought Princess Europa to the beach in the form of a white bull, before turning her into an eagle and flying with her to nearby Gortys where he seduced her.

Approaching Matala today, it is noticeable that the road surface is probably the best I have encountered on Crete, the flat, dark tar-macadam throwing up shimmering mirages in the midday sunshine. On the outskirts of town rows of coaches are parked in designated ranks and when we reach the seafront there is a car park between the shops and tavernas and the beach with not a space to be had. With Mitchell's influence being so important in the recent history of the town it brings to mind another one of her songs, *Big Yellow Taxi*, which opens; 'They paved paradise and put up a parking lot', coincidentally released the year she visited Matala.

Half a century after the first hippies found their paradise, it is their reputation that has contributed to Matala's development as a tourist resort. Eventually driven out of the caves by the police of the military junta and the disapproval of the religious right, the hippies had inadvertently contributed to the establishment of a highly viable destination supporting numerous tavernas, shops and hotels and pensions. Tour guides lead groups of picture-snapping tourists as they clamber through the caves. Occasional street traders sporting 21st-century hippy-chic sell hand-made jewellery or tout henna tattoos and west-coast rock can occasionally be heard emanating from the odd café, but largely the village of legend has been subsumed into just another tourist resort.

Sissi – Paradise Regained

Sissi is a small resort less than seven miles from Malia, but it could be a million miles away. At Sissi Paralia, little over a mile from the main village there is a wonderfully undisturbed small harbour. Surrounded as it is by tavernas and kafenions, it is a mesmeric place to eat a dinner of fish in the early evening as the sun sinks, leaving the lights from the restaurants reflected in the lapping water left by the wash from an outgoing caique departing for a night's fishing in the hidden bays to the east.

Further along the coast road, things get quieter still as you pass through Milatos, a few tavernas sit beside the rocky beach here, one at least with a permanent barbecue ready to cook your choice of fish selected from the kitchens, served whole with lemon juice and oil and a sprig of freshly picked herbs from the mountains that loom as a backdrop to the village.

Milatos may seem nothing more than an unpretentious seaside village, but in Minoan times it was a mighty city from where a fleet embarked to fight in the Trojan Wars. It was ruled by Sarpedon, the brother of King Minos himself. Having fought his brother for the throne, the defeated Sarpedon left Crete to found the city of Miletus, named after his home town, which became the wealthiest Greek City in Asia Minor, near what is now Akkoy in Turkey. There is little evidence of the former splendour of Milatos, although some archaeological evidence has been discovered in an area to the east of the current seafront community. By the time of the Roman occupation there was no record of the settlement still being in existence.

A couple of miles inland up the steep mountain road is a spot that is remembered for a more inglorious chapter of history. Milatos Cave is a series of caverns split across three levels that encroach into the mountainside for thousands of feet. It was here that during an insurgency against the Turks a huge number of Greek Cretans, upwards of 2,500, sought refuge to escape Ottoman reprisals. Hiding out amongst the stalagmites and stalactites in the maze of caverns they were discovered and the Turks laid siege to the cave. With no way out, they accepted an offer of safe conduct from the leader of the besieging troops but, on their surrender, the Ottomans reneged on the agreement and massacred many and sold the others into slavery.

Lassithi Plateau – The Winds of Change

The sight of thousands of windmills in full sail on Lassithi Plateau is one of the most spectacular I have ever experienced. I remember the disappointment of taking a trip there some years later with my children when I returned to the island only to find out that they were gone. Progress had apparently dictated that the pumps drawing the water to feed this fertile plain were now to be operated by electricity, frequently provided by diesel generators. On my most recent visit to the area, I was interested to hear that applications were being prepared for European Community grant money to install wind turbines to drive the pumps since the price of conventional electricity is so prohibitive. The irony of this is not lost on many of the farmers who were encouraged to abandon the old windmills in favour of the less labour-intensive electric pumps, but who are now faced with the subsequent electricity bills.

Putting disappointment aside, the Plateau is still a remarkable place, a flat patchwork quilt of arable land encircled by mountains with small village communities dotted around a road that traverses the highlands marking out the circumference of this extraordinary land of plenty. It is like a lost world, kept hidden from outsiders by the forbidding landscape that surrounds it. In winter the quilt loses its vibrant contrasting colours and is transformed to a pure white counterpane as, sitting at 2,750 ft above sea level it is frequently covered in snow for weeks on end. In this hidden world up in the skies, more than 10,000 white sailed windmills used to utilize the winds which frequently sweep in gusts through the gaps in the surrounding mountains to suck water rich in alluvial goodness to the surface providing nourishment for the abundant crops which flourish here, potatoes and fruit trees laden with apples and pears in autumn and resplendent with blossom in the spring.

Although now inhabited all year around, the plateau can become inaccessible in winter leaving villages cut off for weeks on end. But the flat surface of the soils enriched by run-off waters from the melted snow has meant that this remote area produces high crop yields which have encouraged settlers to put up with the hardships of living there since Neolithic times. Known to have been inhabited since around 6000 BC, its isolation and ability to provide food for troops from the resistance movement led to its depopulation for a period of two centuries from 1293 AD. The ruling Venetians saw the area as a hotbed of insurgency and, in response to frequent rebellions, sent troops to demolish the villages and drive the population out of the region entirely. A death penalty was imposed on any who returned or who cultivated the area, which became known as '*spina nel cuore*' or 'thorn in the heart' (of Venice).

The Venetians did however leave the area with a lasting, and more welcome, legacy. In the 15th Century they allowed it to be repopulated, not with native Cretans, but with refugees escaping from the Turks on mainland

Greece. Mostly from the Peloponnese, these immigrants were allowed to farm the plateau again and, with the help of Venetian engineering know-how, built the huge system of drainage ditches which still criss-crosses the plain taking excess water westwards to a drain hole on the edge of the plateau.

The Ottomans also feared the people from these villages. Twice during their occupation of the island they torched the settlements and killed any locals who could not escape to the safety of the Diktean Mountains. The first occasion for this brutality was in 1823 during the Greek War of Independence and the second in 1867 during the Cretan Revolt. Nowadays the invasion is friendlier, consisting of tourists who contribute a not insubstantial amount to the local income, although this is one of the few areas in Greece which, because of the high productivity of the land, would be economically self-sufficient without the tourist euro.

Many of the coaches that circumnavigate the plateau during the summer months are heading towards the Diktean, or Andron, Cave, which is situated on a mountainside overlooking the plateau in the south west near the village of Psychro.

This cave is a walk or donkeys ride up one of two paths, one fairly steep and rugged, the other a longer, more gradual climb. The cave itself has been made accessible with steps and electric lighting. The path plunges quite steeply down to a depth of 200 ft, and is suitably damp with a natural vaulted roof, in places rising to about 50 ft above head height, covered in menacing stalactites. The cave is split into chambers and within the one furthest from the entrance is a lake. Legend claims that this was the birthplace of Zeus, the god of the sky and thunder and the king of gods and men.

The story goes that an oracle had warned Zeus' father, Kronos, that his own son would depose him. His long suffering wife Rhea, upset that her first five children had been eaten by Kronos to stop them overthrowing him, escaped to Crete and gave birth to her son in the Diktean Cave before presenting Kronos with a rock wrapped in clothes, which he swallowed. From here the young Zeus was later moved to a cave in the foothills of

Crete's tallest peak, Mount Psiloritis further to the west of the island. Here he came under the protection of the fearsome Kouretes warriors who would constantly bang spears against their bronze shields to drown out the baby's cries and keep his presence a secret. When Zeus reached manhood he forced his father to disgorge his other siblings, Demeter, Hades, Hera, Hestia and Poseidon. Angry at having been swallowed by their father, Kronos' children ganged together to overthrow him and the Titans who supported him. After winning the battle, Zeus and his older brothers Poseidon and Hades drew lots to divide the kingdoms of the world they had conquered; with Poseidon winning the seas, Hades the underworld and Zeus the skies and the air.

Whatever the veracity of the legends, the cave has historically been a sacred place with many artifacts, including examples of sacred double-edged axes and bronze-age Minoan statues of both humans and animals, having been excavated from it.

Blinking as we readjust to the light and dry heat of the mountainside in direct contrast to the dark, dank claustrophobia of inside the mountain, we descend to enjoy a beer at one of the kafenions, which together with souvenir shops surround the car park below.

Flying Film Stars

Travelling on Crete's National Highway from Heraklion to Agios Nikolaos we pass out of the coastal plain of Malia as the road ascends into the province of Lassithi. About 25 miles from the capital, near the top of a long climb, the road weaves between two mountains. This is the gorge of Selinari, passing between Anavlohos Mountain to the north and Fonias o Detis to the south. Here the road widens, and an amber traffic light flashes overhead. The signal's just a warning to take care, there's no need to stop. Most people don't, and drive past en route to other destinations in the east.

We had done just that many times until, one day, I spotted an enormous bird soaring above Anavlohos and pulled over in the car. Getting a proper look I could see three of these giants floating on the thermals above the mountain range that stood between us and the sea, less than a mile away to the north.

Unsure, I thought they might be some kind of eagle. Another man, a birdwatcher, was equipped with binoculars and told me they were Griffon vultures.

While standing there I must have counted nearly 20 of these imposing birds, which roost on the south face of the mountain. Now knowing they are there, we frequently stop and, through the zoom lens on the camera, can see them perched beside their nests built on the mountainside. But it is in flight that they are at their most spectacular. About three ft in length, a fully-grown adult has a wingspan of approximately eight ft.

Peering through binoculars or a telephoto lens they are recognizable as having a classic vulture look. With their white, bald, heads, brown bodies and dark flight feathers they look as though they have just stepped out of the Disney *Jungle Book* movie.

From a great height the birds can spot the carrion on which they feed, swooping down to scavenge from the carcasses of dead animals. The living must be good, because these birds have a life expectancy not dissimilar to that of a human, and a captive Griffon was recorded as having lived to 118 years old! Fortunately, these striking birds are protected and are on the increase on Crete, where there are thought to be upwards of 1,000 Griffons that can be seen in any number of mountain locations across the island.

Closer to God

In Crete you do not have to go very far without seeing a church. Often painted white, they can be glimpsed on top of mountains in some of the most inaccessible places. Still a deeply religious country, in Greece the church plays a major role in the lives of most families.

Greek Orthodoxy is noted in the national constitution as the prevailing religion of the country but the freedom to hold any religious belief is also enshrined in that constitution. It is, however, estimated that all but three per cent of the population consider themselves to be of the Greek Orthodox faith.

Families are the building blocks of Greek society, and at the heart of all of these families' life-changing moments and celebrations lies the church. Priests, or papas as they are known, are a common sight, going about their business in the community in their long robes and tall hats.

Although respected as being men of God, this gives them few special privileges in the eyes of the community and they are judged by the same standards as any of its other members. Priests are renowned for standing alongside their flocks. Rather than being aloof they have a long history of fighting with them against the many forces of oppression Greece has faced.

An individual's relationship with the Almighty can be volatile. God can be berated and cajoled, shouted at and pleaded with but ultimately remains the focal point of life. Few Greeks would claim to be saints and, as in most societies, the richer they are the potential for them being less saintly is somewhat higher. As they get older, it is the need of some of these well-to-do sinners to repent, which accounts for the number of churches of various sizes built in the most remote spots.

In an attempt to pass through the eye of a needle, it is believed that by building a church, God will look more favourably on a sinner's repentance. Moreover, the further up a mountain the church is built, the nearer it is to God and the shorter the distance any prayers have to travel to be answered. These places of worship can vary in size from simple tiny chapels to larger, quite ornate, churches. Many of them are only used once a year on saint's days, but they are usually scrupulously maintained, often by local villagers.

A Valuable Resource

Cretans often boast that they have unlimited supplies of water but, although there is an element of truth in this it is somewhat apocryphal. Water on their island is a precious resource and, despite there being plenty for the indigenous population, increased personal usage and the growth in tourism is putting some stress on the supply.

In the mountains there are numerous sites where fresh water is drawn through bore holes from aquifers deep underground. These offer a supply of free, wonderfully pure water to the locals. It is a frequent sight on mountain tracks to see flat-back trucks with massive plastic tanks on the back going to or from these water sources. The tanks are then taken home and hoisted onto the roof to be used as a domestic water supply.

Local authorities throughout the island have offered mains water to many of these remote villages only for these offers to be rejected, as the villagers would then be subject to bills. The recent completion of the Potamoi Dam in Amari, south of Rethymnon, has created the largest lake in Crete. Built with European Union funding it has secured valuable water supplies for domestic and agricultural use.

When I first came to Crete, the water companies controlled usage by only turning on supplies to water tanks once a day. If you emptied your tank you would have to wait until it was filled up again the following morning.

I still hear the odd tourist advising others not to drink the tap water in Greece. What this is based on is a complete mystery to me. Numerous friends and I, as well as of course every Greek, have drunk direct from the water supply for as long as I can remember. Not once have I heard of any ill effects. In my experience it tastes better and looks clearer than that which often comes out of the taps when I am at home in the UK.

Indeed water, '*nero*', is treasured as a drink in Greece. It is something to take time over and savour, just because it is free does not mean that it is not valued. Any taverna or cafenion will supply you with an ice-cold water at no charge. Coffee is rarely served without a glass of water to accompany it, to counteract any dehydration caused by the intake of caffeine and to take any bitter taste from a traditional Greek coffee away.

Spinalonga – The Island of Tears

In 2005 the English writer Victoria Hislop had a number one bestseller with her first novel *The Island*, which tells the story of life on the island of Spinalonga when it was a leper colony. Just off the coast of the village of Plaka in north-east Crete, Spinalonga is a haunting place and Hislop's fictional account of the lives of some of its inhabitants is an ideal *hors d'ouevre* to a visit to the island itself.

Although a novel, this is an authentic account, a fact that enhances its emotional impact. It tells the story of a woman, Alexis, determined to discover more about her family history. Her search leads her to Plaka, where she learns the tale of her great grandmother, Eleni, and a secret past that connects her with Spinalonga. As the story unfolds, so does the tragic history of the island.

You can get a boat to the island from Elounda, Plaka, or take a longer trip from Agios Nikolaos. An early start from Plaka or Elounda is recommended as Spinalonga is a popular tourist destination and when the larger boats from Agios Nikolaos arrive it can get busy.

On a first visit, it is worth getting a tour guide to add the colour and detail, which many of the guide books lack. On one visit we had a guide who, out of season, worked for a charity raising money to help leprosy sufferers around the world. Hearing from her about how an entirely curable disease still afflicts millions of people, whilst standing on ground which had witnessed so much suffering, I found especially poignant.

Just how recently leprosy sufferers had inhabited Spinalonga was brought home to me when I learned that by the time I first visited the island in the 1990s, there were still people alive who had lived there. The condition, also known as Hansen's disease, although eradicated in much of the developed world, is still rampant across India and in some African nations.

Whenever I visit Spinalonga I have an eerie sense of the island's past. Once you get off the boat you pass through the entrance to the colony known as Dante's Gate. The lepers passing here would know they would never leave the island.

Through the gate, the colony looks much like any other Cretan village. Some parts have been reconstructed, others stand in a state of dilapidation, flowers bloom and insects buzz, geckos laze on walls and cats bask in the sun. But the island cannot shake off its past, a lingering reminder of the suffering of those forced to spend their lives here.

Despite the pain and isolation of the islanders, some of the personal stories are life affirming. People fell in love, were married in the church on the island, had children and went about their daily lives in a way that might seem unimaginable. There were shops and tavernas on Spinalonga, and a hospital, where doctors had shown particular selflessness in their dedication to treat the sick.

A walk out of the small village to the other side of the island, leads to the top of a cliff overlooking the sea. Here is the remote cemetery where the villagers were laid to rest. The island became a leper colony in 1903 and the last patients left there in 1957, although the final permanent inhabitant was a priest who remained until 1962. He stayed as, in the Greek Orthodox religion, the dead should be commemorated at regular intervals for years after their passing.

The island is now uninhabited. When the last ferries and tour boats leave before sundown it is left alone, save for the echoes of its eventful history. Prior to the 19th Century, Spinalonga was a pivotal and often disputed fortress defending the bay. The fortifications at its southern end were built by the ruling Venetians in 1579 in answer to the growing threat of the Ottoman Empire.

Even after mainland Crete was ceded to the Turks in 1646, Spinalonga remained impregnable and was only given over to the invaders following a treaty signed in 1715. The Turks, in turn, used the island as a refuge when they felt under threat from Cretan nationalist uprisings. Some of them remained on the island after Crete gained autonomy under the Four Powers agreement in 1898, until it became a leper colony five years later.

Plaka's close relationship with Spinalonga is ongoing, their fortunes continue to be linked as throughout 2010 parts of the village were used as a film set for the shooting of the adaptation of Hislop's book by Greek television.

It was Maria, the owner and ever-present waitress at our bar of choice in the graceful square in Elounda who alerted us to the film set for *The Island*. Like many of the locals she had been taken on as an extra for the filming of the book and was proudly recounting the excitement the arrival a film crew and actors had generated in the small community. The set that had been built in Plaka just a few miles along the road had been struck but another one that had been constructed up the mountain in the village of Pano Elounda had been left to attract visitors and their accompanying cash to the tiny farming community. In our experience the ploy was not working as nowhere was it advertised and as we climbed up the mountain road, there was just one small sign pointing to the heart of the village. Even having found the sign and knowing the attraction was there, it was difficult to find. This, however, was due to the remarkable authenticity of the house facades that had been constructed. They are so incredible that their integration with the real village dwellings is seamless. We had to knock on the walls to discover which buildings were real and which facsimiles. Some were so perfect that only by poking your head inside a window to see if there were any wooden struts supporting the walls could one tell if it was real or part of the set.

As we strolled around the village, an elderly woman in traditional black mufti kept popping up in front of us, asking in gabbled Greek if we would like a drink and gesturing to a small table and two chairs placed outside what appeared to be the front door of her house. On closer inspection we could see crates of Coca-Cola and Mythos beer stacked inside the front room of her tiny dwelling, which had been transformed into a makeshift kafenion to exploit the passing trade brought to the village to see the film set.

An excuse to stop for a drink was welcome, and from the vantage point of this astonishing half-real, part-reconstructed village was the fine view of the bay glistening between gaps in the small houses from where the real Spinalonga could be spotted, The silent trails of foam radiating out from the sterns of the caiques as they plied their way back and forth from the island below.

Refreshed, we took the narrow road back to Elounda to sit and watch the last boats mooring in their berths alongside the village square. We let Maria know that we had taken her advice and visited the set, before heading back to our villa which lies beyond the disused Venetian salt flats, across the causeway and small bridge onto the island peninsula adjacent to Spinalonga. It is the only inhabited building on the island. It is run by the family of the artist Lida Alexopoulou and the magnificent gardens run down to a beach and the sheltered waters of the bay. The property has no mains electricity and is run completely – and very efficiently – by solar power providing a traditional, simple and friendly bolthole to enjoy the beauties of this corner of the bay of Mirabello.

The Dalmatian of Olondi

Elounda itself is considered to be one of the most upmarket resorts in Greece and during the summer there is the regular sound of helicopters landing at one of several five-star hotels on the outskirts of the village, delivering film actors and pop stars who regularly holiday there. It is easy to see the attraction of this secluded spot, which is also close enough to the bustling town of Agios Nicholaos for you to be there in quarter of an hour by car or bus if the mood should take you.

If I say that Boo Boo is the most memorable thing about Olondi, it is not intended to detract from this exquisite taverna right on the seafront at Elounda. Boo Boo is a Dalmatian and, as such, a rarity in these parts.

Before we had ever set foot in the restaurant, she would often come to us for fuss as we walked past when heading for the village. Sporting a rather dashing red neckerchief, she is quite a local celebrity, and no doubt works wonders for the trade at his owner's wonderful restaurant. Not that it needs any help on that front, as the taverna is usually full, particularly in the evening, and the food is some of the best I have tasted.

Often it is the simplicity of the dishes presented that is their charm. Unadorned, they complement the natural beauty of the surroundings in which they are being eaten. They are sympathetic to the spirit of place. A feast of colours meets the eyes when a simple Greek salad of tomato, cucumber feta cheese and olives is placed on the table to be drizzled in oil and vinegar and eaten with a plate of small fried fish and chunks of fresh bread.

The garlic butter or crushed olive paste often provided as an appetizer can also satisfy, often leaving you full before your main meal arrives on the table. With the food perfectly cooked and presented and served with affection, an evening spent in Olondi looking out to the solitary lights from our villa twinkling across the bay is everything you could ask for. During the day the owner's fishing rods lean against the balustrade, lines cast into the transparent water in the hope of supplementing that evening's menu.

The prawns are the biggest I've ever seen, served shell-on and dripping in garlic butter they are the perfect accompaniment to a carafe of the house white, dry, earthy with the scent of all that is best of the island of its origin. There is no rushing here, you can sit talking or just stare out to sea for as long as the mood takes you, or until you can find the willpower to break the spell and leave for bed.

Since I wrote this, the Dalmatian in question has sadly passed away, but I'm pleased to say that his owner's wonderful restaurant is still with us!

Olous – The Town Beneath the Waves

We cast off our small motorboat from a jetty between Elounda and Plaka. It was July and the sun was bleaching the colour out of the island 500 yards off our port bow. Heading south, it was our intention to pass under the small bridge that connects Elounda with the peninsula of Kolokytha adjacent to Spinalonga and out into the Gulf of Mirabello via the small canal.

Through this narrow channel lies the sunken city of Olous. In its prime, 40,000 people inhabited this Minoan port. The seismic upheaval understood to have devastated the island of Santorini is also often attributed as the cause of the sinking of Olous, but it's more likely that its demise might be as recent as the earthquake of 780 AD.

We took the time to moor up alongside the canal and jumped ashore to take a look at a Byzantine mosaic, vibrant with leaping dolphins and fish. This is the floor of what used to be a basilica dating from the 5th Century AD. It is extraordinary, only in Greece would you make such a find. Lying next to a taverna, protected only by a low, stone wall, and free for anyone to view is this priceless piece of original art.

Legend has it that the lagoon itself is the domain of the mermaid goddess, Britomartis, whose likeness is to be found replicated on souvenirs throughout Crete. There are many myths surrounding Britomartis, and the detail of her story may have been changed many times over thousands of years. What is certain is that her image is found on coins that were discovered beneath the waters in the submerged city of Olous.

The most popular version of her story around these parts is that she was the daughter of Zeus and Carme. A nymph whose name means sweet maiden, she was born in Gortys on the island and was the Minoan goddess of hunting and the mountains. So alluring was she that King Minos himself became obsessed with her beauty and pursued her. To protect her honour and escape the randy monarch, she threw herself into the sea and became entangled in some nets set by local fishermen. They rescued her and ever since, as an act of gratitude, she has become the protector of seafarers.

Anchoring 50 yards offshore from the basilica, we dived down with our snorkels to see what remains of the Minoan city. The ruins were clearly visible, foundations made of stone, and the pattern of streets and alleyways that were the town's thoroughfares could easily be made out.

They are enough to stir the imagination into picturing this thriving town that traded with the other great Cretan city states, and further abroad. This was a mighty centre of commerce that boasted its own kings and currency.

As we headed back through the canal to the other side of the lagoon, the afternoon breeze began to cut up rough, and unexpectedly turned into a gale that hit us right on the nose as we headed north back to the quay. It was enough to make our passage distinctly uncomfortable and very wet. But Britomartis was with us and the boat coped admirably, bringing us safely back to shore to dry out in the late afternoon sunshine.

Agios Nikolaos – The Heart of Mirabello

Agios Nikolaos is a gem on a town nestling beside the Gulf of Mirabello on Crete's north-east coast. More self-contained and less sprawling than its larger counterparts, Heraklion and Chania, it retains an effortless beauty, not in the least part aided by its natural location. Looking as though it has always washed its face and brushed its hair, the town sparkles, even on the odd occasion when it rains.

My first visit there was by bus from Heraklion. Even in the early Eighties, before the new main highway was built and when the busses where less sophisticated than the luxury air-conditioned fleet now in operation, the destination made a day trip to Agios Nikolaos worth the discomfort. Nowadays it is little more than an hour's drive from the airport.

The Gulf of Mirabello undoubtedly lives up to its name. It means, 'beautiful sight' in Italian. Rumour has it that during the Venetian occupation of the island, between 1204 and 1669, an Italian ruler looking down from the mountains was asked where this magical place was. Not knowing, but captivated by its beauty, he gasped the words '*mira bello*' and the name has, appropriately, stuck.

The town radiates out from a small inland lagoon, Lake Voulismeni (sunken lake), which since 1870 has been connected by a narrow channel to the old town harbour. Surrounding the lake are tavernas and kafenions and it is the most delightful place to pass the time.

For years we have eaten at Dionysos, a taverna on the edge of the lake. The twin brothers who run it, I look upon as friends and I have certainly been dining there for more than a decade. In my mind I'm convinced that I visited that same restaurant on my first visit to the town, although the twins would not thank me for imagining they could have been working there at the time.

The only trouble with eating at Dionysos is walking past the other restaurants. In Greece it is not unusual for waiters to tout for business outside their tavernas and the more popular the location the more competitive they are. For the most part I am immune to this, saying a courteous *'ochi efheristo'* (no, thank you) usually gets me off the hook. But with our much-loved taverna sandwiched between other restaurants and the water's edge, we have to run the gauntlet of several waiters who have taken it as a personal affront that we only eat in our friends' establishment. I'm sure their forceful selling techniques must put many people off eating in any of the restaurants on the lakeside. Perhaps a less invasive approach would improve business for all.

The restaurants by the lake are the perfect place to people watch, particularly in the evening as Greek families promenade before dinner. Cooked for hours in a low oven, the *kleftiko* is not to be missed. This lamb dish is a Cretan specialty.

It usually has to be ordered in advance and when done properly, as it is in Dionysos, the meat is so tender it just melts in your mouth. The flavours are so unmistakably Cretan and can be recreated anywhere, but rarely does it taste as good as in a Greek taverna. For those who are not familiar with this hearty delight it is essentially a type of lamb stew. The browned meat is slow baked in olive oil with potatoes, onions, tomatoes, garlic, oregano and feta cheese in a sealed oven dish, paper or foil for about four hours.

When the dish emerges from the oven, the smells herald the pleasures to come. Feasting on *kleftiko*, late in the evening with the tiny fishing boats lightly tugging at their moorings, drinking from a jug of dry red Sitian wine, one can't help but think that Dionysos could not have been more appropriately named than after the Greek god of pleasure.

Legend has it that the lake is bottomless, and that the goddess Athena used to bathe in it. In 1853 however, a British admiral had soundings taken and found that it did have a bottom, albeit at a depth of 200 ft. This fact did little to quell the belief that it was bottomless, which in more modern times was a marketable factor in promoting the town as a tourist attraction. This is why in 1976 the highly-respected undersea explorer, Jacques Cousteau, became something of a local villain.

That year the Frenchman and his team of divers came to Crete in search of evidence of the remains of lost civilizations. Taking time out from their underwater searches for Minoan artifacts, he sent a diver into Lake Voulismeni, and he confirmed once and for all that it was not bottomless.

Cousteau's high profile meant that this myth-busting dive made the truth common knowledge, and the Frenchman was blamed for any subsequent loss of trade! In the Noughties he was let off the hook, as the local businessmen transferred their ire to the global recession.

Elsewhere on the island Cousteau is held in greater esteem. On the same expedition his team made some remarkable discoveries. In search of the lost island of Atlantis, they were diving in the waters around the small island of PsClia out in the gulf of Mirabello. Here they found a wealth of Minoan pottery, which was believed to have come from ships that were sunk in the huge volcanic eruption that destroyed the island of Thera (Santorini).

Since then, Greek archaeologist Elpida Hadjidaki has found evidence of a shipwreck in the area. Discovering numerous Minoan jugs, cups and other artifacts on the seabed in 2003, her team has mounted numerous dives and brought to the surface upwards of 200 ceramic pieces. Many of these have been identified as amphorae, used for the transportation of cargoes of olive oil or wine, reminders of the lasting quality of what was valued all those years ago, and how they still remain the heart and soul of Greek culture.

The Lotus Eaters

A popular man in Crete is the late TV screenwriter Michael J Bird. He is attributed with significantly increasing tourist numbers visiting the country from the UK in the Seventies and Eighties. Agios Nikolaos and Elounda certainly benefited from being used as locations for two of his hit series. The first, *The Lotus Eaters* was shot in Agios Nikolaos with two series being shown on the BBC in 1972 and 1973. The second, *Who Pays the Ferryman?*, was filmed about six miles north along the coast in the small fishing town of Elounda.

That *The Lotus Eaters* was shot in Crete at all, let alone Agios Nikolaos was somewhat fortuitous. Bird had conceived the story some time before in Ibiza in the Spanish Balearic islands, which was his original choice of location. But when filming was slated to begin in November 1971 the weather on the Spanish island was appalling so Bird sought out another location. Scouting for this in the warmer climes of Crete he came across Agios Nikolaos and immediately knew he had found the perfect place to shoot the series.

The eastern Mediterranean became a favourite location for his TV dramas, with *Who Pays the Ferryman?* broadcast in 1977 followed by *The Aphrodite Inheritance*, set in Cyprus, two years later. *The Dark Side of the Sun*, a contemporary supernatural thriller filmed in Rhodes, was shown in 1983.

But it was *The Lotus Eaters* that put Bird on the map, along with its location. The title is taken from a Homeric legend in *The Odyssey*. The story goes that Odysseus and his crew were blown off course in a violent storm. Eventually they landed on an island where the locals eat lotus plants that have the narcotic effect of leaving them in a state of such sympathetic apathy that they are content never to leave. Odysseus had to force his weeping crew to forsake the island, fearing otherwise they would never seek to return home. To my mind the selection of Agios Nikolaos as the setting for Bird's series could not be more appropriate.

The Secrets of Katharo

Setting out from Agios Nikolaos, the road makes its way into the Dikti Mountains and the ancient village of Kritsa six miles away. Rattling through the olive groves our four-wheel drive reaches a village that has perched on this rock face nearly 1,300 ft above the sea for 3,000 years.

Kritsa is famous for its traditional woven cloths and embroidery and, despite being away from the coast, is still a destination for tourists. We drive on through its narrow streets, almost touching the intricate tablecloths and small rugs hung up for sale outside the doors of the old shops that line the road.

Elderly women in black dresses with black scarves and knee-high socks sit sewing on chairs in the street. This traditional dress is not so common now in the larger towns, but here in Kritsa it is commonplace. In places the buildings crowd in upon the road forming chicanes, at times making it impossible for two vehicles to pass. Although well worth a visit, the village is not our destination today.

We carry on up towards the eastern end of Mount Dikti. Looking back at Kritsa it is clear that what the locals say is true; the village does look like a scorpion. I have not been up here after nightfall but am told that when the village is illuminated the resemblance is even more striking. Our driver says there are planning regulations that stop building outside the village boundaries in order that it retains its unique shape.

Now we are negotiating a dirt road that, although passable in our vehicle, is littered with potholes. Several times we bash our heads on the roof when we hit one unexpectedly. We are heading for the little known plateau of Katharo, a fertile area of high ground unvisited by most tourists, its only inhabitants being farmers, goatherds and shepherds during the summer months. There are no shops up here; a couple of basic tavernas cater for the needs of the small local community.

At more than 3,300 ft above sea level, we are in one of the most uninhabited regions of the island. But it is in this remote area that the most extraordinary fossils have been found. The dating is inexact, but shows an age range from as early as the middle Pleistocene period some 800,000 years ago to as recently as 100,000 years ago. These fossils are the remains of a number of long-extinct animals.

Throughout the plateau, bones of the Cretan dwarf hippopotamus have been discovered. In one spot in particular, Digenis Anaspa, the remains of a whole herd were unearthed. More remarkable, are the remains of less common dwarf elephants that also roamed here around the same period.

Crete rose from the sea around 2,000,000 years ago, being an island from the start much as it is today, separated from the mainland by large distances of the Mediterranean Sea. During the Ice Age of 540,000 years ago these distances significantly lessened due to giant ice flows. One theory is that it was during this period that a number of hippos and elephants managed to cross to Crete.

Unperturbed by any bigger predators, their populations quickly expanded, leading to the exhaustion of the natural resources that had sustained them. These food shortages were thought to be the factor that caused these creatures to evolve into the dwarf breeds of their respective species. The hippo was about the same size as a sheep, and the elephant a cow.

It is not known exactly what was responsible for the extinction of these animals, although one theory is that following a second Ice Age, 100,000 years ago, herds of deer migrated to the island. More agile and better adapted to surviving off the dwindling food sources, they contributed to creating an environment low enough in sustenance that it was unsustainable for the dwarf hippos and elephants, leading to their subsequent extinction. Many of the fossils collected from Katharo can be found in the impressive Natural History Museum of Crete in Heraklion.

The clear, cooler air up here makes a welcome change from the arid coastal plains and the silence is broken only by the occasional buzz of a honeybee hard at work or the sound of a generator pumping water to an irrigation channel. Here you really are away from it all, lost high up in a mountain world where once elephants and hippos ruled.

Kritsa's Most Famous Daughter

Standing in the main square of Kritsa, a hillside village in the Lassithi province of Crete, is a sculpture commemorating the heroism of a woman called Rhodanthe. Nowadays she is better known as Kritsotopoula, meaning child of Kritsa.

The daughter of a local priest in the early 19th Century, the story that has been passed down is that she was at home with her mother, singing while working at the loom. Hearing the girl's soulful voice, a passing Turkish soldier knocked at the door and demanded to know whose it was.

The frightened girl's mother tried to conceal her daughter's presence but the soldier, who was drunk, grew angry at being lied to, drew a knife and killed the mother and abducted the girl. With the intention of marrying her, the soldier dragged Rhodanthe away to his house in the village. But while he slept she took her revenge by cutting his throat.

Chopping off her own hair and binding her breasts in a bandage, the girl disguised herself as a man and escaped to the mountains to join the resistance fighters. Her identity remained a secret until she was fatally injured in a battle with the Turks in 1823. In a futile attempt to save their comrade, her fellow freedom fighters ripped open her shirt to tend her wounds and discovered her secret.

The main street in the village is named after the local heroine. And, at the very end of the road where it reaches its most narrow point, is the house in which she lived before escaping to the mountains. Carved into the stone above the door is a cross, the sign it was a priest's house.

In 2009 another memorial to Kritsotopoula was unveiled on the road between Kritsa and Lato near the place she is believed to have fallen in battle. The dying girl is being held by a priest, also a resistance fighter, who could have been her father. This imposing life-size stone relief monument was commissioned by the locals and is the work of English sculptor Nigel Ratcliffe-Springall who lives and works in the community.

Cretan Gold

Driving south out of Kritsa into the Dikti Mountains we arrived at the village of Katharo before swinging off onto an unmade track that clings to the side of a plateau which sits about 4,000 ft above sea level. This is Crete at its most splendid, literally off the beaten track where hire cars don't venture.

Sparsely inhabited in summer, the snows make it impassable in the winter months; it is a land where farmers and shepherds survive in their small, basic shelters from April to October. The trees are laden with apples and pears, and grapes ripen on the vines while a myriad of different vegetables grow in abundance. There is no electricity or mains water here. Diesel generators supply what power there is, and water is drawn from natural aquifers that lie on the limestone rock beneath the fertile soil.

Life here has changed little for generations, apart from the farmers' beaten up four-wheel drives that travel at alarming speeds along the tracks, having for the most part replaced the donkeys and ancient MEBEA, Ros and Styl Kar trucks of the past. These strange three-wheeled contraptions, which look like the result of the unfortunate coming together of a moped and a trailer, used to be the vehicle of choice for the Cretan farmer. Occasionally they still can be seen, leaving one bemused as to how they ever managed to reach such isolated spots.

Dotted all around are small, multi-coloured wooden boxes, inside which Cretan gold is created. The island's honey is considered by many to be the finest in the world, and it certainly does have a unique taste. Wild thyme and pine, among other indigenous plants on which the local bees graze, give the honey its distinctive aroma and taste. Rarely is it as good as when eaten in the early morning sun with natural Greek yoghurt and nuts, or oozing out of *baklava* or almond and walnut *kataifi* pastries.

Bee keeping has been an occupation in Greece since prehistoric times and the excavations of Festos and Knossos on Crete have revealed evidence of hives, smokers and representations of bees on jewellery. Apiculture features in the works of Homer and Aristotle and ancient myth has it that Aristeos, the son of the god Apollo, was taught the great Greek triumvirate of agricultural skills: cultivating grapes and olives, and beekeeping. He settled on the island of Kea in the Cyclades and passed on his skills to the natives there.

Nowadays, there are thought to be approaching 30,000 apiarists throughout Greece of which only a fifth are engaged in full-time commercial operations. Nevertheless, Greece produces 17,000 metric tonnes of honey each year, the vast majority of which is consumed by the native population.

Hippocrates, the Greek father of western medicine, advocated the health giving benefits of honey. It is still held to be good for the strength of bones, the health of body cells and neutralizing stomach acidity, as well as having antiseptic and antimicrobial qualities. But most importantly it tastes good.

I was intrigued as to why the hives were painted in so many different, bright colours. When I asked my friend, Yanis, he looked at me incredulous before telling me what I suppose I should have known: it just depends what tins of left-over paint the beekeepers can find in their barns or storerooms.

We drive on along a barely navigable dirt track, which traverses a small valley between the plateaus of Katharo and Lassithi. Commonly known as Goat Valley, I have been here on two occasions, both times by four-wheel drive. The air is so clear it is breathtaking and the only sound above the croak of the cicadas is the musical tinkling of bells around the necks of goats.

Varying in sizes the different tones of the ringing bells provide a harmonious accompaniment to a journey through one of the most deserted and stunning places on Crete. Small stone buildings dot the landscape as summer shelter for the goatherds who bring their animals up to these highlands to graze in the summer months.

Not all the goats wear bells; apparently they are reserved for the animals most likely to wander from the herd. The more recalcitrant the goat is, the larger bell it will wear, its sonorous tones recognizable to its keeper over long distances. The goats have rapacious appetites. If offered food they will even climb on the roof of your vehicle to get at it and, even more amusingly, will climb trees to graze in the upper branches.

The Oil at the Heart of Crete

Olives are the staple crop of Crete and are treated with great reverence. On the island nearly everyone owns a few trees. The plant is the most symbolic of Greece and has been harvested since the early Minoan period, olive trees featuring on some of the frescoes at Knossos. At the ancient Olympic Games, winners were presented with an olive branch and it has since become a universal symbol of peace.

These tough plants can grow in a variety of locations and withstand the hot, arid summers but they are also hardy against winter cold. Everywhere in Greece will claim to produce the best olive oil in the country and, of course, Greek olive oil is always claimed to be the best in the world. There is some evidence to substantiate this claim. Italy imports Greek oil to blend with their own in order to get the acidity levels low enough for it to be marketed as extra virgin.

Greece produces about 12 per cent of the whole world's olive oil and, after Spain and Italy, is the third biggest producer. Having given up well over half of its cultivated land to growing olives, this land produces the largest number of varieties in the world.

But it is the quality of the oil that is so impressive. Most of it is extra virgin. For this reason, it is in such high demand that half of the crop goes for export. Much of that which is sold abroad is used to improve the quality of inferior foreign oils, although frequently, and often illegally, this is not mentioned on a bottle's labelling.

The olive harvest begins in the autumn and lasts through until February of the following year. Nets are laid beneath the trees, and traditionally the branches are beaten with a stick to dislodge the olives that fall into the nets below.

Nowadays rotary poles powered by generators are frequently used to ease the backbreaking work. The olives are then loaded in sacks and taken to the press. Here they are crushed into a paste, usually by steel drums although more traditional operations use millstones.

This paste is then pressed to extract the liquid, a mixture of oil and water. In modern-day production this liquid is placed in a centrifuge to separate the olive oil from the water. In some smaller-scale businesses the slower process of allowing gravity to separate the mixture is still employed.

For olive oil to be virgin it must go through this process with no chemicals added either to help with manufacture or to adjust the flavour. The only difference between virgin and extra virgin oils is the acidity level that must be below 0.8 per cent if it is to make the grade as extra virgin, which more than 80 per cent of Greek oil is.

When you consider that, in other countries, that figure is nearer 10 per cent, it validates the Greeks' claims to have the best quality olive oil in the world; this probably also accounts for the health-giving properties which are attached to the Greek diet, particularly that of the Cretans, who live longer than any other people in Europe.

Greeks personally consume nearly twice as much olive oil in their diet as any other nation. On average, each person uses 500ml every week. High in monounsaturated fats, the oil is linked to a reduction in heart disease and helps lower cholesterol levels in the blood. In addition to its genuine life-enhancing properties it tastes marvellous. Good quality oil poured on a seasoned salad, or bread dipped in oil and vinegar must be one of the most blissful ways of getting healthier.

The oil is also used to make soap to sell mostly to tourists and for export, and olive wood is carved or whittled into salad bowls and chopping boards and many other tactile objects to be found in shops throughout the islands.

A Special Relationship

Sparks flew from beneath our hired Mitsubishi Colt as the boulder-strewn track got worse. The road we had taken headed inland across the island, and it was our naive hope that we would reach the south coast. The 1200cc engine strained as we ploughed on up into the mountains. The road had changed from a serviceable surface to a series of potholes interspersed with small areas of tarmac. Then it transformed into a dirt track littered with rocks, before its final metamorphosis into what could only be described as… a field.

Maps at the time were not terribly reliable, and signposting even less so. My instinct had told me we were heading in the wrong direction, but we continued for several miles hoping the going would get better. Neither were we sure the car would stand up to retracing our steps.

Finally admitting defeat, we brought the car to a halt, and got out the map. It was only then I spotted a man sitting on the back of a cart. He had stopped eating his lunch and just looked our way with an enigmatic stare.

A smile flickered across the edge of his mouth when, map in hand, I asked him where we were. A shrug and gesture made it clear that he was not quite sure of our position on the map. The only certainty was that the only way out was back in the direction we had come.

Until recently signposts and maps were a source of mystery to visitors to the island. Surely such an otherwise civilized people could not be so cartographically dyslexic? It has since been explained that in many cases failure to provide strangers with accurate ways of navigating was a understandable consequence of the island being invaded so often. Knowledge of the mountains was power, and on many an occasion Cretan partisans have been grateful for the exclusivity of that knowledge.

Things are slightly better now. On the main roads signposting is good and spelled out in both Greek and English alphabets. Further off the beaten track, however, there are still some places that, one suspects, the locals would prefer to remain a secret.

As there was no alternative for us but to retrace our tracks we slowly, if not surely, nudged the aging car back along the miles to the tarmac-surfaced road. Abandoning any chance of reaching the coast that day, we headed east into the mountains in the direction of Lassithi.

Although the occupation of Crete by the Germans during the Second World War was 37 years prior to my first visit, away from the coastal resorts, the locals had long memories. In need of some cigarettes following our earlier ordeal we stopped in a remote village on the edge of Lassithi Plateau. I entered the tiny front room of a tumbledown, traditional house that also doubled as a village shop.

So high up, an early spring wind was blowing from the snow-capped mountains and it was bitterly cold. Inside the shop, around a wood-burning stove, sat three elderly men in traditional Cretan dress of wide trousers tucked into tall boots, with black shirts and black headbands, all sporting luxuriant moustaches and inscrutable expressions.

Mustering my best Greek I asked if they sold cigarettes. One man, who I took to be the shop owner, stood up and stared me in the eyes. 'Are you German?' he growled. '*Ochi, ee-meh apo teen Angleea*', I stumbled. A clap on the back almost winded me as all three opened wide smiles and said in unison '*Inglish, katsee*' pulling up a stool for me around the fire.

As requested I sat down, and each of them offered cigarettes and raki was poured. They spoke no English, but I was made to feel extraordinarily welcome and my halting attempts at Greek were widely praised and treated with some amazement.

More than an hour later I had managed to get a packet of cigarettes that my newfound friends refused to let me pay for. I somehow think, at the time, had I been German they might not have sold cigarettes. With time, wounds have healed and an increasing number of German tourists now visit Crete, but these men were of an age to have fought as resistance fighters during the war and to have witnessed the atrocities committed by the occupying army.

British Special Forces had fought alongside these fearsome warriors and, even in the early Eighties, many Cretans held the British in special regard. I still sense a special relationship between the two nationalities in many places I visit on the island.

Not in the slightest bit worried about how long I had been gone, my family had settled in the only taverna nearby and were tucking in to lunch. The south coast had already been forgotten for the day

Sitia – Way Out East

If you should decide to visit Sitia, on the north east coast of Crete, it is best to take your time or take the bus. On several occasions I have suffered by stupidly feeling the need to do the round trip in a day. If you take the bus at least you will not feel the stress of having to drive fast to make a day trip worthwhile. And it is worthwhile.

A small town isolated from the other centres of population along the northern coast, Sitia is a long way from the nearest international airport at Heraklion. A local airport has been built recently and I am told will soon be open to international flights. What effect this might have on an area that has been described as the most hospitable on Crete has yet to be seen, but at the moment the town remains one of Crete's best-kept secrets.

The main coast road is being improved all the time but the drive is still not for those of a nervous disposition. When the coastal resorts to the east of

Aghios Nikolaos have been left behind, there are no towns, and the few small villages and hamlets become less frequent.

Mostly, the road clings to the side of the mountains, which fall away into the sea, but sometimes it has to curl its way inland to navigate an impassable mountain blocking the way. The descent into Sitia is steep and, in between hairpin bends, the whole of the town reveals itself, laid out before you.

I suppose, coming to it cold, Sitia at first appears unprepossessing, but viewed from the sea or looking downwards from the hills it seems to own its place, self-contained and at ease, stretching out along the shore and back into the foothills of the mountains inland. It has a relaxed atmosphere and is as yet unspoiled by the demands of mass tourism. The town has a lively quayside, a fine beach and an impressive garden square, Platia Venizelou, right by the sea.

The town does not wear its heritage on its sleeve in the same way that Chania, Rethymnon and Heraklion do, but its graceful painted buildings hold an august appeal of their own. Sitia's past is most evident in the fortress, which stands inland looking down on the harbour.

This is one of the few historic buildings that remain in a town that has a past that stretches back to well before Minoan times. A settlement was excavated in nearby Petras and Neolithic artifacts were discovered that date from around 3000 years BC.

The Venetians fortified the town and made it their strategic base for trading in the eastern Mediterranean. Unfortunately, Sitia has had to show great resilience over the years. It fell victim to a massive earthquake in 1508, after which it was rebuilt by its Venetian rulers, only to be sacked and burned by pirates led by the infamous Barbarossa brothers in 1538. Rising from the ashes once more, the receding power of the Venetians led to them laying the town to waste to stop it falling into enemy hands following a three-year siege by the advancing Turks.

Having ousted the Venetians, the Turks showed little interest in Sitia, concentrating their energies further to the west predominantly in Heraklion and Chania. It was not until the second half of the 18th Century that any significant repopulation took place there as the town was rebuilt again as a centre for the farmers who made their living off this rugged eastern land.

The fortress is known as Kazarma, from the Italian *casa di arma* meaning barracks, and has stood in one form or another since Byzantine times. Having been repaired following earthquake damage and pirate attack, the current castle is predominantly Venetian. Built on the hill above the seafront it is still a commanding presence, particularly at night when it is floodlit. Carefully restored, it remains the focal point of city life, now playing host to concerts, plays and art exhibitions.

The real beauty of this town lies in its indolent charm. Here there is not the hard sell or the rush for the tourist euro that can be found in some of the other large towns on the island. Sitians are determined that this will not change, but they do face the dilemma of whether to retain their laid back existence which their relative isolation has allowed them, or to fully embrace the opportunities which increased tourism undoubtedly will bring. With the airport set to make the town more accessible to outsiders, I hope they make the right decisions and can balance the benefits with their present way of life.

The Soul of Crete

If olives are the life-giving heart of Crete, then grapes are its soul. Vines abound throughout the island. Although increasingly there are many large-scale commercial growing operations, often the vines are not the cut back, neat varieties seen in serried rows across the other winemaking nations of Europe. Free, untrained, the vines are frequently grown in small quantities to produce wine for personal consumption. This freedom for the vines to grow naturally probably accounts for the wide range of wine available and its variable quality.

The grapevine provides the four drinks synonymous with Crete, wine, raki (or tsikoudia), retsina and ouzo and the vine leaves do not go to waste either, they are stuffed to make a delicious mezze. Filled with rice, herbs, garlic and sometimes feta cheese then drizzled with some olive oil they are the perfect accompaniment to any of the aforementioned liquors.

One of the oldest wine-producing nations in the world, there is evidence of vines growing in Greece going back more than 6,000 years. Archaeologists found the remains of charred seeds and crushed grape skins during a dig on a Macedonian Neolithic site dated around 4500 BC. Ironically, during the time of the Roman Empire, wines from Crete were exported throughout Europe and North Africa. Today their presence abroad is limited, although strenuous efforts are being made to improve their marketability.

The best-known Greek wine abroad is retsina. For many, this is an acquired taste, one I have so far failed to acquire. Best drunk cold, it is usually a white wine, but occasionally a rose, which has pine resin added to it during the fermentation process. To me its smell is reminiscent of turpentine, although I cannot vouch that the taste is similar. However, retsina is a popular drink throughout Greece and is readily available in supermarkets and off-licenses abroad.

A favourite by-product of the wine making process, particularly in Crete, is raki. All the discarded pieces of grape left over from the wine-pressing, the skins, stems and seeds, are fermented in barrels and then distilled to produce this clear spirit which can have alcohol content approaching a very dangerous 90 per cent, but is more usually nearer 70 per cent.

Often raki is offered to guests as a sign of hospitality, served with fruit after a meal. It is also held to have medicinal powers and traditionally has been used as a cure-all for ailments both internal and external.

Most villages on Crete have a couple of people who have licenses to distil the liquor and this is usually an excuse for locals to get together for a celebration. This takes place about six weeks after the grape harvest in the autumn, allowing the fermentation process to weave its magic on the must residue left over from wine making. This is then distilled in copper vats over a bonfire, the whole production cycle frequently taking at least a weekend of sampling, eating and dancing.

Another favourite spirit widely drunk across Greece is made in a similar way to raki, but flavoured with aniseed. Ouzo is distilled from ethyl alcohol frequently made from grape must with added anise and other herbs and spices, which vary depending on the distillery. Its sweet liquorice taste is distinctive, and it can be drunk neat in shots or more usually with ice and water added, which gives the drink a milky colour. Like raki it is best to eat something while drinking as it is more-ish and deceptively strong.

The Greeks love to have a drink and their many celebrations throughout the year are always accompanied by copious amounts of alcohol but it is rare to see a Greek drunk. It is a point of honour to be able to hold your drink and it is unusual for food not to be eaten when out celebrating and for glasses of water to be drunk judiciously throughout.

Vai – A Tropical Heaven?

I knew nothing about Crete before first arriving back in the early 1980s. If I had one image in my mind before I came here it was of palm trees on a deserted beach of golden sand. I don't know what planted this picture in my imagination but it pretty much fits the bill of the palm forest of Vai in the far east of the island. Perhaps I had unconsciously seen a picture of this startlingly mesmeric corner of Crete in a magazine article; or maybe I had confused Crete with some Caribbean idyll – but the pictures in the windows of the travel bureaux along 25 August Street in Heraklion repeated this stunning image.

Unfortunately, at that time, the picture was more of the dream than the reality. In the Seventies, hippies who had been driven out of their previous communes in the caves of Matala on the south coast of the island had appropriated the beach and adjoining forest. Numerous itinerant backpackers joined them, and the lack of facilities led to what had become a giant campsite turning into a rubbish dump.

Carrier bags, cigarette packets, bottles and cans were among the detritus that littered this piece of paradise on top of which was pitched a small shanty town of tents and ramshackle shelters. On my first trip here, after a long, hot, three-hour bus ride to Sitia from Heraklion and a further trip taking the best part of an hour, the state of the beach left me totally disillusioned, my dreams shattered.

The land is owned by the Monastery of Toplou, an imposing building lying some five miles inland of the forest, and the monks and government authorities recognized that something needed to be done. They restored the beach and forest to its natural state and, under an EU directive, it became a protected site administered by the Greek Forestry Commission. All camping along with any activity which is thought could endanger this fragile environment is banned.

Visiting nowadays, it is apparent that the measures taken have been successful. So much so that in the summer the litter lying on the beach has been replaced by thousands of tourists, bussed in from resorts across the island to see what is the largest palm forest in Europe. The 300,000 square yards of Cretan date palms is endemic to the island and have been growing in the area for as long as there is recorded history. The name Vai is derived from the word *vayia*, which means 'palms' in Greek.

To the edge of the beach lie some steps that lead up to a viewing platform. Reaching this point you can see a panorama of the whole beach and forest spread out in front of you. The depth of the blue of the sea is unfathomable as it nudges up to the honey gold sands fringed by the verdant fronds of the palms. A tiny island floats in the middle of the bay wrapped in the encircling embrace of the hot sands and shady palms on the shoreline

The reputation of this spot of outstanding natural beauty is such that it is, like with many other places on the island, best to come out of season. If that is impossible, then visit early or late in the day to avoid the crowds. I made the mistake once of taking some friends who were visiting in late July, after I had sung the praises of Vai's beauty. From arrival at the rammed car park, which was as packed as the beach itself where sunbathing bodies obscured every square inch of sand, it must have been hard for them to relate this to my description of a balmy idyll.

Some quick thinking and a suggestion that we visited Moni Toplou rescued me. *Moni* means monastery, in this case that of the aforementioned order who own the land. We retraced our route driving out of the full car park, navigating past cars now parked in any higgledy-piggledy fashion in anything vaguely resembling a space on the access road. Cars hooted at pedestrians and double-parked coaches stopped to disgorge their cargo of sun-seeking passengers.

Leaving behind the mayhem of the beach we drove the five miles or so back inland to the magnificent monastery. At first sight, the face the monastery shows to the world is not one of a peaceful retreat. It is built for war, and resembles a fortress, dominating the surrounding hot, arid landscape. On closer scrutiny of the history of Moni Toplou or Panagia Akrotiriani (Our Lady on the Cape) as it is otherwise known, it becomes apparent that the building needed to be strong to defend it against any number of antagonists over the centuries. Its very name, Toplou, is derived from the word 'top' in Turkish, which means cannon, referring to weapons which had been employed during Venetian times to defend the order against the marauding Turks. And the monks' history is littered with examples of them being subjected to siege, plundering and persecution.

The outside walls suggest this violent history. There has been a monastery on the site since the 14th Century, but this was thought to have been razed to the ground by pirates. Following its demise it was rebuilt in the 16th Century only to suffer looting at the hands of the Knights of Malta in 1530 before being destroyed again, this time by the catastrophic earthquake of 1612. Undeterred, the ruling Venetians collaborated with the monks to build the current structure to sure up the defences of this remote part of Eastern Crete. Following the demise of the Venetians and their surrender to the Turks in 1646, the monastery fell into disrepair before being resurrected under special privileges obtained from the then ruling Ottomans. This special relationship was not to last. During the independence uprising in 1821 the participation of the resident monks led to their wholesale slaughter by the Turks. With the monastery inhabited again by 1828, the order was once more routed by the Turks in the 1866 revolution. The bloodshed did not end there; during the Second World War the monks continued their proud tradition of independence and gave shelter to both Cretan and British freedom fighters. When a radio transmitter hidden in a cave near the monastery was discovered, the Germans arrested two monks and the abbot. One monk succumbed to torture and died in prison while the other monk and the abbot were both executed.

Outside the fortified walls I turned and looked around this desolate and windswept plain. On a hill in the background turned giant wind turbines, the modern incarnation of the lone mill, its sails long since gone, which remained the sole building outside the main monastery walls, apart from the small chapel which marked the monks' graveyard. I turned back to the imposing gates above which openings in the walls through which boiling oil was poured on attackers can be seen. On entering, the monastery showed a different, more benign face. The interior courtyard that stands in the shadows of the 33-foot-tall fortified walls is paved with pebbles, smoothed by the sea before being layed here and being further burnished by centuries of the monks to-ings and fro-ings. The cloisters surrounding the central courtyard are bedecked with pottery urns from which flourish an abundance of flowers of every conceivable hue. A stairway leads up to the cells where the three blue-robed monks and the abbot now in residence retire when they are not working, dining in the refectory or at prayer in the church which is topped with the imposing square bell tower with a domed belfry standing 110 feet tall. Inside is an icon by the 18th-century master Ioannis Kornaros, his 1770 work, *Great Art Thou, O Lord, and Wonderful Are Thy Works*, comprises four central pictures surrounded by 57 individual miniature biblical scenes illustrating a line from the Orthodox prayer of the icon's title.

Leaving the dark interior of the church, our eyes blinking as they readjust to the blinding light, we notice an inscription in the wall of the church. This, I later discover, is the verdict handed out by a court of arbitration in Asia Minor called Magnesia, which had been called upon to rule on a dispute over land rights during the Roman occupation of the island in the 2nd Century BC. The factions involved were Cretan tribes from nearby Itanos and from Ierapytna further to the south west, now Ierapetra. For what it's worth, the ruling went in favour of the local Itanos clan but the inscription itself had been discovered by the British classicist, mathematician and writer Robert Pashley in 1834 who found it being used as a headstone in a graveyard and suggested it be given pride of place set in the wall.

The monastery also has a small museum containing engravings made by monks from Mount Athos on mainland Greece and exhibits a number of 15th-century icons of the Constantinople School. Although only four members of the order remain living here, the wealth of land, over which the monastery presides, produces wine, raki and olive oil, all of which are available for sale in a small shop on site.

Making Modern Greece

The beginnings of modern Greece as we now know it can be traced back to 1832 when, following a successful uprising against the Ottoman Turks that lasted between 1821 and 1828, the British, French and Russian governments recognized the legitimacy of the Greek state. The Treaty of London ratified this in 1932, making Greece an independent monarchy.

This newly emerging country then consisted of Central Greece, the Peloponnese, the Sporades and the Cyclades but did not include Crete. Some might see it as incredible that there was, and still is, such a force for unity especially now in an age where many nation states are disintegrating. What was it that held the Greeks together for so long without a recognized geographical homeland? The three most important factors in that cohesion are ancient history, religion and language.

The great civilization of Classical Greece between 505 BC to the death of Alexander the Great was followed by the Hellenistic period that lasted until the Greek heartlands were conquered by the Roman Empire in 146 BC. As the power of the Roman Empire in western Europe waned, it was followed by a strongly Greek-influenced Eastern Empire centred on Constantinople. This Greek speaking Byzantine Empire lasted until the Ottoman Turks overran it in 1453 AD.

Whether colonized for their own protection or conquered by an aggressive force, the Greeks as a race continued to speak their own language and worship in the Greek Orthodox faith. They also proudly held on to the knowledge that they were the living ancestors of the Ancient Greeks and that their rightful homeland was the 'cradle of civilization'.

Despite this powerful pull towards unity, it seemed that differences over politics, the constitution and even language could tear the newly-reunited nation apart. If there had not been an overriding hatred of the Ottoman Empire and an ambition to achieve the *megali idea* (great idea) of reuniting all Greek lands to their Byzantine boundaries, modern Greece might still remain nothing but a dream.

Two crucial arguments raged within the new Greece. Firstly, the fundamental political and constitutional differences between the monarchist right-wing nationalists, and the republican, liberal left who saw Greece's part in a wider European and world context. This became known as the national schism. Secondly, there was the language question.

Most Greeks spoke a form of the language called *dhimotiki*, which had developed naturally through everyday usage over the centuries. Many of those in the educated elite perceived this language as a peasant tongue. They believed that if the glories of Ancient Greece were to be restored, then what was effectively a pastiche of Classical Greek should be spoken. This completely different language was known as *katharevousa* and was adopted in official documents and newspapers. This was divisive, in that few of the uneducated masses could understand it.

Monarchs came and went, military coups overthrew kings and governments alike and ultimately this inner turmoil put paid to the dream of the *megali idea*. Greece's internal struggles were responsible for it losing territory it had gained after the First World War following defeat by Kemal Ataturk's forces in 1922. This led to the great population exchange in 1923 where 1.5 million Christians and 500,000 Muslims were uprooted and moved to land within the redrawn borders of Greece and Turkey.

I think it is fair to say that the country only put to rest the two issues of the national schism and the language question following the declaration of the current republic in 1974. Two years later *dhimotiki* was finally declared the official national language.

With the question of the country adopting a constitutional monarchy or being taken over by military rulers now unlikely, the political high-ground of modern Greece has, at least until the recent economic crisis, largely been contested by the right-wing New Democracy Party and the left-wing Pan Hellenic Socialist Movement (PASOK) who have operated a revolving-door policy in Government ever since.

Zakros – The Forgotten City

In many ways Kato Zakros is the forgotten Minoan city of Crete. It is also its most complete example of a Bronze Age settlement. It lies literally at the end of the road, where the tarmac trail that has weaved its way through olive groves and banana plantations from Palekastro through the small town of Ano Zakros eventually peters out about five miles further on near the sea at the extreme eastern end of the island. This is a wonderful drive, which looks more daunting on the map than it actually is. It is well worth the visit, not least because so few other people travel here, giving it a wonderful tranquility that belies its resplendence and importance.

Zakros is a relatively recent find, which didn't reveal its secrets until 1962 despite having been the subject of archaeological interest since the beginning of that same century when the discovery of the palace itself eluded archaeologists by a matter of feet. Both Arthur Evans and Federico Halbherr both harboured suspicions that there was an ancient settlement hereabouts. Their tentative digs uncovered little. In 1901 an archaeologist of the British School, David Hogarth was more successful, unearthing a number of houses and artifacts. These at first were believed to come from a small Minoan port but, like others before him, he had missed his mark.

The ancient city was reluctant to give up clues to its existence lightly. It showed more of itself in the 1930s when a local doctor bought some artifacts from a farmer who was a patient of his. A bull's head pendant, which can now be seen in Heraklion's Archaeological Museum, was the most significant of the items found under the plough. Its discovery gave rise to the belief that there just might be something more down there. In 1961 a Greek archaeologist, Nikolas Planton, convinced there was more to the site than met the eye, began a painstaking dig in the area and the following year discovered the magnificent Minoan palace.

Kato Zakros lies near the sea at the bottom of a ravine known as 'The Valley of the Dead'. If time allows, the ideal way to approach it is by foot, taking the five mile walk through this stunning gorge from near the enchanting little town of Ano Zakros. The gorge is so named because along its length a large number of caves have been discovered containing Minoan burial tombs. The walk can be done in as little as two hours at the right time of day, but to rush it would be to miss out on the abundance of flowers and wildlife which share this place with the dead. Wild flowers flourish in spring under the watchful eyes of eagles, buzzards, and vultures that hover in search of food, floating on the thermals high above. Before leaving the gorge, at the bottom take the time to spin around and bellow 'Ha!'. It soon becomes apparent why modern day locals have renamed the 'The Valley of the Dead', 'Ha! Canyon'.

Experiencing the seclusion of this walk heightens the experience of visiting the palace as it contributes to an unperturbed state of mind ideal for ruminating on the Minoan civilization that existed here 4,000 years ago. The thing is that, because of the relative seclusion of the site and the surrounding mountains, it is rare in providing the peace to provoke such thoughts.

Whether approached by car or on foot the journey in itself is rewarding. The first site of the remains of the palace standing apart from a pebble and sand beach in a sheltered bay takes the breath away. The site only covers about 12,000 square yards of which less than half is the palace, the rest being the town. Remarkably it has yielded a valuable artifact for almost every one of those square yards. Many of these finds are displayed in the archaeological museums of Sitia and Heraklion. It is a fair old way back to Heraklion which houses the most important of these objects but if you have the inclination it is worth the visit, context is all. Putting the magnificent reconstructed ceremonial vessel made of quartz mentally back in the treasury where it was discovered, or finding the jar from the courtyard which contained olives preserved in water lends much to the experience.

As you first look down on the extensive remains, you can see what is left of the second Minoan palace. It was built on the site in 1600 BC to replace the first palace, which had suffered extensive earthquake damage. In the years that followed, until its demise in 1450 BC the palace was the seat of monarchy in the far east of the island from where produce from the fertile land hereabouts was traded for gem stones, ivory, silver and gold from Egypt and the Middle East.

The palace is built around a courtyard. Corridors and rooms squirrel out from the communal centre. On its eastern side a thoroughfare known as 'Harbour Street' led from the palace's main portal to the all-important port. Just off the courtyard near the Treasury Room, hundreds of fragments inscribed with Linear A script were found in a number of wooden chests. Unfortunately, only the top layers had survived as water had damaged the lower levels, and these could have been invaluable in the ongoing attempts to decipher the language. And water is still a problem. As the whole of the eastern end of Crete is sinking, the rising water table poses a threat to the site and fear of flooding makes it difficult for archaeologists to dig deeper. The circular water tank in the cistern hall in the east wing, which may have been used for fish storage or indeed as an early example of a swimming pool, retains a water level which is much appreciated by the wild terrapins which have adopted it as their home.

That no human remains were found in the palace or the town somehow further confuses the ongoing debate about the demise of the Minoan society in 1450 BC. Academic thought had been swinging towards the idea that marauding Mycenaeans had driven the citizens from their homes. However, Platanos, who died aged 82, believed that the discovery of walls uplifted by extreme force on the site indicates they may have been caused by volcanic eruption or tsunami damage caused by the episode near Thira. The debate continues, but one thing is certain, it was the complete demolition of the palace and its subsequent disappearance beneath tons of earth, which makes it such an important find. As the site had eluded archaeologists, so had it escaped the attentions of casual looters. This meant that all its treasured remains lay in situ and as such were able to reveal more to the scientists who subsequently excavated here.

Walking along Harbour Street, crossing the scrubland between the palace and the coast I see a snakeskin, dried and discarded by its owner. The result of this sloughing is so well camouflaged in silver with terracotta and black markings that I step on it and almost jump out of my skin too before regaining composure. When I realize what I am seeing I slink away to cool my feet in the sea. Reaching the beach there is a small taverna with rushwork umbrellas and small fishing caiques moored off, anchored astern and bow lines brought ashore secured round boulders on the beach. On a rock sits a fisherman, his yellow nets laid around him, checking for snags and holes. A few people sunbathe on the beach or swim in the sea. Looking east to the horizon there is nothing to see but the Mediterranean stretching away, the next land mass in that direction is Cyprus, some 300 miles distant.

Ierapetra – To the Edge of Europe

Ierapetra is the most southerly town in Europe. Lying on the south-eastern coast of Crete, it experiences some of the hottest temperatures on the island. Washed by the Libyan Sea, the town is the heart of Crete's flourishing market garden industry. On the plains inland stretch rows of massive greenhouses in which tomatoes, beans and bananas among other fruit and vegetables grow in abundance. These structures are just made of large wooden frames covered with plastic sheeting, but they do the job.

Ierapetra is often, rather unfairly, described as unexceptional, but I love it. Even at the height of the tourist season it manages to retain its own unique identity. The south west of the town, stretching inland from the harbour and guarded by its ancient Venetian fortress, is a mish-mash of old, Turkish-style architecture, traditional Greek houses and newer small apartment blocks, connected by narrow streets ablaze with climbing clematis and potted geraniums. The alleyways are too narrow for speeding cars, and the peace here is in stark contrast to the hectic, newer part of town.

This old region of the city is called Kato Mera, and has the footprint of the earlier Venetian and Turkish settlements. It is home to the old mosque, a reminder of the former Ottoman occupation. Situated here is the church of Agios Georgios from where priests can often be heard broadcasting to the faithful through loudspeakers mounted on lampposts.

Snuggling among the ramshackle buildings is a faded, two-storey house with crumbling stucco and bare-wood shutters, unexceptional except that Napoleon lodged with a local family here on his way home to France in 1798, following his Battle of the Pyramids campaign in Egypt.

The modern part of the town, known as Pano Mera, encircles Kato Mera and is still growing. It is a bustling commercial sector that reflects the relative wealth of the town – said to have the highest standard of living on

Crete. This is in no small part a result of the success of the market gardening industry. The 14,000,000 square yards of agricultural land covered with those plastic greenhouses produces a massive crop, much of which is for export and contributes a considerable boost to Greece's balance of payments.

A Dutchman called Paul Kuijpers is celebrated around these parts for his contribution to hothouse cultivation. A horticulturalist, he settled on the island in 1966 and was instrumental in introducing the greenhouses to the area. Tragically he was killed in a motoring accident near his home in the town. He died in 1971 aged just 32 years old. A bust celebrating his contribution to the local society stands at Gra Lighia on the road between Ierapetra and Myrtos.

The marble-paved promenade on the sea front is a relaxing, if sometimes windswept place to sit and enjoy a drink looking out over the Libyan sea towards Africa. The waves that lap against the man-made sea wall ripple in over a gently shelving seabed that remains shallow in places for several hundred yards out into the ocean. This is not a natural phenomenon. The promenade was built over a beach, and the waters offshore now deposit sand over a wider area further out to sea, creating the shallows.

To the west of the town there remains a long, sandy beach, which was used as the location for Anthony Quinn's famous sirtaki dance scene in the film *Zorba the Greek*. But even this has not been immune to the interventions of man. Large quantities of sand were removed both officially and unofficially to be used as bedding in the area's thousands of greenhouses.

Off the coast of Ierapetra, is an island that has been designated an area of outstanding natural beauty. Chrissi, meaning 'golden', is a small island that lies seven miles offshore and is now uninhabited. There are boat trips which leave the town quay every morning to this beguiling place which was once a Minoan, and later a Byzantine, settlement. Now its brilliant white sands and pine trees bear witness only to the tourists who visit daily during the summer but must leave before nightfall on the return ferry.

As the only town of any significant size on the south coast of Crete, Ierapetra has been nicknamed the 'nymph of the Libyan Sea', but it is by no means the only destination worth visiting along this part of the coastline. Leaving town going west through industrial estates selling cars, agricultural equipment and supplies, the road narrows and traverses the rows of nurseries and orange groves that lie between the higher, olive-lined hills inland and the sea.

Little more than six miles away, above the coast road in the hills, is the site of the early Minoan settlement of Fournou Korifi, dating from the third millennium BC. From the remains of this labyrinth of small dwellings, numerous artifacts have been excavated and can be seen in the archaeological museum in Agios Nikolaos. The most celebrated of these is a vessel crafted in the shape of an ample-bodied woman with a long neck and small face. She is carrying a jug through which libations, most probably of oil, wine or honey, would be poured onto an altar as an offering to appease the gods.

A mile or so further on along the main road, if you stop and walk up a dirt track to the top of a hill, the remains of the palace of Myrtos Pyrgos reveal themselves. Destroyed by fire in about 1400 BC, its rooms, courtyards and stairs are still clearly defined and can easily be made out.

Interesting as these sites are, to me the real treasure lies less than a mile further on and is the current settlement of Myrtos. This village occupies the site of a former small port. Most of the dwellings here were built following the Second World War during which German soldiers torched the old houses when the inhabitants refused to abandon their homes.

A hippy haven in the late Sixties and early Seventies, Myrtos is now a more mainstream, if small-scale, tourist destination for those who enjoy the peaceful life. There are plenty of rooms and apartments to rent. Sitting along the narrow streets are tavernas, a bakery and a few shops, and the long, immaculately clean beach is never more than a few steps away. Time spent here, walking through the winding alleyways of whitewashed, shuttered buildings among tubs of vibrant red geraniums is like a distillation of the essence of Cretan life.

The Wedding Venue

Leaving behind a small village, Ano Viannos, in the south, we drove into the mountains following a deserted road around the hairpins, which overlooked the fertile valleys below. The occasional ramshackle farmhouse came and disappeared from view and the fields were deserted in the middle of the day.

It was lunchtime and we were not optimistic of finding a taverna such a long way from any village. We should have known better, in Crete you are rarely far from somewhere to eat and drink. But in this instance the source of sustenance was somewhat surprising.

Cresting the mountain pass we saw a huge, white-painted, concrete building raised up above the road with a large, covered terrace looking down into the valley. The blue and white of two Greek flags fluttered on their poles either side of the entrance to an enormous empty car park.

On the terrace was a man eating alone, at another table a couple drank coffee. When I asked if they could serve lunch they replied 'of course' and gestured us to sit at a table. A girl appeared from inside and told us what was on the menu; '*katsiki che horiatiki salada*', goat and Greek salad.

Not spoiled for choice, we gratefully ordered what was on offer. Grilled with herbs, the goat was served with chips and a salad of olives, tomatoes, cucumber and feta cheese dressed in olive oil and vinegar. The meal was delicious.

Maybe the silence and the stupefying view enhanced its taste. Looking down into the valley it was dotted with small beehives painted in a multitude of bright colours. Terraces of fruit trees and innumerable varieties of vegetables ran between irrigation pipes and channels, and the scent of wild sage and oregano drifted in on the barely discernible breeze.

Inside, the building was immense with a slightly-raised stage at the front and tables and chairs set out in rows, which could seat upwards of 1,000 people. It seemed strange that such a large building should serve a handful of people so far outside a village or town. I later learned that this was one of the venues that plays host to the massive Cretan wedding receptions. And in Greece, weddings really are big, lavish occasions, celebrated in the grandest style.

From the time a child is born, the parents start saving to pay for when they get married. It is also tradition that, where possible, the parents provide the newly-married couple with a home. This is one reason so many buildings have an unfinished additional storey above the lived in accommodation. It is in readiness to be completed for when the owner's children get married. So, for many couples, they start married life with a home to move in to.

And that is not all. Most wedding gifts are of money, and at the wedding reception there is also a tradition of pinning bank notes to the bride and groom's clothing or throwing cash at them as they dance. Considering that often the whole village is invited to a wedding and it is not unusual for there to be 1,000 guests, it can give the happy couple a good financial start to their married life together!

Greeks are very family-orientated. It is unusual for a child, particularly a daughter, to leave home until they are married, unless they go away to university or are doing national service. The parents look after their children, supporting them as much as they can and, in return, their children look after them in old age.

Marriage is enshrined in tradition and religious orthodoxy. It is still tradition for the man to ask his intended's parents for their daughter's hand before he proposes. After the match has been agreed, an engagement party is held where the rings, blessed by the local priest, are placed on the couple's left hand ring fingers in front of their families and friends.

The church is strict as to when weddings can be held, and without special dispensation from a bishop, a wedding cannot take place during religious festivals or times of fasting. Prior to the wedding, guests are invited to the couple's new home where gifts are presented to wish them good luck for their future together.

A day or two before the wedding ceremony any young unmarried friends of the family take part in the bed ceremony called *to krevati*. In this traditional ritual, the bed at the couple's future home is made by any young girls visiting, then the sheets are ripped off by the other guests and the girls remake it.

This is repeated several times and then a baby is rolled over on the bed in a gesture of good luck for the couple's future fertility. Sometimes money and rice are thrown on the sheets to wish them a prosperous future.

The wedding service lasts for about three-quarters of an hour. A profoundly sacred occasion, it can seem somewhat informal. Guests walk in and out of the church during the service, groups of men leaving to smoke outside or women to have a chat. This is not disrespectful in any way, but is usually because so many people want to attend that there is an unofficial rota operating so that everyone can witness a small part of the service.

The groom awaits his bride alongside his best man at the entrance to the church and she arrives, usually a few minutes late with her best woman. The groom hands her the bouquet as they enter the church. During the ceremony the priest blesses the rings that are then placed on the couple's right hands.

Two crowns joined together by ribbon are put on the heads of the couple by the best man who swaps them over their heads three times. After drinking wine from the same cup together, the couple walks around the church three times and guests shower them with rice. Sometimes the best man will follow holding a plate on which guests can place gifts of envelopes containing money.

The congregation and the couple then leave for the reception to be joined by even more guests and the celebrating continues until dawn. The bride dances all night, first with her husband, then her family, next with her husband's family, then her friends followed by those of her husband - all this is accompanied by a lavish feast.

For anyone who has attended a Greek wedding celebration it is unlikely they will ever forget the experience, even if the details may prove just a little bit hazy.

Rethymnon – The Serene City

There are few things as pleasurable as taking a walk around Rethymnon old town (Palia Poli). More than any other of Crete's historic cities it has managed to retain much of its original Venetian and Turkish heritage.

The town sits midway between the major cities of Heraklion and Chania but maintains its own very individual character. If Heraklion, 50 miles to the east, exhibits the restless metropolitan swagger of a capital city and Chania, 37 miles west, a pride in its distinguished past, Rethymnon displays a unique serenity.

Built by the Venetians as a staging port between its two larger neighbours, its smaller size makes it more intimate and less inhibiting. Although you can wander for hours in the narrow streets and alleyways you will never be far from the wonderful harbour, lined with fish tavernas and cafes where tourists and students from the university alike wile away hours chatting or feeding fish in the crystal clear water.

Retaining most of its architectural integrity, walking the streets reveals much of the story of the town. Fortifications, fountains, domes and minarets all stand testimony to its ancestry, indeed there is archaeological evidence that a small settlement has been on this site since Minoan times.

The town's name is derived from the flourishing Mycenean centre of Rithymna, which was large enough to mint its own coins. For some unexplained reason the town went into decline, although the discovery of both Roman and Byzantine mosaics does reveal that the site remained inhabited.

It was in the early 13th Century, when Crete became a Venetian colony, that the city as we know it began to develop. As a centre of commerce, Rethymnon had its own council, nobles and a bishop. They built the city walls and the castle, the harbour, the Loggia and many of the churches and houses, which remain today.

With the decline in Venice's power and influence, the city was captured by the Turks in 1646 and became part of the Ottoman Empire. Minarets and domes were added to former Christian churches, which were transformed into mosques in which the new Muslim population could worship. The solid, stone walls of classic Venetian houses were adorned with wooden balconies and the waterfront cafes were built as places for the men to congregate and drink coffee.

The harbour today makes the most of its stunning location, and competition to attract business is fierce among the waiters in the dockside tavernas. Just a short stroll inland to the Platia Petihaki where restaurant tables are scattered around the pavements that surround the graceful Rimondi Fountain is probably a better bet for a reasonable meal without the hard sell.

The fountain is, needless to say, Venetian as its three lion heads spouting water might indicate. It has been a focal point for locals since it was built as a source of clean water by the rector of the city, A. Rimondi, in 1626. The water runs into three sinks that support four Corinthian columns above which the latin words *liberalitatis* and *fontes* (generous and fountain) can be made out.

In the streets and alleyways around the fountain are shops selling handmade jewellery, leather goods, embroidery and lace. Wandering there you catch glimpses of the towering minaret of the Mosque Neratzes. Now a music school, the Turks converted the Christian church of Santa Maria by adding the galleried minaret and three small domes.

That the city has kept so much of its architectural integrity and is a centre for cultural and academic pursuits lends much to its air of relaxed confidence. I have visited Rethymnon as often as I have visited Crete itself, its lure being hard to resist if I am on the island.

Arkadi Monastery – A Religious Experience

One particular morning the usual smell of floor polish tinged with sweat had been replaced by something different. As I climbed the stairs towards the school, the sweet smell of pine hung in the air.

'*Kalimera*', I greeted the secretary and went into the staff room, where the smell got stronger. '*Kalimera professor*' Manolis welcomed me as he did every morning, carrying on smoking and marking books. I couldn't fail to notice; walking around the room was a priest, swinging an incense-burning censer and muttering a prayer.

After making sure the incense had penetrated every corner of the staffroom he moved on to the classroom next door. My eyes followed him. Seeing that I thought this was somewhat unusual Manolis offered up an explanation. The local priest, for a suitable donation to church funds, came in once a year to bless the school, his prayers rising with the smoke from the incense towards heaven.

Dressed in a fading grey robe and tall drainpipe hat, such priests, or papas, were seen all over the town. Although, as in many countries, congregations are declining, the Orthodox religion still lies at the heart of most Greek people's lives. The priests are very much a part of the community, and have a proud heritage of resistance against forces of occupation throughout Greece's history.

It is this tradition of Orthodox religion standing alongside the faithful that has created a strong bond between church and state. An example that epitomizes this relationship is legendary, and was instrumental in changing the course of the island's history.

Twelve miles to the south east of the coastal resort of Rethymnon stand the buildings of Arkadi Monastery, now a national sanctuary to members of the resistance movement. The story of the monastery is an unforgettable reminder of the bravery of the freedom fighters and the role of the church in their defiance in the face of the oppressor.

In 1866 the monastery became the centre for the local resistance fighters who had risen up against their Ottoman rulers and carried out attacks against them in their stronghold in the city of Rethymnon. Eventually Turkish troops tracked the partisans and their families down and, surrounding the monastery, demanded their surrender. The abbot, Gabriel Marinakis, refused and the Turks lay siege to Arkadi for three days, suffering horrendous casualties.

Eventually the superior numbers of Ottoman troops broke through. Rather than surrender the abbot ordered the survivors to retreat into a wine store where they kept their barrels of gunpowder. As the Turks advanced he gave the order to shoot into the casks, causing a massive explosion, killing the Cretans and hundreds of their attackers. Nowhere is the Cretan belief in 'freedom or death' demonstrated better than in this historic moment.

Although the Turks regarded the storming of Arkadi Monastery as a victory, it was to prove a turning point in international opinion. Their assault on this holy place and the atrocities that followed, enraged public opinion abroad and supporters of an independent Crete became more vocal. The Italian military hero and politician Garibaldi voiced his support for the Cretans, as did Victor Hugo, the French romantic poet and human rights activist.

Outrage at the slaughter of the Cretans by the Ottoman despots did not immediately lead to autonomy, but it signalled the beginning of the end of Turkish rule as the great powers began to put political pressure on Turkey to withdraw. It took a further 30 years, until 1898, for Crete to finally gain independence, but it was the atrocity at Arkadi Monastery that was the catalyst which brought about the end of 230 years of Turkish rule.

Amari Valley – A Place to Linger

Leaving behind the sombre Arkadi Monastery we head inland to a place often sited by lovers of the island as their favourite – the Amari Valley. Yet word has obviously, and fortunately, not spread. It is cooler here by some degrees than on the coast, which is just as well as this is lingering country. Everything about it winds back the clock to a pace that is human, and if you submit to its laconic lifestyle, the valley will reward you with its riches. It is hard to believe this place could have borne witness to some of the most violent reprisals taken by German troops during the Second World War. I can only imagine the aggressors in that macabre episode were not of this world, so preoccupied were they with bringing death that life passed them by. But the theatre where that historical obscenity was played out has been reborn in the shadow of Crete's greatest mountain, Ida or as it is otherwise known, Psiloritis.

Its history aside, things are less extreme here in the Amari Valley. Even in summer it has a carpet of flowers beneath the shade of trees laden with fruit. It is not difficult to get to this playground of Zeus, but most pass by either side en route to Agia Galini or Gortys in the south. The beauty and colour of this gentle valley is in stark contrast to the mountains that surround it. The burnished colours of oranges and cherry blossom, white tinged with pink in spring, or the deep red of the cherries themselves which grow in the orchards here alongside apples, olives and grapes above a panoply of wild flowers of every imaginable colour are echoed inside any number of unassuming small white churches. These simple places of worship so often belie the sumptuousness of the strong-coloured frescoes that lie within. These magnificent works of religious art, although common all over Crete, somehow seem more prevalent here, their artists possibly inspired by the strong lines of the mountain ranges exerting their power over the vivid hues of the valleys they patrol.

Some of these chapels are open, but at others you will need to ask for a key, the caretakers are usually close at hand if you enquire of their whereabouts from the locals. We are some 1,800 ft above sea level. This is not a place to plan a visit to carefully, it is somewhere to wander, explore, discover. You cannot get lost as the surrounding mountains will hold you in check. In the village of Amari itself we climb to the top of a bell tower built during the Venetian dynasty and can take stock of the whole, surrounding valley.

A good road circumnavigates the region, which is criss-crossed by other roads and paths of varying calibre. We are heading for the village of Thronos at the northern end of the valley where we have booked rooms for three nights. As its name suggests it was probably the seat of a bishop of some considerable standing. There is evidence here that it was a place of importance, judging by an early Byzantine mosaic that runs underneath the current tiny church of Panagia (All Holy Virgin Mary), presumably having been the floor of another much larger church that stood on the same site. Inside the frescoes date from the 14th and 15th Century, in the nave a depiction of the dead Jesus being cradled by the Virgin and St John.

Sitting outside a taverna we spend the evening watching the sun go down before tucking into a meal of grilled kid and *horta* salad with potatoes braised in olive oil and tomatoes. As the night wears on we remark on lights twinkling high on the slopes of Mount Psiloritis. Our host explains they are the fires of climbers who took the trek at night-time under the full moon to avoid the heat of the day. He says he can organize a climb if I want to go the next night. It looks an awfully long way, but he explains the first part of the trek is undertaken by four-wheel drive. Persuaded, though daunted, I agree.

The mountain is the highest on the island, just, and nestling in its folds lies the Nida Plateau. Psiloritis means 'large one' but the mountain's real name of Ida is thought to stem from the word 'da' meaning mother of all gods, so it is appropriate that Rhea, the mother of Zeus, is connected to the mountain by way of the Idian Cave, which overlooks the plateau. Legend has it that, following his birth in the Diktean Cave in the mountains surrounding the Lassithi Plateau to the east, Zeus was brought into hiding in the Idian

Cave to escape the notice of his murderous father, Kronos, who had an insatiable appetite for eating his offspring to prevent them from killing him. Luckily for the young god, Rhea placed him under the protection of a goat named Amalthea and the benevolent but warlike Kouretes who were reputed to have performed a war dance bashing their swords against their shields whenever Kronos was likely to hear his son crying. This ploy by his unconventional babysitters worked as Zeus, as we know, grew up to become the king of all gods, and went on to overthrow his murderous father.

From within this dank cave numerous finds of pottery shards, gold jewellery and statues have been discovered which date from the Minoan period and are exhibited in the Archaeological Museum in Heraklion. There is little else hereabouts apart from a small chapel near the mouth of the cave and small piles of stone which on closer inspection appear to be shelters, presumably for the shepherds and goatherds who graze their animals here in the summer months.

The wisdom of climbing the mountain at night by the light of a full moon soon becomes apparent. The trek, even during hours of darkness, is still warm in the summer heat, although we carry layers of warm clothing in our packs as, if the wind gets up, it can turn bitterly cold. We have also been advised to take a sleeping bag to get into at the summit as we await dawn. Before setting off we tuck in to a hearty meal of souvlaki at a small taverna and although wine is on offer I abstain, the summit does seem an awfully long way off.

The path is relatively untaxing, but I welcomed the decision of our guide to take the trek under the illumination of a full moon as it would be easy to turn an ankle on the uneven surface and loose rocks. One thing I am also sure of is that if I had undertaken the climb without the assistance of a guide I would now be completely lost. We walk at a steady pace. Every forty minutes or so we stop to take on board some water and energy-giving chocolate and, as we get higher, the conversation between climbers gets less and less. It feels as if we are all deep in a collective reverie – that we are about to witness something spectacular. The silence is punctuated by the low tinkling of goats' and sheep's bells, although I cannot see them and cannot estimate how far away the sound is coming from.

Less than an hour before dawn we make the summit, which is a flat plateau of rock with the tiny stone chapel of Timios Stavros that, amazingly, is the highest point on the island and is named after the summit of Mount Ida. Inside the chapel some candles are burning. I settle down on the cool rock with my back to the wall to have a rest before sunrise, and rustle round in my pack for some sustenance. As the bright ball of fire rises over the mountains to the east, it seems as though the whole of Crete is suffused in light and lies beneath my feet. The sky is a clear blue so this place, which so often stands above the cloudline, now offers up a panoramic view of such radiance it commits all who are experiencing the moment to silence. Only the occasional click of a camera shutter breaks the moment. To the north I can see all the way down to the coastal plateau segueing into the opal water of the sea.

We stand, drinking in the magnificence of this view, aware that we are unlikely to experience much like it again. When we have drunk our fill, we begin our tentative, dizzying descent, intoxicated by what we have seen. It is wise to get well under way before the sun rises too high and makes the climb uncomfortable, and our guide is keen to head down. We stop for a break at one of the stone shepherds' huts similar to those I had seen on the Nida Plateau. Our guide informs me these are called *mitado* and in this one we were invited to try the goats cheese, which is made there from milk straight from a herd grazing the mountain. Slightly off white and smelling of the beast of its origin, the smooth but strong flavour resonates with the smells, sites and sounds of the mountain and is extremely welcome after our exertions. We arrive back in the late morning and I settle down to a plate of eggs fried in olive oil with the thinnest rashers of crisp bacon and chunks of freshly baked bread and a cold beer before heading back to my room to sleep.

We meander our way home around the villages that cling to the mountains on the western side of the valley. They seem timeless. In reality they stand testament to the human spirit's will to regenerate itself. These tight-knit communities have been rebuilt from the ashes after being burned by German troops who murdered all of the people they could run to ground on 22nd August 1944. This barbarism was in reprisal for the audacious kidnap of the German Commander on the island General Kreipe who was captured by Cretan partisans and British special agents and moved across the island under cover of night on shepherd's tracks in the mountains. Their sacrifice has not been forgotten and is marked in every village by a memorial, with a particularly poignant large sculpture of a lone woman chiselling the inscriptions of the names of the dead into a plaque just outside the village of Ano Meros. It is hard not to consider the hell that was once perpetuated in this Garden of Eden.

On our way home we take a diversion to take a look at the new Potamoi Reservoir. This was created by a man-made dam paid for by an EU grant. Prior to its construction there were ructions among different factions worried about the effect this dam might have on the environment. It is finally now full and, as the water glints like a mirror dropped at the feet of Psiloritis, I can only say that the aesthetic of what is now Crete's largest lake is immensely pleasing. It's incongruous to have such a large body of water in this environment giving the area an almost Alpine feel. It must have been tough for locals who had lived and grazed their herds and flocks in this valley for generations to have their land flooded. I understand, however, the compensation was generous and the new wetlands have created a diverse environment where wildlife can flourish as well as harvesting a new water supply for Rethymnon and the surrounding area.

The dam is named after the legendary gods of the rivers, which were depicted in mosaics, paintings and sculptures as bulls with the head of a man or alternatively a man with the head of a bull and the tail of a fish. They were the sons of Okeanos, the great body of water that encircled the known world, their sisters were Okeanides, goddesses of clouds and rainfall and their daughters were nymphs, the Naides who danced in the freshwater springs.

Water is still a revered resource in modern-day Crete and I suspect that now the lake and dam are here the benefits will be appreciated.

Margarites – The Potters' Village

Perched precariously on the edge of a ravine in the foothills of Mount Psiloritis is an exquisite spot. Its appearance eloquently expresses everything that is captivating about Crete. This quintessential village, which I first visited with a friend of mine, David, a potter, back in 1983 has changed little over the years. The blue paint on the shutters and doors may be a bit brighter and the whitewash might sparkle more in the luminous mountain air, but the essence of Margarites has remained unchanged.

Famous for its pottery, this small, rambling village is bursting with studios, kilns, wheels, glazes and other paraphernalia. The speed and skill of the potters never ceases to amaze me. The alchemy that turns umber or shale-coloured clays into works of art, whether small, highly-glazed tourist trinkets or giant storage jars, or *pithoi*, which have changed little since the days when they would have graced the larders of Knossos storing oils and wine, is tantalizing.

Open doors along the winding labyrinthine streets reveal craftsmen at work sitting at their wheels. Some of these are still operated by treadle as skilled hands coax moist clay into their vision in the blink of an eye. The creation is then sliced from the turntable with a wire and set aside for first firing. Some of the potteries lie on the hills just outside the village looking down on Margarites with views of the coast shimmering in the distance.

Examples of the finished work are everywhere. Walking uphill along the main street there's a chance to view the fruits of the artists' labours. Highly glazed or in a functional matt finish, pots of all shapes and sizes are here to be bought. Sometimes it's hard to resist a purchase and I have any number of oil and vinegar jars and wine jugs at home waiting to be filled. They always bring me back here whenever I catch glimpse of them, which is perhaps a more useful function. With a cruet set lovingly wrapped in red and white striped paper, it is time to return to the pretty square or admire the 14th-century frescoes in the small church of Agios Ioannis Theologos, Saint John the Theologian, with its single-arch belfry suspending a lone bell beneath a cross at its apex. This simple, stone church holds some faded but extraordinary works of art depicting religious scenes starting with the nativity itself.

The history of this ancient village is steeped in the art of the potters' trade. The locals have set up an exhibition showing the history of pot making in all its stages and the results of their craftsmanship throughout the ages. I had always wondered how the giant *pithoi* were transported in the days before motor vehicles. Here I learned that the potters from the village were, at one time, itinerant workers who would ply their trade around the island. The artisans' wheels and kilns, along with their talents, were transported by donkey. Pots were turned and fired as near as possible in situ. Nowadays it is not unusual to see these giant pots swaddled in blankets and roped onto the back of a four-wheel drive as they are taken away to be deposited as a planter at the doorway of a villa or taverna down on the coast near Rethymnon

Celebrations of Life

In Crete Easter is a much bigger celebration than Christmas and name days are far bigger than birthdays. Before I understood the concept of the name day, I was amazed at why so many pupils arrived at school in a state of high excitement all apparently celebrating their birthday on the same day.

I expressed my surprise to Manolis who explained that most Greek children are named after saints, martyrs or legendary figures. Consequently, throughout their lives, they celebrate their name days alongside other people similarly named. So if christened Giorgos or Giorgia, on St George's Day they celebrate with a host of other people who share the same name.

Easter is the most important single festival in Greece and is a time for much solemn contemplation preceding some serious feasting and drinking. In spring, the weather is warm and the countryside full of promise, lush and bathed in colour. It is a perfect time that is wholly appropriate for the celebration of the resurrection of Christ.

Many Greek Orthodox Christians still fast throughout Lent, eating no meat or animal products. By Holy Thursday the sense of expectation of the coming celebrations is tangible, and families prepare by dying eggs red as a symbol of life, ready for them to be eaten on Easter Day. In the evening of that same day, women go to church and decorate a casket with flowers ready to receive the icon of Christ on Good Friday.

The following day is one of mourning the crucifixion of Christ. The Priest will take down the icon of our Lord from the cross in the church and wrap it in linen before placing it in a casket that is symbolic of the tomb in which Jesus was buried. In the evening the casket is carried at the head of a procession around the village to the accompaniment of hymns.

After the procession, people retire to a local taverna where they eat a dinner of seafood but still no meat. Shellfish, squid, taramasalata and salads bring welcome respite to those who have been fasting.

By the evening of the following day the churches are packed for the service of the resurrection, which begins an hour before midnight. In villages with small churches, the people spill outside where the service is relayed to them through loudspeakers. During the service the lights are turned out and the congregation light candles they have brought with them from the Holy Light passed round by the Priest. Just before midnight the Priest leads his flock outside the church and as the hour strikes he chants 'Christos anesti', Christ is risen.

The announcement is the cue for fireworks to be set off and in some places guns are shot into the air, while families and friends wish each other well before heading home. Keeping your candle alight is supposed to be a sign of good luck for the coming year and making a sign of the cross above a doorway with the soot from the flame is said to protect the family who live there.

With that, the fast is over. Traditionally families will eat a soup made from the organs of the lamb they will roast for the following day's feast. The dyed eggs are then cracked against those of others and the person whose shell smashes last will have more good luck!

Easter Day itself is one of huge celebration; a lamb or a goat is roasted, often on a spit, and a massive outdoor party ensues with music, drinking and dancing well into the night.

The Rhythm of Life

Out in the countryside the overwhelming sound of summer is that of the cicada. The clicking noise is not, as is often thought, the sound of them rubbing their wings or legs together, but the result of the male insects vibrating membranes in their abdomens which act like tiny echo chambers creating the distinctive sound.

The buzzing is a mating song used to attract females and is competitive in nature. When one male starts his call all the others in the surrounding area quickly join him until the noise reaches a crescendo. The name cicada is Latin, and literally means 'buzzer'. The Greek word for them is the more onomatopoeic *tzitzikas*.

Although the rasping of cicadas is commonplace, strangely absent in Crete is the sound of birdsong. Wild birds, except the larger protected species, are often hunted and eaten in rural areas, leaving the numbers of songbirds in the wild considerably diminished. Strangely, it is in the towns, where people frequently keep caged birds, that you are more likely to hear birdsong. From many a balcony, resplendent with blooming flowers the sweet sound of singing birds softens the roar of the traffic below.

To Agia Galini by Sea

It was still daylight as we spun the wheel round and headed up into the wind to drop the mainsail before heading for a stern in mooring in the small south coast harbour town of Agia Galini. *Endeavour* had made good time reaching along the coastline, healing under full sail in front of a robust south westerly on a gently rolling sea. Our early start from Paleochora had rewarded us with a simple daylight entry to our mooring with still plenty of space left in the busy little harbour.

With the mainsail secured and genoa furled we coasted under engine to our chosen berth and the village revealed its true glory. Cliffs rise up to either side of the settlement, which peers out onto the stage of the gulf of Messara like a captivated audience from an auditorium. It had changed from when I first visited by bus in the early Eighties. Back then Agia Galini, which quite literally means 'holy calm' was little more than a sleepy fishing village starting to awake to the possibilities of tourism. On going ashore at the town quay it is clear that the village has seized the opportunities presented by its imposing natural location and developed into a bustling small resort.

Such change has been sympathetic and sits well here. The constraints of the surrounding mountains have meant development has been dense but often this adds to the surprises held in its shadowed streets. Yes it is busy, because it is popular and the locals wouldn't have it any other way. It retains traditional Cretan charm, which mirrors the smiling faces of the brilliant white buildings cascading with Mediterranean blooms of every hue.

Right on the quayside is the town car park but other than this, for the most part Agia Galini is pedestrianised. Its narrow streets which step up as you ascend inland are crammed with tavernas, shops, small hotels, rooms for rent, car hire firms and travel agencies all going about their seemingly booming business. A long, if unremarkable, beach stretches away to the east and hire boats ply their trade along the coast to the likes of Matala and Preveli.

Tired from an early start we settle for seats under the awning of a taverna near the waterfront. We share an early evening meal, a platter bursting with fresh fruits of the sea and a white wine so dry it catches the throat, before returning for a nightcap in the cockpit of our yacht. In silence we stare at the remarkable display of stars unveiling a magnificent bedtime story of constellations before being rocked to sleep by the gentle ebb and flow of the sea.

The Dashing Horses of Chania

Don't get me wrong, I love my old hometown of Heraklion where I lived for a year; but if I were an impartial observer I would have to say that what it lacks in charm, Chania makes up for. The capital of Crete between 1898 and 1971, the Old Town retains much of its former grandeur. Alongside its historic architecture, abundant flowers and magnificent vistas, both out to sea and to the spectacular mountains inland, there is something else that is etched on the memory – horses in hats.

Whether as an adornment, or to protect them from the sun, the horses which pull small carriages in which people can tour the Old Town, wear hats! This is not just peculiar to Chania and, indeed, I have since seen donkeys in Kerkyra in Corfu similarly adorned.

When I first saw these horses I didn't know whether it was incredibly kitsch, practical or endearing, I suspect all three but the sales pitch works, particularly when children are involved. Don't be embarrassed, just go with the flow and it isn't a bad way to see the area around the old harbour.

I have heard it claimed that Chania is the most beautiful city in Crete, even in Greece. These are quite some claims to make, but that anyone would consider making them should tell us something about the town. It is effortlessly sublime. The Old Town stretches inland from the harbour with its long defensive wall running parallel to the coast with the splendid Venetian lighthouse standing as a sentinel at its entrance. Surrounding the boundaries of the old Venetian settlement is what is regarded as the New Town, a more vibrant, noisy area of apartment blocks, shops and offices.

Chania has been continuously inhabited for more than 5,000 years. Only a select few cities around the world could boast such credentials. And the city wears the ravages and adornments of its historic past with pride.

The most recent invaders were the Germans during the Second World War, but before them the Turks and Venetians had colonized the town in the centuries succeeding the decline of the Byzantine and Roman Empires. Even before the Romans, Chania was an important settlement for civilizations stretching back through the ancient Hellenistic and Mycenean to the Minoan.

Not only does the city boast a proud ancient heritage, it was also the birthplace of the greatest Greek statesman of the 20th Century. In Chania it is difficult to escape the name Eleftherios Venizelos, the leader who, more than anyone, was responsible for *enosis*, Crete's unification with Greece, in 1913.

Venizelos was born in Mournies, a village just a few miles to the south of the city and is buried in a grave on the Akrotiri peninsula on a spot looking down on his beloved Chania. The son of a Cretan revolutionary, Venizelos trained to be a lawyer and became prominent in Cretan politics following the establishment of a semi-autonomous Cretan state by the four 'Great Powers' of Britain, France, Russia and Italy.

Prince George of Greece was imposed as High Commissioner of the island. Venizelos, as both a rebel leader and skilled diplomat who was instrumental in releasing Crete from Ottoman control, was made Minister of Justice in 1899, but it soon became clear that his opposition to Prince George's rule made his position untenable and he resigned in 1901.

Venizelos remained a continual thorn in the side of Prince George and his successor Alexandros Zaimis and was central to the unofficial unification of Crete with Greece in 1908 and the establishment of a revolutionary government. The unification was internationally recognized on 1 December 1913, and the Greek flag was raised at the Fircas Tower in Chania in the presence of King Constantine of Greece who stood alongside Venizelos at the ceremony.

Before his death in 1936, Venizelos held the office of Prime Minister of Greece no less than seven times between 1910 and 1933, and has been called 'the maker of modern Greece'.

Pride in Venizelos is evident everywhere around the city with a square, street and numerous statues in his honour and of course his grave on the Akrotiri peninsula is a point of pilgrimage for many Greeks.

However, for the casual visitor, the city is special for its faded richness. A walk or ride in a carriage around the harbour reveals the grandeur of its past. Both inner and outer harbours are protected by the long, stone sea wall with its lighthouse that has provided a beacon to guide generations of seafarers home.

The Venetians were responsible for building the Firkas Tower, which now houses the naval museum. They also built the vast arsenals that stand beside the coast road to the south of the harbour and again at its eastern end. These were where the warships and trading vessels were built that allowed the Venetians to so dominate trade in the eastern Mediterranean for nearly 500 years.

When the Turks stripped the waning Venetian empire of the city, they were not slow to signal their dominance by building the domed Mosque of the Janissaries alongside the harbour. Behind here lies the Kastelli quarter, the oldest surviving part of the town, which is thought to be the place of the original settlement, excavations having uncovered a bounty of Minoan artifacts as well as fragments of Roman columns.

The Venetians built a wall around Kastelli, turning it into an impregnable fortress. This wall originally had four gates through it, but German bombing during the Second World War left two of these in ruins.

Exploring the narrow streets that surround the Kastelli quarter, it is a treat to escape the scorching sunlight reflecting off the water on the seafront and get lost in your thoughts among the labyrinth of golden-coloured buildings. Men wearing traditional dress are still a familiar sight on the streets. Sellers of lottery tickets call out to anyone who feels lucky, and around most corners there is a reminder of Chania's colourful past. The Turkish baths, a minaret, the fortifications; but perhaps the most popular place away from the seafront is the covered market.

Built in 1911 it is a cool, if not tranquil, haven from the heat outside. Based on the market in Marseilles it is built in the form of a cross with immense, high ceilings. Painted stalls and shouting traders advertise their goods, which vary from everyday foodstuffs to tourist trinkets. In the quieter corners are small kafenions and restaurants from where you can watch the theatre of the market while enjoying a refreshing drink.

I have never exhausted the delights Chania has to offer, always discovering something new to enrich the experience. Getting around the old town is easy on foot, although finding a way out through the new town's congested and confusingly signposted streets can be a challenge. There is no point in hurrying; sooner or later the traffic will spit you out back onto the national highway from where you can regain your bearings.

Samaria – The Longest Gorge

The early start had taken its toll and I was fighting with my eyes as we approached the foothills of Crete's White Mountains in the west of the island. I had walked the Samaria Gorge before, but the experience had been somewhat spoiled by my own bad planning. First I had gone on an organized trip, second it was the height of summer, neither of these factors proved an ideal way to experience walking what is claimed to be the longest gorge in Europe.

The walk in itself is not too taxing if you are reasonably fit but, as I discovered, a 10-mile downhill trek in 35 degrees heat is uncomfortable, and when surrounded by hundreds of other walkers it is difficult to ponder on this towering natural phenomenon.

This time I had experience on my side and was determined to enter the National Park the moment it opened at 7.00am. It was the end of September, when the sun, although still hot in the middle of the day, would be more forgiving.

My taxi had arrived to pick me up from my *pension* in Chania at 5.45am to ensure I was in good time to be ahead of the coach tours. I needn't have worried, my driver put me in no danger of being late – that is if I was to make it at all. He swung the silver Mercedes enthusiastically around the hairpin bends in the dark as we threaded our way up into the White Mountains.

No longer able to doze, I was torn between staring out into the void of the sheer drops just inches from the car's screeching wheels and closing my eyes in terror at my proximity to an early grave. And there were grounds for my nervousness, as born testament to by the increasing number of roadside shrines which appeared, caught in our headlights, as the going got steeper. At each little chapel erected in memory of previous motorists who had succumbed to the precipitous nature of our route, my driver would take one hand off the wheel and cross himself.

Now wide awake and in excellent time to start my walk, my taxi driver probably mistook my effusive thanks for gratitude rather than relief when we arrived at the head of the gorge at Xyloskalo. His haste to get me to my destination at least allowed me time to appreciate the most radiant sunrise which began to fill in the colours of the trees and rocks and played a breathtaking accompaniment to the silence which restored my composure and whetted my appetite for the walk ahead.

Right on 7 o'clock I paid my entrance to the park and set off along the path which almost immediately turned into a steep drop down steps into a valley densely forested with pines and cypresses trees. This is the start of a spectacular descent of some 4,000 feet from the Omalos Plateau to sea level at the small village of Agia Roumeli on the south west coast.

Along with Knossos, this is widely regarded as a must-see by many visitors to the island, and in the peace and quiet of this early morning in late September it was living up to its reputation. The gorge has been carved out of this spectacular limestone and granite landscape by a river that runs between the White Mountains and Mount Volakias.

Over thousands of years the chemical reaction between the water and the rock has created this wonder of nature in the shadow of the spectacular

White Mountains, or Lefka Ori. The range is so named because its colour never changes. The mountains are snow covered in the winter months and when the warmer weather comes they glow white as the sun reflects off the limestone.

The mountain range is massive, and the largest on the island, covering more than 300 square miles. It is the most remote area on Crete and is home to the renowned Sfakiots, named after Sfakia, the capital of the region, a small port on the south coast.

Sfakia is famous for being at the heart of the evacuation of Allied troops from the island during the Battle of Crete in the Second World War. For the Sfakiots, living has been tough and this toughness is reflected in their temperament. Throughout Cretan history they have been at the centre of the fight against oppression.

The Sfakiot qualities are typified by the man known as Yannis Daskalogiannis, after whom Chania's international airport is named. His real name was Yannis Vlachos. The son of a wealthy merchant in the 18th Century, he was educated abroad and nicknamed Daskalogiannis, meaning John the Teacher because of his wisdom. He became a rich ship owner and chairman of the council of Sfakia.

In 1770, after being promised support by the Russians, he led a force that rose up against the ruling Turks and had many successes in liberating parts of the region. But, with the Russians reneging on their promise, he was eventually overwhelmed by the sheer numbers of Turkish troops and surrendered at Frangokastello Castle near the region's capital of Hora Sfakion. Yannis was taken to Heraklion where he was skinned alive in public in front of the harbour fort.

The highest peak in the White Mountain range is Mount Pachnes, at 8,045 ft it is just 12 ft shorter than Mount Psiloritis, the tallest mountain on Crete. I have not been to the summit but am told that there is an ever-growing pile of rocks there, deposited by proud locals in an attempt to make their mountain stand taller than its rival to the east.

The Samaria National Park was set up in 1962 to provide a protected haven for the significant numbers of species of plants and animals indigenous to the area. In the same year the last villagers of Samaria left their homes to accommodate the park that bears its name and which, in turn, was named after the small, white 14th-century church of Saint Mary or Ossia Maria.

There was still a chill in the air as I got into my stride, the smells of wild marjoram, pine and eucalyptus infused the atmosphere as I criss-crossed over the small, burbling stream that runs through the gorge. It seems hard to believe that this benign trickle could have been partly responsible for creating such an imposing formation. But throughout the winter months, swollen with rainfall and melt waters from the snows on the mountain peaks it shows its true colours, and during this period the park is closed to visitors as the massive flow of water makes walking too dangerous.

Well before 9 o'clock I must have descended about half the height of the gorge as I passed the small stone church of Agios Nikolaos standing in self-reliant solemnity beside the trickling river. Another hour and I was approaching the abandoned village of Samaria.

Here is a good stopping point to sit for a time and take on some food and water. This is supposed to be a favoured haunt of the *kri-kri* or indigenous Cretan ibex, which is an endangered species and a major factor in the establishment of the National Park as a wildlife reserve.

These unique animals are extremely agile, and are able to leap vast distances and cling to the most precipitous of rock faces. Their numbers were estimated to have declined to fewer than 200 in the 1960s, partly as a result of them being one of the only sources of food available to partisan soldiers hiding out in the mountains during the Second World War. Although still endangered, their numbers are rising as a result of the strict conservation laws. At the turn of the century there were more than 2,000 *kri-kri* living on the island.

These goats are important to Cretans because they are the living embodiment of a link to the past. It is believed that their Minoan ancestors imported the *kri-kri* as farm animals to provide both milk and meat. A number of frescoes and pieces of jewellery depicting the Cretan goat have been discovered by archaeologists and dated as coming from the Minoan period. Similarities between these archaeological finds and the *kri-kri* with their long, curved, swept back horns are clearly discernible.

On that occasion I was unlucky. I had seen some of these rare beasts higher up the Gorge on my previous visit when the park was heaving with people. But now, all alone, these allegedly timid creatures were nowhere to be seen. I don't know what that says about me!

Despite the seeming attraction of the crowds for the *kri-kri*, I was still determined to stay one-step ahead of the guided tours. After a snack of bread, olives and feta from my backpack, I set off again downhill for the second half of the trek towards the coast. This is the most spectacular part of the walk as the gorge narrows, closing in on me and emphasizing the sheer nature of the vertical rock faces on both sides, stretching upwards and at times obliterating the sun.

I was approaching the famous *sideroportes*, or iron gates, where I felt I could almost touch both sides of the canyon at once. I reached out to try, and fell short by some six feet, looking upwards the rock faces towered above me for 1,000 ft at least.

This was breathtaking. I stood in awe, breathing in the majesty; alone, a tiny dot at the bottom of this natural canyon.

From here the path flattened out as I followed the river out of the park along the course of its final few miles to the Libyan Sea. An elderly goatherd in traditional Sfakiot dress stopped to watch me, chin resting on his crook as his herd tinkled their way across the rocky lowland between the end of the Gorge and the sea. He nodded enigmatically at my greeting of '*kalimera*'.

It was the middle of the day and the sun was beating off the large rocks that gradate to stones before forming a pebble beach as my journey matched that of the river and reached the sea at Agia Roumeli. A regular boat service runs to Sfakia from here, there is no way out by road.

From Sfakia there are frequent bus services travelling back up into the mountains on one of the most dizzyingly dramatic routes in the country, which makes its way north across the 40 miles back to Chania. It is worth preserving enough energy to remain awake and, for those who travel well, try to get a window seat on the bus.

Crete's Greatest Fight

Back in the Eighties, many older Cretans still remembered the Second World War. Many of them had fought against the German occupying forces and remembered the atrocities perpetuated by them.

Outside the tourist areas, Germans were not always welcome. The Cretans are conservative by nature and have long memories, although time and their need for the tourist euro has more recently allowed these memories to fade and, in most cases, let the past lie.

It was British and Commonwealth troops, predominantly from New Zealand and Australia, who had fought alongside the Cretans in their ultimately doomed attempt to hold off the German invasion in May 1941. Crete's position in the Mediterranean was seen both by the Allies and Axis powers to be strategically crucial. The Germans had air supremacy in the area and the Allies were dominant at sea. This led to the German decision to stage the largest airborne invasion that had ever been attempted.

Codenamed Operation Mercury, the Germans launched their invasion on the 20th May, heralding 10 days of brutal combat. Using paratroops followed by gliders, the Germans launched an attack on Maleme airfield near Chania in the north west of the island. They suffered terrible losses but crucially managed to land enough troops near the airfield to keep the defending forces deployed.

Later the same day similar assaults took place further east near Rethymnon and again near Heraklion. The Cretan civilian population also joined in the battle, attacking the invading forces with whatever they had to hand.

Despite fierce resistance and the massive losses sustained by the invaders, a breakdown in communications led to the Allied troops, who had been containing the Germans at Maleme, to withdraw from the airfield, allowing the enemy to secure a vital strategic advantage. More invading troops could now pour onto the island and, with the German army breaking the defensive cordon around Heraklion, the Allied and Greek troops were now in retreat.

Some were evacuated by the Royal Navy from Heraklion, but others had to take the long trek across the mountains to the south of the island. Over the four nights of 28-31 May 16,000 troops were taken off the beaches by Royal Navy ships from Sfakia and escaped to Egypt, leaving 9,000 troops behind fighting an impossible rearguard action.

In total the battle accounted for around 11,000 lives. Four thousand died from each of the opposing forces along with 3,000 of the civilian population. Seventeen thousand soldiers were taken prisoner by the invading army, although many of the troops left stranded on the island were later evacuated by submarine and small boat. Some remained and others were later landed in secret to support the bands of resistance fighters which had set up camp in the mountains.

Among these was the late Patrick Leigh Fermor. Now regarded as an outstanding travel writer, he was at the time an officer in the Special Operations Executive, sent to Crete to help organize the resistance against the occupying forces.

Leigh Fermor became the subject of the 1957 film *Ill Met By Moonlight*, which tells the story of how, under his command, a group of resistance fighters audaciously captured the German Commanding Officer on Crete, General Heinrich Kreipe, and smuggled him off the island as a prisoner of war.

Following the evacuation of troops, members of the resistance movement lived mostly in the mountains and were supplied by small boat or parachute under the cover of darkness. Their activity was crucial in keeping the occupying forces tied down, but also led to terrifying reprisals by the Germans who shot civilians and razed whole villages to the ground.

In June 1941, the village of Kandanos in the south west of the island was the subject of German reprisals when they massacred all the inhabitants they could find and burned down every building. Following the kidnap of General Kreipe, the mountain village of Anogia was likewise destroyed. But the Cretans and the British Special Forces continued their campaign of resistance undeterred for the three years that followed the invasion.

Eventually the Germans resigned themselves to being unable to subdue the islanders, and retreated to a heavily defended enclave around Chania until withdrawing from there in June 1945, three months before the end of the war.

The celebrated writer, George Psychoundakis, told his experiences of this dark period in his classic book *The Cretan Runner*. A shepherd, Psychoundakis acted as a dispatch runner for the Cretan resistance movement and later for the SEO under the command of Leigh Fermor, often operating behind enemy lines. It was Leigh Fermor who translated his manuscript into English and helped to get it published in 1955. Psychoundakis died in 2006, aged 85; Leigh Fermor five years later in 2011, aged 96.

Sfakia – A Proudly Isolated Place

My long journey from the east came to an end in a small square right beside the sea. I had long wanted to visit the capital of the wildest region of Crete, Hora Sfakion, its name literally meaning the main town of Sfakia. This rugged corner in the South of Chania province is renowned for the extreme beauty of its landscape and the inscrutable locals whose nature has been moulded by the toughest of existences eked out of the unyielding environment. With the exception of the nearby Samaria Gorge this part of Crete is the most unspoiled and unvisited, perhaps because it is a long journey from the resorts on the north coast and there are no significant long stretches of beach or enough flat land to build hotels on.

There are still plenty of places to stay, my room in a small pension was basic but adequate as a base to explore the region, it even had an en-suite shower tray into which luke-warm water dripped constantly from the leaky shower head with only slightly less pressure than when the shower was turned up full.

I had left Heraklion at dawn, a low October sun reflecting off my rear-view mirror as I turned the rental car west onto the national highway skirting the coast out of the city and into the mountains. As the sun rose, the sea revealed itself benignly calm whenever the road met the edge of the cliffs and the sky matched it in colour before it was gradually bleached whiter as the sun reached its zenith.

Just past Georgioupoli at a place called Vrysses I turned off the main road and headed south into the White Mountains (Lefka Ori). The road soon steepens as it leaves the north coast behind and the temperature noticeably drops. It passes through ravines, which hold secrets of the violent struggles that have taken place in these inhospitable mountains. This is the least inhabited place on the island with fewer than 3,000 people living in a vast area of 180 square miles. It is this very remoteness that has resulted in their violent history. Traditionally the proud families from these parts have sorted out disputes with vendettas, which certainly raged well into the 20th Century and are rumoured to continue still.

It was through these mountains that Allied troops retreated during the Battle of Crete in 1941 with Cretan guerrillas bravely fighting a rearguard action to buy them time. It is the only part of Crete that has never come totally under the control of an invading force and was the scene of the ambush and massacre of two armies of the ruling Turks in the uprisings of 1821 and 1866. It was as a reprisal for the 1821 uprising that Hussein Bey landed with a joint army of Turkish and Egyptian soldiers some 12,000 strong. Charged with subduing any revolt they burned all the villages on the plateau of Askifou, which now lay before me. The name comes from the ancient Greek word *skyphos*, which means cup. The base of the cup is a fertile plain, a tapestry of cultivated fields overlooked by the remains of a Turkish fortress, which bears witness to the region's turbulent past. The plateau itself is about 2,400 ft above sea level and is surrounded by the towering peaks of Kastro in the west, Agathes to the south and Tripali in the east. Sheep and goats graze in the pastures, which are thought to lie on the site of what was, in prehistoric times, a natural lake.

In the village of Kares it is worth stopping to take a look at a place that appears to have escaped the notice of most guide book writers, this is the incredible War Museum of Askifou. The collection was the work of the late Georgios Hatzidakis who felt passionately that the sacrifices made in the Battle of Crete should not be forgotten. Now the collection is curated by his children and is kept in a private house, which is splitting at the seams with every imaginable sort of war memorabilia. Predominantly concerned with the Second World War there are exhibits dating back to revolts against the Turks in the 18th Century. Although the museum is of undoubted historical interest, appeals by the late Mr Hatzidakis for some financial aid from the Government were consistently snubbed; despite this the exhibits can still be viewed for a voluntary contribution.

It would have been easy to while away a few more hours here but I wanted to get to Hora Sfakion in time to find myself a room, so took off on the road which follows the pass through the mountains enclosing the southern side of the plateau and past the entrance to the Imbros Gorge, a seven-mile long canyon cut out of the limestone rock which runs from Imbros village at its head to Kommitades.

The road to Hora Sfakion itself is a good one, and it needs to be as it spirals down the south side of the White Mountain range towards the sea. The views are spectacular but I have to concentrate hard on my driving as I pass a number of coaches coming the other way swinging well over onto my side of the road as they navigate the sharp bends. Hora Sfakion is the landing point for boats from Agia Roumeli at the foot of the Samaria Gorge and thousands of tourists pass through there to catch busses and coaches to return to the resorts in the north of the island.

Some tourists come here to stay. Most leave on the last buses after the final ferries from the Gorge have docked and the village returns to its sleepy self, leaving its 300 inhabitants to go about their business. After booking in to my pension, I find a taverna by the harbour and settle down with a mezzes of delicious cheese pies drizzled with honey and a carafe of sturdy red wine to watch the sunset and plan my next day's trip to the castle at Frangokastello.

A castle on a small plain beside a golden beach, Frangokastello itself and the small village which also bears its name has an other-worldly quality and lies less than 10 miles to the east of Hora Sfakion. Meaning 'fortress of the Franks' the subtext of the name is Castle of the catholic invaders, which was how locals referred to this immense redoubt completed by the ruling Venetians in 1374 as a bastion against pirates and the unruly local Sfakiot population. The Venetians had called it the Castle of St Nikitas after the nearby early Christian basilica of Agios Nikitas, the ruins of which can still be discerned nearby.

Although an impressive structure, *in situ*, standing beneath the towering peaks of the Lefka Ori, it must have been an isolating experience for any garrison billeted there. It stands four square with a serried tower at each corner of the rectangle. Four straight walls all topped with battlements connect the towers, the fortification in the south-west corner is taller and more substantial than the other three. This was the tower used to protect the main gate and also the final bastion if the walls were penetrated. On closer inspection it is clear that what remains of the castle is the outside shell. At a distance the fortress is almost incongruous having a rather Arabic feel as, if you view it with your back to the sea, it appears almost to stand in a small oasis on desert sands with a rocky backdrop of mountains. The light plays tricks with the stone as the walls change from pink early in the day to a sandy colour blending with the beach to orange as the sun sets over the mountains in the west.

Looking up above the main entrance I can just make out a carving of the winged lion, the symbol of St Mark, which was emblematic of the Venetian republic. It reminds me of the fort guarding Kerkyra, the capital of Corfu way to the north, which also had the emblem above its portal. The Venetians built the fort not only for their own protection, but in response to requests from the ruling warlords in the area. Feuding between the two most powerful families had led to discontent among the rest of the incumbent Sfakiots and, in an effort to restore some sort of order, they called upon the Venetians for support. Persuaded to build the castle they sent soldiers to guard the tradesmen as they worked. Feeling vulnerable to attack during the night they left the site unattended. It is said that, during the hours of darkness, locals would destroy the work done on the previous day. This game of cat and mouse continued until the Venetians brought in extra troops and the leaders of the wreckers, the Patsos brothers from nearby Patsianos just north of the plain were betrayed, caught and executed.

Despite the erection of such a formidable castle, the building did little to subdue the local population and its bloodthirsty history continued under the rule of the Turks, who left Frangocastello unmanned for long periods of time. In 1770 the celebrated freedom fighter known as Daskalogiannis was captured there before being taken to Heraklion where he was flayed alive in front of the fortress, as an example to other would-be revolutionaries.

In 1828 the castle was again at the centre of Cretan revolt when a Greek revolutionary arrived on Crete from Epirus in northwestern Greece attempting to spread the Greek war of independence to Crete. The forces of Hadzi Michalis Dalianis together with an army of Cretan freedom fighters garrisoned themselves in the abandoned castle. Some 650 men came under siege by the army of Mustapha Pasha, the island's Turkish governor who marshalled some 6,000 troops on the plain beneath the castle walls. Needing to break out Dalianis led his troops from the castle to do battle in a brave but ultimately doomed attempt to escape. He was killed along with more than half his army, the rest surrendered. Mustapha Pasha, determined that the castle should never again be used as a refuge for rebel forces, ordered that it be blown up, a move later regretted when 38 years later a successor had to order it to be rebuilt to defend his own army from the marauding armies of Cretans during the revolt of 1866.

Legend has it that the only things that inhabit the castle today are the *Drosoulites* or Dew Men. The story goes that in May, around the time of the anniversary of the massacre of Dalianis and his army, their ghosts rise up from the sands that buried their bodies and their shadowy forms walk in file towards the castle before disappearing into the sea. There have been many eye-witness accounts of this phenomena which always takes place around dawn, leading to the belief that the soldiers are a mirage caused by bright early-morning sun shining low in the sky being refracted by the damp air caused by the dew, hence the name Drosoulites.

The unfortunate ghosts of the soldiers are said to have had more success than their flesh and blood selves. When the apparitions were spotted by a detachment of Turkish troops in 1890 they turned and fled from the castle. Some years later during the Second World War, in what has more than a hint of a *Bednobs and Broomsticks* moment about it, a unit of German soldiers on the look out for resistance fighters opened fire on the *Drosoulites* in error, no doubt revealing their true position to the real special forces hiding out in the surrounding mountains.

Following the route of the spirits, I walk across the gently shelving sand to the water, which laps warm and inviting from the shallows of this sheltered spectral spot. Looking back, the effulgence of the castle is clear to see, shimmering in the sunlight the image pastes a picture in the mind's album forever. A small fishing caique moored to a rock bobs in the bay, its painted eye warding off any evil spirits, the sand slowly bakes my bare feet, the mountains soar behind this deserted reminder of the island's turbulent history. Because of its remoteness few visitors are in evidence, allowing this idyllic spot to retain the full integrity of its heritage. Long may that continue, for it is a magical place.

Loutro – Carefree and Carless

Being in Hora Sfakion it is the ideal opportunity to take the trip to Loutro. This coastal village is unique in this day and age in that it can only be reached by boat or on foot across rugged terrain. As ferries can be boarded a short walk from my pension, I select this option and embark on one of the boats which ply their route west along the coast, dropping passengers off at Loutro on their way to Agia Roumeli at the bottom of the Samaria Gorge. The journey takes all of 20 minutes and, approaching the village by boat, it is easy to see why Loutro turns its face towards the sparkling blue waters rather than inland to the stark backdrop of the mountains to which it clings. Loutro is the only safe natural harbour on the south coast of Crete.

The bay is semicircular with a tiny, pebble beach, and the settlement is compact. We cruise past a tiny island in the bay and a small lighthouse. The bay, with the arms of the coastline wrapped around it, is like a sheet of deep blue glass, the only things disturbing it the bow wave and wake of our small ferry. White houses with their blue doors and window frames give this hideaway a Cycladean feel reminiscent of Santorini. Tavernas, and a few shops and rooms for rent stand only a few steps from where we disembark on the village's single jetty.

There is little to do here except enjoy the peace and quiet, eat, drink and swim – and for that we should be grateful. The lack of the sound of motor vehicles at times makes the silence deafening and for any visitor carrying residual stress it may take some time to adjust.

This gem of a natural haven has been used as a harbour since Hellenistic times when it was the port of Anopolis, a settlement the best part of a strenuous two-hour walk away up a mountain track on a plateau in the White Mountains. In those days it was known as Phoenix, a name still held by another village close by. Pirates and slave traders operated here until the

Venetians sought to civilize the locals and built a small castle. The ruins of this are still visible, as are those of a later Ottoman fort built high above the village in the 1860s as part of the Turkish strategy to pacify the area which was continuing to be a thorn in the flesh of the occupying powers.

And it is easy to see why they were uneasy about the native palikari or freedom fighters. The 1821 Cretan revolution emanated from here. The village was central to the famed, but doomed, Daskalogiannis uprising some 50 years previously. The aforementioned Ioannis Vlachos was so called because he was an educated man, which led his friends to nickname him Daskalos or teacher. He was born in Anopolis and operated his four merchant ships from the port of Loutro. A statue of the ill-fated hero stands in the town of his birth and Chania airport is named in his honour.

I had a choice; I wanted to retrace my steps eastwards to the renowned Glyka Nera beach. Its name means sweet water beach, because of the cold fresh water drained from the mountains that wells up here on the beach or into the bay from beneath the seabed. To walk it would take an hour each way, which even in the early autumn sun would have been exhausting. Small ferries also make the trip or I could hire a kayak. With time on my hands and the sea beyond the confines of the harbour still benign, I opted for the latter. With no tide or winds blowing in from Africa it was a neutral paddle and taking a leisurely pace with frequent breaks to drink from my bottle of water and splash my face with handfuls of sea I reached my destination in 40 minutes.

From the sea the beach appears the very epitome of remote, a narrow strip of grey pebbles pressed in upon by dark brown cliffs, rising imperiously skywards, their almost vertical faces casting shadows on its western end. Getting out of the kayak to haul it up the beach I notice how unusually cold the water is, particularly as it is so shallow. It is a result of the icy, fresh water springs bubbling up from below and mingling with the warmer waters of the Libyan Sea. Almost anywhere on the beach you can dig down with your hands through the pebbles and locate a supply of cool, clear drinkable fresh water.

There are few people here in the bay, but several tents are pitched towards one end and there is a small shack that sells a limited supply of food and drink. From the boulders strewn across the pebbles near the base of the cliffs it is clear that rock falls here are not unusual. This is Crete at its most unspoiled; there are no sun loungers or umbrellas here, just a bucolic calm only broken by the whisper of the sea as it caresses the pebbles on the waterline.

The sun is blisteringly hot and there are few places to escape that do not require getting close to the unstable cliffs so I lie down beside the Kayak to read until the temperature moderates and I can have a more comfortable paddle back to Loutro.

The welcome spray splashes down the paddles and onto my arms as I set out. Somewhere out to sea, about 25 miles away and hidden by the haze is the island Gavdos and its acolyte Gavdopoula, the most southernmost extreme of Europe – after that it's Africa.

You can catch ferries to this outpost from Hora Sfakion or Paleochora, but even though the weather inshore was perfect it would be foolhardy to try and paddle the distance as the waters between the coast of Crete and its tiny satellites can cut up rough when the winds blow in from Africa, turning what now is a silken sheet of azure blue into a churning grey, charging rhino spitting spumes of foaming spray.

The fierceness of the sea and Gavdos' exposed position has eroded the cliffs. At the south-eastern tip of the island as the rocks tumble into the ocean there is a spectacular arch, formed over thousands of years by the pounding of the elements. This is Cape Trypiti and atop the cliffs stands a statue of an enormous chair.

Over the centuries Gavdos has gradually seen its population decline from thousands to less than one hundred people who are resident throughout the year. Although still relatively quiet as a tourist destination, during July and August these numbers can swell to around three thousand and there are rooms to rent and a number of tavernas to serve the growing tourist industry. During the 1950s many natives of the island took advantage of a state-run plan to exchange their land with that on Crete around the area of Paleochora, contributing to the general *diaspora*. The islanders settling on that fertile isthmus on the south-east coast formed a community there which came to be known as Gavdiotika.

Despite its small size of approximately 14 square miles, historically Gavdos punches above its weight. It has been inhabited since Neolithic times and the 2nd Century BC Greek Libyan poet Callimachus held it to be the Ogygia of myth where Odysseus was held captive for seven years by the nymph Calypso in Homer's *The Odyssey*. In Hellenistic times, under the auspices of the great Cretan city of Gortys, it was a base for shipwrights and chandlers for the fleet and the production of cedar oil for medicines. During the Roman occupation the island was known as 'Clauda' and is referenced in the Acts of the Apostles as the island St Paul was blown past in a storm on his way to being shipwrecked far to the west on Melita (Malta). In more recent times, the island was used in the 20th Century for the internment of political prisoners by a succession of dictators. Gavdos also found notoriety in 2002 when the leader of November 17, a terrorist Marxist group who had been responsible for 23 assassinations, was arrested on the island where, apparently, he had been living and working as a beekeeper.

For any visitors to the island, the very isolation that makes living there so difficult is one of its joys as it can offer a seclusion that is difficult to find these days. When the winds are not blowing, the summer sun can blaze up to a staggering 40 degrees centigrade. When it does there is little for it but to swim from the white sandy beaches in a sea so clear it reveals the wealth of life that inhabits it for many feet deep. When this gets too much, settle under the shaky rush awning of a taverna for a frosted glass of Mythos and a plate of seasoned snails, lightly sautéed in olive oil with a garlic, onion and tomato sauce, bread and olives.

Today for me this was not to be, but no doubt Loutro could provide a suitable place where I could satisfy my appetite built up by the paddle back.

Old World Charm – Paleochora

At the end of the main road from Chania to the south coast that passes through the olive-laden valley of Kandanos and then west of the Samaria Gorge leaving the peaks of the White Mountains, lies a narrow peninsula feeling its way into the Libyan Sea. Paleochora has a unique atmosphere for a resort town. It appears to have managed to stay stuck in a time warp. The small town faces out two ways to the large sandy beach looking west and in the opposite direction east over a more sheltered pebble shore.

Approaching down an avenue of eucalyptus trees, we leave a small plain covered with olive groves, greenhouses and polytunnels with large tomatoes ripening on the vines. The road then trickles into the small town packed with tavernas, shops and small hotels.

After dark the town bustles but doesn't shove, it retains a well-mannered charm which is appreciated by those who come to enjoy its simple pleasures. Paleochora doesn't shout about its history but, as the main street of Venizelos peters out, you'll find the unspectacular remains of a castle after which the settlement got its previous name of Kasteli Selinos. The castle then leant its name to the surrounding region, which became known as Selinos; which was originally the area surrounding the ancient city of Kalamydi. This was in 1278 when the Venetians were incumbent and the village was established largely to support the needs of the fortress.

Through the centuries, Paleochora became the focus of many battles and the castle was repeatedly routed and rebuilt, most famously by the forces of the infamous Ottoman corsair and slave trader Hizir Hayreddin Barbarossa in 1539. When he passed on to plunder elsewhere the Venetian rulers painstakingly rebuilt it, only for it to be taken over by the Turkish invaders in 1645.

The Turks were not always the most enthusiastic at property maintenance and the castle fell into a state of terminal disrepair under their patronage. Had they been more meticulous in retaining the integrity of the fortress, history may have taken a different turn. In 1866 during a revolt against the ruling Ottomans, the British navy evacuated hundreds of women and children from the peninsula in an humanitarian action that was viewed by the Turks as tacit support for the Cretan revolutionaries. The Russian navy followed suit and the resultant incident led to the cause of Cretan independence moving up the international political agenda.

Nowadays there is little to see except the ruins of walls, but a walk among the remains on this slightly-raised piece of land is a good vantage point to take in the view of the labyrinth of tiny streets in the town and both sides of the promontory with its harbour at the southern end incorporating the relatively recent yacht marina.

During the daytime, when most people are on the beach or on boat trips to Sougia, Gavdos, Elafonisi or Agia Roumeli, is a good time to wander in the shade of the close-packed buildings of the town. Bougainvillea tumble from the balconies, and glimpses of tamarisk shaded courtyards interrupt thoughts of the Fifties when many of the inhabitants of this small town on the edge of Crete left the much harsher environment of the island of Gavdos to the south in exchange for a better life here.

Loaves and Fishes

A common site in small grocery stores in the villages of Crete back in the Eighties were baskets full of what looked like stale bread and others containing unappetizing looking grey pieces of dried fish. In a country where many of its people have historically had to live from hand to mouth, waste was not an option. Although the packaging and marketing of these products has improved, both these essentials are still widely available here.

When the climate is hot, food scarce and refrigeration at a premium, it is understandable that such ways of preserving food staples is common. The unpromising looking fish can easily be reconstituted and made into a hearty fish stew just by adding stock and a few vegetables and simmering on top of the stove.

The bread is not in fact stale but has been purposely dried out to preserve it. Called *paximadi* it was traditionally made of barley or chick pea flour by families who would bake only once a month. The bread is baked twice and then dried to preserve it and remove any moisture. It can then be moistened again with olive oil, wine or water when it is ready to be eaten.

Off the coast of Crete, to the south of the small resort of Agia Galini in the Libyan Sea, lie two small uninhabited islands named Paximadia, named after their resemblance to these once vital bread rusks.

Elafonisi – Crete's Desert Island

Wading knee-deep through the water towards the small islet, it is hard to imagine anywhere more resembling the south Pacific than this remote corner of Crete. The sand is smooth underfoot, almost white beneath a sea so perfect in colour it is the very definition of turquoise. Looking back at the beaches encircling the lagoon the white sands are tinged with the pinks and reds of tiny shells eroded over the centuries. This is the famed Elafonisi that I had been told about, claimed by many to be the most stunning beach in Crete. Standing in warm, shallow water on the sandbank that crosses to the small islet also named Elafonisi it would be hard to disagree. Right on the south-western corner of the island it is the last stop off for many species of birds as they make their way south to Africa. The island is a protected area as a nature reserve and there are no buildings here. Its name derives from the word *elafos,* meaning deer, although I haven't caught sight of one yet.

The sand bar is no more than 900 yards long and, because there isn't any significant tide, there is no chance of getting trapped by rising water, just keep an eye on the wind as the sea around here can get rough, a fact to which a lone wooden cross on the island stands testament. It was just off this coast in 1907 that the Austrian passenger ship, *Imperatrix,* ran aground in a storm, killing 39 people who tried to reach the shore in a lifeboat. The wreck of the ship can still be made out and scuba divers explore the site to this day. Following the tragedy a lighthouse was built but this was demolished by the Germans during their occupation of the island in the Second World War, no doubt to hinder any attempts by allied shipping which frequently plied these waters dropping off men and supplies to aid the resistance. At the western tip of the isle the lighthouse has since been replaced with an unprepossessing, utilitarian steel structure resembling an electricity pylon with a light on top.

Walking towards the centre of the islet the creeping roots of rock samphire, exuding the smell of wax, line the beach alongside the white and green leaved false dittany and Mediterranean saltbushes. Paths are marked so people do not stray onto the delicate environment beneath the juniper trees. On reaching the highest part of the island, looking out over the Libyan Sea and back into the lagoon gives one the feeling of being on the edge of the world. Here there is a plaque remembering a sobering incident, which besmirched this beleaguered part of paradise.

During the Greek War of Independence in 1824, a group of some 40 armed resistance fighters along with families numbering a further six or seven hundred, including women, children and the elderly, holed up here awaiting rescue by a ship to take them to the safety of the Ionian islands. Across the bay the pursuing Turkish troops, unable to locate their enemy pitched camp on the beach. Unfortunately one of the Ottoman army's horses broke loose its tether and wandered through the water to the island. In an effort to retrieve the escaped horse some men followed it across the sand bar and discovered the hideout and without mercy the army attacked, slaughtering most and selling the few who survived into slavery.

Despite its history, this spot is a good place to escape to and hide except in July and August when, alongside the tourists, families from Chania escape city life and take the short wade across the channel laden with hampers, inflatable dolphins and all sorts of other beach paraphernalia. As the beach is protected there are no sunbeds and umbrellas or buildings and on weekdays slightly out of season it is the perfect getaway. We lie down on the sand watching the golden sun setting as its last rays pick out the glinting pinks and reds on the white sand like fireflies in the snow.

Phalasarna – The Ghost Harbour

More than 100 yards inland from the shoreline on the far northwest coast of Crete lies the ghost of a harbour. No ships weigh anchor here, or run for cover from gales blowing in from the Adriatic far away. The quays sit empty, the tower unguarded and the warehouses deserted.

This is Phalasarna, an ancient harbour perched on the side of Cape Gramvousa that, at one time, dominated the western gateway to the Aegian. Before the days of compasses and clocks it was the only Cretan port from which, or so it is alleged, navigators could find their way by sight all the way to the Peloponnese by eyeballing their way via Pontikonisi, Antikythira and Kythira. I don't know if this is possible and we will never know – because this extraordinary port is landlocked.

It was discovered by the British classicist and explorer Robert Pashley and the Royal Navy's pioneering archaeoseismologist Captain Thomas Spratt on their travels around the island in 1859. What surrounds us now has mostly been revealed recently, with excavations beginning in 1986 and continuing even now under the supervision of the celebrated marine archaeologist Elpida Hadjidaki, herself a native of Chania.

There has been a settlement here since the 6th Century BC and it is considered to be the oldest known port in Crete. Its heyday was probably the 4th Century BC and the remains that are currently visible have been dated to that period. The impressive nature of the towers, buildings and walls suggest that a sizeable and wealthy population lived here, possibly flourishing on profit from piracy and the slave trade after gaining independence from the nearby town of Polyrhenia. Having made a healthy profit during the Hellenistic period, the piratical nature of the locals was anathema to the invading Romans in the first Century BC who vowed to rid the

Mediterranean Sea of pirates and blocked off the channel to the manmade basin and sacked the town in around the 1st Century AD.

By the time the Venetians occupied Crete, Phalasarna had already been declared a 'lost' city, which it remained until Pashley and Spratt uncovered evidence of its existence. Following this discovery little was done on the site until the work of Hadjidaki and her team finally put to rest some of the questions about what lay beneath the earth.

What can currently be seen is a large harbour basin surrounded by walls connecting four large towers. Inside the walls are the remains of substantial quays supporting large mooring stones. From this enclosed port runs a narrow channel that would have led to the sea. I say would have, because even if the Romans had failed to shut down its activities, a natural disaster which took place in 365 AD put paid to its future. That year the largest earthquake ever known in the region drove a huge wedge of lava under the whole of the west of Crete, lifting the deserted port 25 ft into the air and pushing it inland.

This same event also made the town that stood between the harbour and the acropolis uninhabitable. The temple dedicated to Artemis, the goddess of the wild and animals, looked down on the disaster from the hillside behind. The area surrounding the old port is one of great natural beauty, particularly the curving beach of pristine white sand as you head towards Platanos passing through a valley of olive groves and greenhouses bursting with tomatoes, melons and cucumbers. At Platanos itself we pull over at a taverna beside an old watermill for fresh juice and grilled goat and potatoes, fresh with the fragrance of mountain herbs and the smoke of the grill. We head back towards Chania before the day starts to draw in as the road in places can prove challenging and I do not relish driving it in the dark.

Santorini

A Journey to Atlantis

If you have the time while in Crete's capital city, Heraklion is the ideal place to board a boat for Santorini and, believe me, it is worth the journey if only for a day trip. It is magical.

Shimmering white, perched atop sheer cliffs overlooking a cerulean sea, the villages of Santorini, or Thera as it is classically known, sum up so many people's visions of a Greek island. Cats bask in the sun under blue shuttered windows as multi-coloured flowers cascade from terracotta urns. Even the capital, Fira, the hub of the island's commercial and tourist trade, manages to retain this picture-postcard charm.

Not much more than 60 miles north of Crete, the first time I took the journey it lasted four hours. Nowadays it can be done considerably quicker by hydrofoil, but I still prefer the conventional ship. The slower approach to this spectacular island allows more time for the appreciation of its unique views, which are the dramatic result of a history of volcanic activity.

The main crescent-shaped island and its five smaller acolytes are all that remain of a once much larger land mass, which was destroyed by a massive volcanic eruption in the second millennium BC. This explosion blew a hole in the island that now constitutes the Santorini lagoon. What once was dry land now lies submerged 1,300 ft underwater.

The consequences of this volcanic event, one of the largest eruptions in recorded history, were monumental. The lagoon covers about 50 square miles and butts up against sheer cliffs that rise up out of the water to a height of 1,000 ft. The seismic activity that created this dramatic geological feature also completely destroyed the Bronze Age Minoan civilization that had prevailed there.

For me, contemplating the magnitude of such an event as your ship sails across the deep, calm waters of the caldera is one of the great pleasures of taking this journey. As the ferry coasts towards its mooring on the very edge of the crater's rim, the cliffs thrust skywards to form the current island, where the small villages of white houses glimmer in the sun as they cling precariously to the summit.

As on other islands, competition to sell rooms was fierce. Walking down the gangplank we were met by hoards of islanders hustling to sell us accommodation. Having only come for a day trip we pushed our way through the scrum and made for the awaiting bus. Cases and crates, rucksacks and boxes were being stowed in the luggage compartment or on the roof, tied down tight in preparation for the winding ascent up the precipitous side of the caldera to the island's capital.

Huffing and puffing, the bus took off in a cloud of dust and exhaust fumes. The ascent is not for the faint-hearted. The road when I first visited was not bordered by crash barriers and, on each hairpin bend, the bus would alarmingly hang its front end out over the sheer drop to the sea below.

Smoking and with music blaring from the speakers, the driver would wrestle the wheel around the sharp bends, sometimes taking a hand away to cross himself three times whenever passing one of a number of none-too-reassuring roadside shrines.

As the coach neared the top of the cliffs, for the braver of the passengers who looked out and down over the lagoon, the view was breathtaking. Our ship below tied up to its pier and, further out to sea, small fishing caiques plied their trade across the lagoon, leaving a web of wake trails breaking the glassy surface. The occasional pleasure boat was taking visitors to the other inhabited island in the archipelago, Therasia.

From here it is easy to see why Santorini is thought by many to be the inspiration for Plato's lost island of Atlantis. Although this might be the fanciful romanticizing of a myth, such opinions have been given some credence by frescoes depicting the island's shape prior to the eruption having been found by archaeologists beneath the volcanic ash.

The wall paintings are considered to have more than a passing resemblance to the Atlantis written about by Plato in his *Timaeus* and *Critias* dialogues. These tell the story of a mighty, all-conquering state that spread its influence throughout North Africa and what is now Europe, before catastrophically sinking into the sea.

Such dreadful devastation has created this spectacular landscape, which is now the destination for so many visitors. Its beaches reveal this turbulent geomorphological past, consisting of black, red and white sand depending on which geological layer has been exposed by the erosive action of the sea.

As recently as 1956, the island suffered a sizeable earthquake and volcanic eruption that did significant damage to many buildings and resulted in the desertion of several of its villages. Despite this, a permanent population of about 15,000 people remains on this flawed paradise, making a living out of tourism, wine production, fishing and market gardening.

The climate is especially arid and water is in short supply. A desalination plant supplies water for washing and watering crops, but it is not suitable for human consumption. However, looking out across the bay, it is easy to see why people stay, risking all to remain on this island heaven.

Rhodes

Rhodes – The Island of the Knights

With a fair wind, the island of Rhodes is but half a day's voyage by ferry from Piraeus. Athens' seaport lies some 250 miles to the north west of this jewelled island that nestles little more than a stone's throw away from Asia and the Turkish coast. At 11 miles from the natural homeland of the old Ottoman Empire, Rhodes, the largest of the Dodecanese archipelago, has for millennia been subject to the push and pull of the tides of political fortune in this south-eastern corner of the Aegean Sea. Although the fourth largest of the Greek Islands, it is small enough to be easily explored, its landscape benign, yet abundant enough in variety to hold the attention for a lifetime.

If that vista exudes a timeless quality, the intervention of buildings and archaeological finds betrays the island's turbulent past. But in the context of modern Greece, Rhodes and the other islands of the Dodecanese were the final piece in the jigsaw, the last part of this intricate picture to be put into place. It was not until after the Second World War, in 1947, that the defeated Italian rulers were officially made to hand over the islands. Rhodes and its satellites were finally reunited with the newly reformed, independent Greek state that had been pulling itself together for the previous 135 years.

Lawrence Durrell, in *Reflections on a Marine Venus*, his classic memoir about post-war Rhodes, writes of the difficulties of expressing the essence of the Island: 'In Rhodes the days drop as softly as fruit from the trees. Some belong to the dazzling ages of Cleobulus and the tyrants, some to the gloomy

Tiberius, some to the Crusaders. They follow each other in scales and modes too quickly to be captured in the nets of form.'

The difficulty lies in trying to find an identity that fits. The island has changed its clothes so many times throughout history that it is hard to identify the fashion which best reflects its character. Inhabited since the Neolithic period, the Minoans came here in the 16th Century BC, but did not leave their mark in the same way that they had further to the south west in Crete. The Telchines are held in some legends to have been the first inhabitants. The offspring of Gaia and Pontus, they hailed from Crete. These children of the gods had magical powers and were skilled metalworkers who created Poseidon's trident, and a sickle for Cronos. In certain accounts their children were Ialyssos, Lindos and Kamiros. This theory is at odds with another that claims these boys, who gave their name to the triumvirate of early Rhodian cities, were the sons of Danaus. To make it more confusing, the poet Pindar wrote down the myth that is perhaps most widely accepted. He claims that the aforementioned children were the fruit of the union between Aphrodite and Helios, and it was their daughter, Rhodes, who lent her name to the island.

It is almost impossible to find any two accounts that concur. Frustrated by the failure of my research, I am forced to recall my friend Theo's thoughts on the matter. Usually adroit, he would frequently remind me with a certainty that only a few glasses of ouzo can engender, that the ancient Greeks were promiscuous in their interpretations of the myths, so it is reasonable that we too can pick and mix our legends.

Pindar was something of a revisionist himself, however. On the flimsiest of evidence, he cites Helios as the father of our eponymous heroes, who himself was worshipped across the island and was celebrated by the magnificent Colossus, one of the Seven Wonders of the Ancient World. Bearing this in mind, Pindar just edges it. That Rhodes' airport is named after the Olympic boxer Diagoras, in whose honour Pindar wrote the *Seventh Olympian Ode* that recalls the myth, further reinforces the case!

The subject of the poem epitomizes the glories of sporting achievement and the joy in sharing the success of others. In the 5th Century BC, Diagoras won the boxing event at the Olympic Games twice, but at the 83rd Olympiad in 448 BC, two of his sons also became champions. In celebration, they hoisted their father aloft and carried him around the arena. This was held to be the most contented a man could be and, from the standing crowd, a spectator is believed to have shouted, 'You can die now Diagoras, as Mount Olympus you will not climb', with which the proud father did indeed drop dead, a happy man, we are led to believe. The occasions I have arrived at the airport named after the famed boxer have often been far from happy though – bomb scares and delays of Herculean proportions, along with the resulting exhaustion, have influenced my decision to arrive on the island by boat.

My ship cast off from Piraeus in the early evening. By the time dusk fell, the breeze created by the ferry pushing south left a chill on the spring air. The lights of Athens rode the waves like a giant cruise liner disappearing over the horizon. The sky was ablaze with stars given full licence to shine their brightest in the darkest of blue-black skies. Occasionally a cluster of lights from some small island would appear like a mystical galaxy adrift in a watery universe.

Pulling on a jumper and sitting in the lee of a lifeboat, the moment was laced with anticipation, the regular drumming of the engines beating out the only accompaniment to my thoughts. Eventually letting the cold get the better of me, I descended the steel steps to the saloon and claimed a spot where I could stretch out for the night. Some cheese pies, a sweet Greek coffee and Metaxa lulled me into a sound sleep on my bench seat, until a hint of sunlight through the overhead porthole shook me awake, calling me on deck to see the emerging dawn. Off our starboard bow the lights were going out as Rhodes Town rose from its slumbers.

From several miles out it was already showing off its full pomp, the crenellations of battlements and its minarets and domes silhouetted against the encroaching dawn. It is an enticing sight. But one that only welcomes those who come in peace, for the defences of the town are formidable and the history of the island is one of siege. We coast along past the imposing city walls and the ancient windmills which grace the harbour of Mandraki before turning hard to starboard; winches grinding we come alongside in the commercial port just to the east of the old town.

It is an overwhelming, medieval aura that distinguishes Rhodes from its island cousins; it is not the sun-bleached, dusty antiquity of ancient Greece, but the gothic that takes precedence here. And for the old city of Rhodes, which is now a World Heritage Site, it is reluctantly Mussolini's black-shirted revisionists and their unhealthy preoccupation with the chivalric traditions of the Knights that we must credit for much of the restoration of the town.

To access it now from the harbour is simple. A stroll through any of the vast gates that punctuate the walls delivers you into a different world. The Knights themselves took the island after a two-year siege in 1309, succeeding where the great Macedonian King Demetrius I had failed some 1,600 years previously. Known as Poliorcetes (the siege maker), he turned his attentions to the strategically important centre of Rhodes in punishment for them not having supported him in his successful campaigns against the Egyptians and Cypriots. His flagship led a massive fleet of warships, carrying an invasion force of more than 40,000 troops, double what the Rhodians could muster to defend their birthright.

With an impressive armoury including a battering ram – at 180 ft long so huge it took more than 1,000 soldiers to wield it – and a siege tower called Helepolis (conqueror of cities) weighing little under 200 tons and standing 125 ft tall, he led an assault on the town, which proved futile. A year of huffing and puffing was enough, after which Poliorcetes turned, weighed anchor and set sail for Athens. The bravery of the islanders had left such a mark on the Macedonian that he deserted Helepolis as a token of respect for his worthy adversaries, making him an unlikely benefactor. The melted down scrap was used in the building of the great Colossus of Rhodes, dedicated to the god, Helios, who, Rhodians believed, had restored their fortunes in the war.

On the run from the Knights Templar following infighting between the chivalric orders, the Knights Hospitaller dragged their wounded rump from Cyprus to Rhodes. Seeing its potential as a stronghold for the beleaguered order, they set siege to the island in 1307 and prevailed after two years of bitter conflict. Reinventing themselves as the Knights of Rhodes, they set about further reinforcing the island's already prodigious defences, building a city in the image of their gothic ideal. And it is mostly the Knights' heritage which has been restored, firstly by the Italian invaders and, since then, by various more empathetic archaeological practitioners.

If the magnificent buildings were beautiful manifestations of the Hospitaller's arrogance, their longevity on the island surviving two great sieges is evidence that not all their swagger was misplaced. In 1444 the Sultan of Egypt tried his luck but was comprehensively repulsed. Thirty-six years later the Ottoman leader Sultan Mehmet II, or 'The Conquerer', failed to live up to his name and was driven back into the sea by the cavalry of the Knights commanded by Englishman John Kendal. Eventually in 1522 the Ottomans under Suleiman the Magnificent gained the territory they had cherished for centuries.

A force of some 100,000 finally prevailed over just 640 Knights and their ragbag band of supporters who had found themselves in the city and its surroundings at the time. By December the embattled Knights realized they were beaten and negotiated safe passage for the surviving 180 members of the order. On the 1st January 1523 they set sail for Crete before finally settling in Malta some six years later.

This began another era that left an indelible mark on the city. For almost 400 years, until 1912, Rhodes came under the panoply of the Ottoman Empire. Greeks were banished from within the great walls of the capital. This left behind only a Jewish settlement pitched under the defences to the east, and the Turkish settlers who set about the Islamification of the town, turning all churches to mosques and erecting public buildings, of which the hammam or Turkish baths (now called Dhimotika Loutra) is a fine example. In this 17th-century Byzantine edifice in the south of the old town, with the sunlight streaming through star-shaped apertures in the towering cream dome of the baths, any visitor can still gain relief from the heat and dust of city life. A few euros can see you sweating it out by the olive wood fires, sitting on the same marble slabs as the Pashas did centuries before.

These days I prefer to take my refreshment in the *Nea Agora* (new market), a place I remember as being more open and light than it now appears. When I first visited here it was a dusty, airy space with random scruffy tables set out beneath the odd tree which emerged through dirt gaps in the squared paving slabs. The imperious domed entrance to this heptagonal building opposite the old harbour of Mandraki looks like the work of the Ottomans, which had spilled outside the walls of the old town. In fact it was the musing of Italian architect Florestan di Fausto, employed as an urban planner in Rhodes between 1922 and 1926 who was also responsible for the Governor's Palace further north along the coast road.

That the city developed outside the walls of the old town was a result of the expulsion of the indigenous citizens following Suleiman's ousting of the Knights. The Jewish settlers, however, were given leave to remain. They did so in peace for 422 years until the Gestapo rounded up most of the community and sent them to the death camps in 1944.

Much of the new town is a legacy of the Italians whose neo-Gothic and Venetian reveries make a pleasing, if on occasion incongruous, juxtaposition to the earlier medieval and Arabic styles. The archway supporting di Fausto's dome is resplendent in gold decoration and dominates the forefront of the harbour side. Looking back seawards, the defensive circular tower of the Knight's castle of Agios Nikolaos stands sentinel at the harbour mouth. In its shadow rise the two columns supporting a bronze stag and a doe on either side of the entrance to the old port. In times of conflict the harbour could be defended with underwater chains strung across its entrance to arrest the progress of invading ships. Inside the Nea Agora's walls the courtyard closes in on you. The tavernas and ouzeries of old have been supplemented by souvenir shops, flower beds and mature trees, all of which conspire to make it a pleasant place to sit on one of the many tables which spill out onto the centre of the courtyard. On my first visit I ate snails with a garlic aioli to dip, bread to tear and steely cold wine to drink, today we settle for a pizza and beer, which was just as welcome.

The Lost Wonder

Before visiting Rhodes in the mid Eighties, the thing that resonated most about the island was the Colossus. It seems ironic that for many this island is famous for something that no longer exists, even as ruins, particularly as there is still much debate as to where it stood.

Built in the island capital of Rhodes Town, one of the Seven Wonders of the Ancient World, it took 12 years to construct and was finished in 280 BC. The statue was of the Greek sun god Helios and stood more than 100 ft tall. It was created by Chares, a local sculptor from nearby Lindos, commissioned to celebrate the islanders' successful defence of an invasion in 304 BC.

The giant statue was built largely from recast iron and bronze left behind by the besieging 40,000 strong army of Demetrius Poliorcetes when it was seen off by the forces of the ruling Ptolemy. The statue stood on a huge stone pedestal and was made of individually cast bronze plates held together by rivets and strengthened inside by iron rods. The legs would have been filled with rocks to ballast them.

The romantics among us would love to believe that the giant statue straddled the harbour entrance of Mandraki, between the walls where the deer of Rhodes now stand atop their columns, but this apocryphal story has been discredited as being impossible for any number of practical reasons. It is more likely that the statue was built somewhere near the port, although some archaeologists have suggested it may have stood as part of the Acropolis, situated on a hill overlooking the city.

Unfortunately the great statue, although a tremendous feat of engineering, only stood for 56 years. In 226 BC Rhodes suffered a massive earthquake that the Colossus, along with many of the island's buildings, was unable to withstand. Although the ruling Ptolemy III offered to fund its reconstruction, the people feared that they had in some way upset the god Helios and preferred to let the matter lie.

That the Colossus actually existed is not in doubt, there are numerous documented accounts of the remains of the statue which lay on the ground for a further 800 years. They disappeared at the time of Rhodes' occupation by Arab forces in 654 AD. There are stories that the remains were sold for scrap to a Jewish trader, but this has never been verified.

The architects who designed New York's Statue of Liberty were strongly influenced by the idea of what they believed the Colossus looked like. It is referenced by the Emma Lazarus poem *The New Colossus*, which is inscribed on the plaque inside the newer statue's pedestal. In an attempt to bring more tourism to Rhodes the idea that the Colossus should be rebuilt has often been mooted and in 2008 it was agreed that this was to happen, although it is likely, considering the financial constraints that Greece is now under, that the realization of the project may be protracted.

Lawrence Durrell – Rhodes' Great Advocate

To the north of Mandraki Harbour, in the part of the town inhabited by the fine administrative buildings erected by the Italians during the thirty-odd years they held sway here, is a little dwelling made famous as the house rented by the writer Lawrence Durrell. The celebrated author lived here for two years immediately following the end to hostilities with the Germans after the Second World War in 1945. The house nestles near the Grande Albergo Della Rosa hotel. Built in 1925, the hotel now houses the Rhodes Casino, but at the time was the headquarters of the British administration on the island.

If the Roses Hotel is famous for the signing of the treaty which saw the ceasefire between the newly created Jewish State of Israel and their Arab neighbours in 1949, this small gatekeeper's lodge in the secluded cemetery of the Mosque of Muraid Reis, being Durrell's erstwhile refuge, has its own, not insignificant, claim to fame. The road outside bustles with cars now. But it does not take too much of a leap of faith to imagine the small house with its courtyard garden as a secluded bolthole. Here Durrell could relax with his then partner, Eve Cohen, away from his job as the public administration officer for the island in the transitional period between its liberation in 1945 and *enosis* in 1947.

Durrell had spent the war years in Egypt, which was to be the inspiration for his most heralded work, *The Alexandria Quartet*, published between 1957 and 1960. But it is during his time here that the author claims to have been happier than at any other period of his life and on which he based his book, *Reflections on a Marine Venus – A Companion to the Landscape of Rhodes*, first published in 1953. A hidden hibiscus garden became Durrell's private space to entertain his friends and muse on the past and future of the 'Island of Roses'. He called his home Villa Cleobolus after the 6th Century BC governor of Lindos, one of the seven sages of great Greek thinkers heralded by Plato and Herodotus.

In his exquisite book *The Greek Islands*, published later in his life in 1978, Durrell writes of his time spent on Rhodes with less passion but no less affection than he does of his books about Corfu and Cyprus. The affable nature of the people and the beauty of the landscape affirm a sense of abundance. His contentment in his relationship with the island is more like that between good friends than passionate lovers, and it is easy to see why. Like no other Greek island, Rhodes has absorbed the vicissitudes of its past and proudly displays all its heritage, just as the Knights might have flown the Maltese cross from the highest ramparts of the Palace of the Grand Master. Perhaps the comfort of Durrell's wonderfully languid descriptions of the island have led to him being heralded here less than elsewhere in Greece. In Corfu he and his brother, Gerald, have a Garden in Kyrkyra named after them, here a plaque on the wall of Villa Cleobolus suffices.

'For two lucky years I was able, by virtue of my job with the occupying force, to swim at the Albergo Della Rosa beach and to inhabit a tiny studio buried in flowering hibiscus hard by – at the shrine of Murad Reis which still exists, though the old Mufti is dead and the cemetery terribly unkempt.'

Lawrence Durrell, *The Greek Islands*

The title of his book on Rhodes does not revere the great Colossus or indeed the Temple of Apollo that looks down on the old city from Monte Smith, the hillside acropolis incongruously named after a British admiral. His Marine Venus is coyly hidden away in the city's Archaeological Museum. With details of its provenance and history unclear, she has nevertheless been immortalised by Durrell as a symbol of the island, raised from the depths to find new hope after the dark days of war.

This is not the famed Bathing Aphrodite of Rhodes, who crouches nearby in the museum, drying her hair in the sunshine after emerging from the sea, but a real escapee from beneath the waves, or so local folklore would have it. Durrell's Venus was a smoothed Aphrodite Pudica, thought to be a cult statue from the temple to that same goddess which lies near what is now the commercial harbour. She was landed by fishermen in their nets, sea worn and battered; a catch that became imbued with lasting value. Buried for a second time, this time in some underground vault to hide her from the ravages of war, Durrell witnessed her re-emergence into the light again, liberated at last, and invested the statue with its timeless significance.

'So long as we are in this place we shall not be free from her; it is as if our thoughts must be forever stained by some of her own dark illumination – the preoccupation of a stone woman inherited from a past whose greatest hopes and ideals fell to ruins. Behind and through her the whole idea of Greece glows sadly, like some broken capital, like the shattered pieces of a graceful jar, like the torso of a statue to hope.'

Lawrence Durrell, *Reflections on a Marine Venus*

Durrell left the island in 1947, some years before he found international recognition as a writer, before moving to Cordoba in Argentina and on to Yugoslavia and Cyprus, on which he based his award-winning 1957 book *Bitter Lemons*. Forced out of Cyprus by the troubles between the Greek Cypriots who wanted *enosis* with Greece and the British administration, a disillusioned Durrell settled in the South of France where he lived until his death in 1990. But even after having left the eastern Mediterranean he remembers Rhodes with great affection.

'There could be no pleasanter place to buy a cottage for the summer; I venture to think that of all the island climates I know, the Rhodian climate is the best in every sense... It was always with a pang that we took ships to leave Rhodes; the farewell siren echoed up there on Monte Smith and among the green glades of Callithea and Rodini with heartbreak in it.'

Lawrence Durrell, *The Greek Islands*

The City of the Knights

Approaching Rhodes Town from the sea on *Birba*, it was easy to imagine what confronted Sultan Suleiman the Magnificent's 100,000 troops aboard their 400 ships as they approached to lay siege to the city in 1522.

Shadows of the town's medieval fortifications loom defiantly over Mandraki Harbour, exuding romantic notions of chivalric knighthood. Today, aboard the little sloop silently cruising towards harbour it is one of the most beautiful island vistas in Greece but, to the Sultan's men, the picturesque lustre of the approach must have been outweighed by a terrible apprehension.

Much of the current town was built to meet the vision of the chivalric ideal by the crusading order of the Knights Hospitaller who renamed themselves the Knights of Rhodes after taking control of the city in 1309. We pass between the two pillars on top of which stand two deer, one male and one female, symbols of the island. This is the entrance to the harbour which some believe was, at one time, straddled by the Colossus.

Mooring up stern first we head ashore into the old city. In the heat of the day the alleyways and squares are deserted. We walk along the Street of the Knights where the warriors used to train and pray, from the New Hospital that now houses the archaeological museum to the magnificent Grandmaster's Palace. The medieval buildings are so well preserved that walking among them it is difficult not to imagine that you have been taken back in time.

Despite inflicting massive casualties on the invading Turks, the Knights finally faced the inevitable and agreed terms by which they would gain free passage from the city with all the wealth they could carry. In return the Greek population would be allowed to continue their Christian worship outside the city walls without retribution.

On departing the island, the Knights found shelter on Crete and Sicily before moving to Malta and Gozo. The taking of Rhodes by the Turks was of tremendous strategic importance to the Ottoman Empire, giving them a staging post for their eventual rout of the Venetians in Crete a century and a half later in 1669.

Unlike Crete, there was no great physical resistance to the Turks, which probably accounts for how well the old town is preserved. The Greek population was forced to move outside the city walls where they continued to worship in Orthodox churches and made their living in the predominantly rural economy.

Within the city itself most of the churches were transformed into mosques; with domes and minarets being added to the existing structures. The Turkish baths, which still operate, were built, and existing medieval houses were augmented with the traditional enclosed wooden balconies much favoured in Ottoman architecture.

The Turks held Rhodes for nearly four centuries, but in 1912 their power was in decline. Whilst defending the Ottoman Empire in the First Balkan War against the league of the Christian states of Greece, Bulgaria, Serbia and Montenegro, Italy took its opportunity and seized the

Dodecanese. Although a blow to any ambitions the islands had for *enosis*, or union with Greece, it did, however, keep them out of the traumatic exchange of population with Turkey following Greece's ill-fated campaign in Smyrna in 1922. In this year millions of Greeks and Muslims were uprooted from the country of their birth and relocated within the newly drawn borders of Greece and Turkey.

The signing of the Italian armistice following their defeat by the Allies in 1943 led to the occupation of Rhodes and the rest of the Dodecanese by the Germans. The next year they sent 1,673 of the island's Jewish community to the death camps. Only some 150 survived. The islands were finally united with Greece after the signing of the post-war peace settlement in 1947.

As night falls, we sit drinking in the cockpit of *Birba*. The town again becomes the City of the Knights. The walls of their stronghold, now illuminated, dominate the skyline. Solid and impenetrable, it is difficult to see what other memory of this unique place at the far east of the Mediterranean could take precedence.

Icons – Prayers Made Visible

Something that set Greece aside from anywhere I had ever visited before was the profusion of dimly lit, cavernous shops selling icons. In the back of these ateliers, artists sat hunched over easels creating works of art in a style with which I was to become familiar. Although the profusion of these studios is no longer so apparent, every town has a shop selling these religious works. It seemed strange to me that such art was so often created in darkness, unlike the paintings and sculptures of Western artists, which celebrate the light. But having learned more about these religious works I now understand that light is not required as these are not likenesses of worldly things or representations of the artist's imagination, but they are prayers made visible. *Eikon* in Greek means image, and just as Christians believe that Christ was created in the image of God, these representations of religious figures are analogous rather than realistic.

On chapel walls, in private homes, on church iconostases throughout Greece these radiant gateways to the Lord can be seen in all their stylised solemnity. Rumour has it that the first physical records of icons relate to pre-Christian times, to when Roman Emperors were venerated as divine beings and pictures of them were displayed around the empire for people to show their obeisance by burning candles and scented oils in their presence. Indeed, it is this link to the pagan past that throughout history has created rifts in the church about the veneration of images. Some faiths allude to the Old Testament view that such things went against the commandment of making 'graven images'. In fact the flattened nature of the work traditionally goes back to the belief that in three-dimensional, realistic sculptures lurked demons with supernatural powers, not unlike those powers held by the gods of Greek legend. Icons in the Greek Orthodox faith are usually portrayed on flat panels. If they are ever sculpted or carved, icons will always be less obtrusive than bas relief and as such will have considerably less depth to the figures than they would have if they were proportionately to scale.

Here icons are a constant presence in daily life; they hang in corners in the poorest of homes, adorn the walls of the most inaccessible chapels on mountain tops, emblazon the iconostases of city cathedrals or comfort the loved ones of those killed in accidents in roadside shrines. But all these religious works, whether they are in the simplest of forms or drawn by a grand master hold one thing in common: they all adhere to a strict set of conventions.

Christ and the saints are always represented with halos, as are angels who are also adorned with wings, as they are the messengers of God. This symbolism accounts for a style that is self-consciously the antithesis of realism. Golden backgrounds represent the incandescence of heaven, blue is used to colour humans while red illustrates beatific divinity. A stylized letter convention is also incorporated to help identify the scene and the characters that enact it.

These conventions not only serve to take the icon out of the temporal world of human reality, but also act as a code which could be understood by even the least literate members of society. They became a direct way for an uneducated society to learn the gospels; indeed, icons were used as a way of converting people to the faith after the declaration of religious tolerance following the conversion of the Roman Emperor Constantine the Great himself in 313 AD. They were a *lingua franca* that could be exploited, as the iconic form had been used from the earliest of times for the veneration of ancient gods and former Roman emperors themselves. The most famous of the Greek Orthodox schools of iconography was based in Heraklion in Crete. By the 16th Century this was an established centre for post-Byzantine art, and El Greco was a Master of this renowned painters' guild before leaving Greece to work in Venice and Spain. But Rhodes has some outstanding representations of the icon painter's art, examples of which can be found in two churches on the island, that of the Assumption of Our Lady in the narrow lanes of Lindos and the more remote but no less meritorious Church of the Dormition of the Virgin in Asklipio. But similar work is to be viewed across Rhodes and sometimes in the most unlikely of places. Wherever it turns up, it is always a joy.

Monolithos – A Fairytale Castle

I don't know why I had not heard about Monolithos before actually stumbling upon it on a drive around the south west of Rhodes. It is sublimely peaceful, and is none the worse for hiding its light under the proverbial bushel. The first reason we stopped there was hunger. Every day I try not to eat a sizeable lunch in an attempt to preserve my appetite for dinner, and on this particular occasion I failed spectacularly. Driving up from the southernmost tip of the island one Sunday, the road from Prasonissi Cape and Apolakkia happens upon an unpretentious gem of a restaurant. Sited at the point where the road arrives at the outskirts of Monolithos before heading northwards, playing hide and seek with Rhodes' spectacular western seaboard, a third road peels off and heads into the village itself. At this meeting of the ways stands Christos' Corner Taverna.

As the first lunchtime customers, we had the pick of the outside tables. Not long afterwards a string of locals were arriving. Soon all the tables, in a no doubt prescient way, were full to busting. Christos led us to his kitchen, if that's what you can call a large fridge next to a charcoal grill beneath a flimsy shelter in the middle of the jumble of tables. This was where most of the cooking was done, and he proudly showed us what was on offer. Any hope of having a light lunch was extinguished in the face of a mouth-watering display of refrigerated *souvlaki*, chicken, chops, and numerous fish.

The smoke from the recently-lit grill gave off an enticing aroma of herbs from previously cooked delights and all resolve was abandoned. I ordered pork chops and a Greek salad. When it arrived at the table I was left wondering from which behemoth of an unfortunate pig these cuts had been butchered. Two succulent, giant chops overlapped the sides of my plate barely leaving room for two foil-wrapped jacket potatoes. A roughly hewn loaf of bread was squeezed onto the table between two enormous salads, a bowl of fresh tzatziki and an earthenware jug of red wine. The creamy potatoes dripping with butter and the melting chunks of meat brushed with oil and all manner of herbs from the surrounding hills made the challenge of eating such a quantity all too achievable.

Having finished and requesting the bill we were brought glasses of a clear spirit called souma. This is made locally, and is a distillation of dried figs. Slightly sweet and strong, it has a taste distinctive from its better-known cousins Raki and Ouzo, but its capacity to slow down the system is much the same. Not wanting to waste the rest of the day sleeping in the sun, we headed for the village centre.

From the tranquil air that pervades this small place, it is clear this must be a well-kept secret. There is little to do here except inhale the beauty and atmosphere, which I consider one of the most perfect spots on the island. Beyond the classic white houses, their courtyards ablaze with the ubiquitous bougainvillea and geraniums, lies the sea, sanguine beneath the towering cliffs dominated by a dazzling outcrop on which languishes the remains of the striking castle for which the village is famous. The isolation is reminiscent of King Arthur's legendary fortress at Tintagel in Cornwall, but this redoubt was more recent, built by the Knights of St John in 1480 to protect from invaders and pirates.

What is left of the castle stands upon the rock that gives this charmed spot its name *mono lithos*, meaning 'lonely rock'. It can be reached by way of a narrow, steep staircase hewn out of the cliff face. Parking at the bottom of the crag we began the trek upwards. A lighter lunch might have been sensible, but the breathless hike to the top is worth it, not least to take a look around the ruined walls that encircle the remains of two small chapels and the cisterns, which would have provided for the basic needs of the garrison stationed here. The real reward for the climb, however, is the view. Beneath the vertiginous, 300-ft cliffs tiny, secluded beaches burrow into their secret coves. Out to sea, peeking through the heat-haze of breathless air, are two small islands moored offshore, and inland a lush pine forest floods the foothills of Rhodes' second highest peak. Mount Akramytis rises some 2,700 ft above the tiny village glimpsed beneath us inland. The forest is so different from much of the landscape elsewhere on the island. It comes as a shock after the barrenness of the south from where we have just come.

We return to the car and drive back to the outskirts of the village and stop to buy from one of the many honey sellers who have set up shop alongside the winding road. The woman is proud of her produce, telling me it comes from her brother's hives that sit in the vast acreage of pine forest. She lets me taste the different honeys on offer, explaining the provenance of each batch. Savouring them together, the difference in flavour was incredible.

The pine honey was especially surprising as I was tasting something redolent of Christmas, sweet but infused with the taste of the trees from which the bees reap their harvest. Darker and thicker than the other honey on display, its heaviness chimed more readily with this image of wintertime. The bees' harvest is not directly from the trees themselves but from honey dew, which is a sugary secretion deposited on the trees by insects that live off sap from the pine. In the heat of a Rhodian afternoon, in that brazen sunshine overlooking the most sedate of cerulean seas, the taste of that honey was endowed with a purity that seemed only achievable when a food is enjoyed in its natural environment.

It was intriguing to experience the difference between the varieties of honey deriving from a range of plants and herbs. The thyme honey was a natural antioxidant, so the stallholder told me, and others had the scent and taste of wild oregano and rosemary. I bought more than enough to enjoy with my breakfast yoghurts throughout my stay.

We were right on the verge of the pine forest. Instead of heading back to the village we took a detour along a road that delved into the trees. The air cooled under the shade of the fronds of the thousands of pines, which stretched for miles inland. In clearings stood stacks of felled trunks awaiting their journey to the sawmill. Everywhere dotted among the vast evergreens, resting on a carpet of cones, seeds and needles were multicoloured hives. I have never seen more beehives in Greece, or anywhere else for that matter. The air hung limpid in the forest, the silence only broken by the odd worker bee going about its business in the heat of the afternoon, most of their co-workers perhaps had taken the wise course of action and were indulging in an afternoon snooze. After driving for several miles, the road became a track, which gradually got more rutted and threatened to overwhelm our tiny hire car. We retraced our steps leaving the forest behind, emerging once more into the full strength of the light reflecting off the sea some hundreds of feet below our meagre road that desperately clung to the sheer cliff.

Feta – A Taste of Victory

Membership of the EC may be a contentious issue in Greece these days, but one thing the Greeks will always be grateful to the Brussels' bureaucrats for is their landmark ruling in 2005 giving protected designation of origin (PDO) status to that cheese which crowns the ubiquitous Greek salad, feta. No longer can inferior grade products be passed off as the cheese that lies at the heart of so much of Greece's cuisine.

Not only does this crumbly, tangy, brined cheese – with an unmistakable aroma of the ewe's milk so essential to its authenticity – glisten with golden oil as it crowns *horiatiki salata* it is also a key ingredient in so many other Greek staples. Its use in *tyropita*, small filo pastry parcels stuffed with cheese, omelettes and a wealth of *saganaki* dishes, to name but a few, contribute to making the Greeks the biggest consumers of cheese in Europe.

The battle over the right to call a cheese feta was fierce, the main protagonists surprisingly being the northern European countries of Denmark and Germany. Both produced large quantities of soft, brined cheeses made from cow's milk. The Danes were the Greeks' largest competitors producing some 25,000 tonnes for export with the Germans manufacturing a not insubstantial 20,000 tonnes. The Danes started to make the cheese in the 1930s and the Germans as late as the 1970s, although they only jumped on the bandwagon and marketed their versions of the cheese as 'feta' in 1963 and 1985 respectively.

Feta is the Greek word for slice. Whether this refers to the way the cheese is sliced on top of salads, or how the cheese is cut up to be put into the wooden barrels in which it is traditionally matured has been lost in the sands of time as the cheese has been referred to by its current name since the 17th Century. Greek claims to the cheese go back even further than that. An Italian traveller to Crete wrote of seeing such a cheese being cured in baths of brine as early as 1494. Being of Byzantine origin it would clearly see off the foreign interlopers, but legend has it that such cheese dates back some

2,000 years earlier still, the museum at Delphi exhibiting artifacts from early cheese making from the 6th Century BC.

The battle raged from 1996 when the EC first gave protection to feta, the name only being allowed to be used for cheeses produced in certain parts of Greece and made from a minimum of 70 per cent sheep's milk, the remaining percentage being goats' milk. It was also ruled that the cheese must be made using certain traditional methods. Challenges from other countries were not finally fought off until 2005 when the EC's highest court, the European Court of Justice eventually ruled in Greece's favour.

For lovers of this sublime cheese that, at its best, combines a creamy texture while remaining crumbly, and a salty taste that still has hints of sweetness coming through, this was the right decision. The best feta has been matured in wooden barrels. It feeds off its own juices for weeks before being stored for months more, maturing until ready to eat. For real connoisseurs I am told the best time to eat the cheese is July, as feta bought straight from the barrel at this time will have been made from the milk of ewes which grazed on the best of the new spring herbs and grasses, imbuing the cheese with the scents and flavours of the hillside.

The cheese is made by heating pure sheep's milk or a blend of sheep and goats' milk in a vat before rennet is added to induce the separation of curds and whey. The curds are then cut into small pieces before being put into perforated moulds and left for more of the whey to drain off. Sprinkled with salt and left overnight for this to absorb the curds are then cut into pieces and squeezed into wooden barrels where they sit in any more whey which has been expelled.

After several days the barrel is sealed tightly, any air inside is pumped out so the cheese is in a vacuum where it remains for up to 20 days fermenting on its own yeast and bacteria. After this time the barrels almost explode open, at which point they are checked for taste before water is added and the barrels are resealed and refrigerated for three months or more. At that stage the cheese is ready for market.

This is an age-old process that has changed little over the years and the end product is a world away from the bland thin, watery cheeses masquerading as feta and often marked 'Greek style' in supermarkets outside Greece. Nothing is wasted in the traditional manufacture of feta. The small pieces of cheese that are produced when it is sliced are called *trimma* (crumble). This is often given away and ideal for using in cheese pies or sprinkling into an omelette or on a chunk of oiled bread and herbs. Even the separated whey does not go to waste. It is blended with skimmed milk and heated up again with rennet and formed into a hard cheese which, after aging for more than a year, is perfect for grating over dishes. It is possible to make something resembling this cheese at home – just as long as you remember not to call it feta...

A Journey Back in Time – Palia Poli

Ten gates punctuate the sturdy walls of the Palia Poli, or Rhodes Old Town. To pass through any of them is to enter into another world. Within the two and a half miles of fortifications built by the Knights Hospitaller on top of earlier Byzantine defences lies an intriguing snapshot from which the inquisitive visitor can glean much of the island's turbulent past. The whole of the old town is a World Heritage Site, designated as such by UNESCO in 1988 and, spending any amount of time meandering within the walls of this medieval fortress town, it is easy to see why.

Cultural edifices from Hellenistic, Roman, Byzantine, Medieval, Ottoman and Italian periods of the town's history are all represented here. Those who seek evidence of the earlier heritage of Rhodes will need to go further afield, to the ancient capitals of Lindos, Ialyssos or Kamiros which held sway until a pact between their leaders paved the way for the creation of the original Palia Poli in 408 BC.

For most though there is plenty to satisfy here, and the architectural style that pervades at first would appear to be that of the Knights. But some of this is pastiche, the work of heavy-handed Italian ideologues trying to create a long forgotten chivalric era in the image of the crusaders. The Italian influence came crashing down under the marching heels of the jackboots of their erstwhile allies the Germans in 1943, an echo of the eventual capitulation of the Knights some four hundred years earlier to the Ottoman forces of Suleiman the Magnificent in 1522.

The folly of that ill-conceived Italian dynasty may have restructured parts of the town in a cold, stern idealisation of what they held to be medieval, but things could have been so much worse. To the untrained eye, the flying buttressed lanes of the original city segue effortlessly into the reconstructed facsimile and, in passing, it is difficult to see the joins.

Nowhere more is this true than in the *Anaktoro ton Arkhonton*, the Palace of the Grand Masters. This lies at the heart of the higher part of the city, to the north west, the Knights themselves having constructed their castle, the Collachium, on earlier Byzantine fortifications. The Palace was the epicentre of Hospitaller governance, housing the offices of state and the most senior denizens of their chivalric society. Outside of the Collachium lies the *Hora*, where the working population of the city lived and went about their business.

The palace sits on the *Ippoton*, the aptly named Street of the Knights, which has a pleasing sense of relaxed stateliness befitting its heritage. This is maintained by the absence of shops and restaurants along its length. In these reconstructed buildings, which have been set aside by the great and the good of the modern administration to house administrative and cultural offices, used to reside the Knights.

For the Hospitallers, Rhodes was the safe haven they had been seeking after centuries of conflict. The Order can be traced back to 1048. It was then that it was founded in Jerusalem to administer to the needs of pilgrims visiting the city. As tensions rose with the crusades, the Knights of Saint John succumbed to the militarisation of their number and were charged by the church to defend the Holy Sepulchre in Jerusalem to their last breath. Evicted from the city by Saladin in 1191 they wandered the region before

settling in western Galilee in the city of Acre before fleeing to Cyprus in the
face of Mamluk forces in 1291. Infighting between The Hospitallers and the
incumbent Knights Templar led to the order being driven off that island in
1306 when, desperate for a new home, they attacked the Byzantine fiefdom
of Rhodes, prevailing in 1309 after a protracted siege.

In the ground floors of these buildings on the Ippoton where clerks now
sit drinking coffee and idling over spreadsheets, horses used to be shod, fed
and watered as squires and farriers tended to the needs of their master's
mount and armoury while, in the chambers above, the Knights would make
plans to exploit the wealth of, and defend, their new-found home.

Members of the Order came from all over the Christian world, and were
divided into units called Tongues, dependent on their nationality. From
Spain, Italy, Germany, England, Provence, The Auvergne and the rest of
France, Knights joined this new order that had found favour and support
from the papacy. Along this street can be found, among others, the turreted
and gargoyled Inn of the Tongue of France. Like the other groupings of
Knights this enclave would be presided over by a bailiff and the Knights
would elect a leader for life from their number who became the Grand
Master. The original palace built by the Knights survived the siege of
Suleiman which ousted them from the city in 1522, but failed to weather an
accidental explosion when it was being used as an ammunitions dump by the
Turks in 1856. The cool, sand-coloured lines of the present incarnation of the
building are an Italian architect's interpretation of the original, brought to
fruition in the 1930s.

The palace encloses a beautiful arched and cloistered courtyard, and
houses two museum collections, one of Rhodian artifacts and another
specifically medieval. Elsewhere the exhibits are more eclectic. Climbing the
grand staircase to the upper chambers that look out across the inlaid grey and
yellow squares of the inner sanctum, there are mosaic floors from both
Hellenistic and Roman periods, incongruously laid down in this 20th-century
homage to the medieval. But it would be churlish not to acknowledge the

magnificence of this building, whatever its dubious heritage, which in a way encapsulates a wider pantheon of Rhodian history than it might have done if it had remained neglected.

The *Hora* is less grand but more authentic and serendipitous, the streets of sandstone and lime-washed buildings with iron-fortified windows and blazing blue doors weave their cobbled ways between hidden *chochlakia* (pebbled) courtyards, tiny cracked churches and crumbling mosques. A snatch of modern pop music emanating from an open window can do little to break the reverie this magical place engenders, a hotch-potch of Gothic, Turkish, Byzantine buildings buttressed against potential earthquake as they meander from shaded square to hidden residences resplendent with summer blooms. On Sokratous Street the old rubs shoulders with the new. Traders and restaurateurs lucky enough to own a piece of this popular piece of history go about their business, catering to the needs of the thousands of tourists who prefer the hustle and bustle of this one deeply flowing street and its tributaries.

I have often been pleasantly surprised at how it is still possible to find an authentic and reasonably priced meal right here at in the centre of Rhodes' cultural heartland. There are few other places imbued with such an atmosphere where you can enjoy watching the world go by to an accompaniment of a plate of flash fried *kalimari* with lemon juice.

Lost in Lindos

Picture perfect, Lindos is the epitome of the classic Greek island town. So much so that in recent years it has carved out a niche for itself as a popular wedding destination. The labyrinthine lanes weaving their way between the sturdy, brilliant white walls of family dwellings and shops, and the delights of numerous rooftop restaurants have seduced many an engaged couple. All this in the shadow of the imposing citadel of the acropolis which tops the spectacular spur of rock which has stood guard over the tiny town for all remembered time.

Heavy bare-wood doors, dressed in uncompromising black ironmongery, stand open to reveal the mosaic *chochlakia* floors of a thousand courtyards. These intricately laid black and white beach pebbles set in symmetrical shapes that allude to Lindos' maritime past or even just to the aesthetic whim of a master craftsman are said to massage the bare-footed stroller in much the same way as pressure points in acupuncture or chiropody. Whether this is true or not, they provide a striking location for families to eat, drink and siesta as cats doze in the shade of potted pink, purple, red and yellow hibiscus, barely opening one eye to the swallows busying themselves building nests in the gnarled old beams above.

Had I not glimpsed these delights for myself some years earlier, I would have been unaware of what awaited me, as a 12-hour delay in our flight from the UK had left us struggling to find our accommodation at three o'clock in the morning, with little idea where we were going. A little apartment hiding in the old town, away from the bustle of the centre, but within easy reach of its attractions, is to be highly recommended, if you can find it in the first place. With the streets deserted and some rather inexact directions this turned into something of a mission. After toying with us for long enough for us to consider returning to the car and awaiting sunrise, the gods of the maze revealed our accommodation. We stumbled over the threshold, across the courtyard sweeping aside fronds of potted palms that brushed our faces before we tumbled into bed.

I was awoken by the clamour of bells, which had scant regard for the sleep of exhausted travellers, the wavelength of which stirred the old walls of our flat like a burgeoning earthquake. Flinging open the shutters, the sound came flooding in on the coat tails of the brilliant light that seeped into every nook and cranny, dispelling any annoyance at the untimely reveille. Flattered by its invitation, the delicious sun drew me outside in search of the makings of a simple breakfast; coffee, bread, yoghurt and honey. Foolishly the lessons of the following night had not been learned. Tracking down a shop selling the required provisions was easy but retracing my steps was not so simple.

By the time I got back to our rooms, I was more than ready to enjoy the not-so-recently acquired fruits of my labour.

Lindos is built on a spot of supreme natural beauty, and over the years its inhabitants have, for the most part, been in tune with their surroundings, leaving a sympathetic legacy that satisfies on so many different levels. Split into two distinct areas, the lower town is the commercial and residential sector, whereas the upper town, which encompasses the older settlement, is the acropolis built on top of a rock that towers some 400 feet over two natural harbours to the north and south.

It is easy to see how settlers favoured such a location as early as the 12th Century BC, when the Dorian King Tlepolemus decided to put down roots there. Its natural attributes and geographic location far to the east in the Mediterranean made it a natural stopping place where Greeks and Phoenicians could do trade, and it became the most important of the three ancient Dorian cities on the island. Until 408 BC these three great centres of Ialyssos, Kamiros and Lindos, competed for trade until the elders took the unusually pragmatic approach to combine their resources, revoke their independence and build a new city – that of Rhodes Town. This unification was called the *synoecism*, but although government moved to the new city of Rhodes, Lindos remained an important religious focal point and important seaport with her own colonies as far away as Asia Minor and Sicily.

As the temple celebrating the cult of Athena Lindia, built as long ago as the 10th Century BC, attests, this site has been one of profound religious significance since the earliest of times. The original Doric temple was probably erected in celebration of the local ancient cult of the goddess of Lindos sharing devotions with the Dorian goddess Athena, which settlers brought with them from overseas and assimilated with the existing local beliefs. What can be seen today, however, was built in the 4th Century BC around a new temple constructed there following the destruction of the original building by fire in 392 BC.

Just as they have been for the past 30 centuries, people are still drawn to the summit of this sheer promontory. The ascent is not for the faint hearted as the stairs rise steeply enough to catch the breath; although an alternative of taking a donkey ride to the summit is a possibility. As a rule I shy away from such things as I have been to some places in Greece where I have been concerned for the animals' welfare. Having said this the 'Lindos taxis', as these working donkeys are affectionately known, do seem to be well cared for. Their ancestors no doubt have plied this route hauling goods, building materials and travellers for a succession of Greeks, Romans, Byzantines, Knights of St John, Turks and Italians, all of which have left their mark on the plateau at the summit of this outcrop.

Legend has it that the founder of this blessed place was the eponymous Lindos, a grandson of the sun god Helios. Others hold that Danaus, the first leader of all the Hellenic peoples, was first to step foot here en route from Egypt to Ancient Greece, naming Lindos after one of his three daughters, before going on to found Ialyssos and Kamiros, named after the other two girls – all three of his offspring were worshipped as goddesses. The Greek poet and chronicler, Homer, talks of these three cities being founded by the Dorians and of how Lindos under King Tleptolemos was a major contributor of ships to the fleet in the Trojan Wars of which the king took personal command.

After climbing the medieval steps that ascend from the entrance to the archaeological site, it is worth stopping at the first level where the magnificent carving of a Rhodian warship bears witness to the island's maritime heritage. Although more recent than the Trojan Wars – dated around 180 BC – this relief of the stern of a trireme is believed to be the work of the sculptor Pythokritos and formed part of the base to a statue, which an inscription on the ship's side tells us was of Admiral Agesander, son of Mikion.

Staring at the graceful, swanlike neck of the aft quarters of this galley it is easy to be transported back to the Peloponnesian War of the 5th Century BC where, as members of the Delian Confederation, Rhodes supplied ships for the Athenian fleet, before swapping allegiances to the victorious Spartans not long before their victory. Three tiers of oarsmen numbering some 160 could propel such ships more than 60 miles a day. They were used for ramming the enemy or transporting troops and supplies for land battle. In the true spirit of Athenian democracy of the time, they were not crewed by slaves, but by an assortment of free men either fulfilling their military service or paid hands. The ships would only travel by day and were of light enough construction to be beached by the crew overnight.

Lindos continued this seagoing tradition and its dependency on trade led it to establish shipping laws. These developed through the period of the Roman Empire and became Rhodian Sea Law around 600 BC. During the Byzantine period these became the naval laws that in turn became the basis for modern maritime law dealing with shipping regulations and the responsibilities and liabilities for cargo.

I am standing beside the three underground cisterns which were used since the Hellenistic period for the essential storage of water, reminding me it would be wise to take a drink myself as the early morning heat is already winding itself up to fever pitch. Even at this height, the view out to sea is breathtaking. Some of the boats below announce themselves with the bass tones of their engines singing through the still air while others sail silently, leaving behind a ribbon of white as the only evidence of their passing. I could sit here for hours, but am aware that the tourist traffic up the medieval stairs is already increasing and I am determined to enjoy the acropolis in relative solitude.

Dragging my gaze from the sea I focus on making footfall up the steep and uneven staircase that leads to the Governor's Palace, which is identified by the coat of arms of the ubiquitous Grand Master Pierre d'Aubusson high up on the wall. The leader of the island's ruling Knights of St John was also responsible for the building of the magnificent hospital in Rhodes Town, among other architectural gems, between 1476 and his death in 1503 AD. This building augmented the fortifications and the settlements already established by the Knights, overlaying much of the Hellenistic and Roman remains that had fallen into disrepair prior to their settlement of the island in 1309 AD. Built with its outfacing walls rising from the precipitous cliff side, this naturally impregnable building has been restored and now houses the offices of the archaeological teams dedicated to the ongoing restoration work of the acropolis.

Unlike most of Greece and its islands, it is the Gothic architectural style brought here by the Knights Hospitaller for which Rhodes is perhaps most remembered. It is the inclusion of such architecture into the ecumenical mix of historical buildings that contributes greatly to the island's fascination as a destination. And, as I continue uphill, nowhere is this more in evidence than on the acropolis at Lindos. From the 15th-century medieval archway, the domain of the knights gives way to the remains of a Byzantine church dedicated to St John some two centuries earlier.

Turning right up a stairway I pass what is signed as a storage area from around the 1st Century BC, before entering the stoa. Built in the 2nd Century BC this area was once a large covered walkway, which provided respite from the pounding midday sun. It also provided a dramatic approach to the grandiose great stairway, built on the original ascent, dedicated to the pre-Socratic philosopher king, Cleobolus, who ruled the settlement in the 6th Century BC and was responsible for discovering the underwater springs which provided the water to sustain it. His tomb is on the hillside to the north of Lindos. Cleobolus was one of the Seven Sages of Greek thinkers feted by Plato to whom the words 'meden agan' (nothing in excess) inscribed in the Temple of Phoebus Apollo at Delphi are attributed.

Today, less than half of the original 42 Doric columns remain, but their surprising resilience is more than enough to paint a picture of the magnificence of the stoa, which pre-empted the ascent to the Temple of Lindia Athena which crowns the plateau at the summit of the hill. The impact of the temple, set to the left of the plateau poised upon a dramatic sheer drop to the sea beneath, belies its relatively small size which, at some 72 ft in length and 26 ft wide, is considerably smaller than that of the stoa below. Built in the 4th Century BC, what can be seen today replaced a previous older place of worship, which was destroyed by fire in 392 BC.

The honey-coloured, limestone columns appear almost to grow from the dust, allowing them to blend in with this solemn place of contemplation. The ones that stand here now are mostly the result of restoration work originally done during the Italian occupation in the first half of the 20th Century.

That the Italians were often more concerned about making the grand gesture rather than strict authenticity has led to criticism of them by modern archaeologists, and the scaffolding, which is frequently a feature of the acropolis, alludes to a more thorough and wholesale restoration under the aegis of the Greek Ministry of Culture, which is a perpetual work in progress.

The original excavation of the site was carried out by Danish archaeologists under the direction of Christian Blinkenberg and Karl Frederik Kinch between 1900 and the beginning of the First World War. Looking over the southern precipice of the promontory, gazing down at the cobalt blue waters of St Paul's Bay, I couldn't help thinking that for those archaeologists from the Carlsberg Institute, going to work on a Monday morning could not have been too daunting. This natural shallow harbour has the smallest of entrances in its north-east corner making it an ideal anchorage and, legend has it, one which was taken advantage of by St Paul when he landed here to fulfil his mission to preach Christianity to the islanders. Turning around looking north across the Grand Harbour you can see for miles along the coast in the direction of Rhodes Town.

Back in the lower town I headed out from the centre wherever my weary legs would take me. This happened to be an unassuming courtyard restaurant just opening for lunch which served me *bakaliaros skordalia*. These small chunks of salted cod are soaked in water then dried, floured and seasoned with pepper before frying in olive oil until golden and then doused in a thick sauce made of pureed potatoes, olive oil, almond and copious bulbs of crushed garlic. I followed this with an *avgolemono* soup, dipping the chunks of bread from the basket in a bowl of zesty lemon chicken broth taking the salty edge off the ice cold Amstel I had ordered.

Wandering down the path to an almost deserted St Paul's Bay we found a shady spot to siesta away an afternoon in the shadow of the acropolis before an early evening swim as the lights illuminating the columns and ramparts above against a star-studded sky signalled time for dinner on a rooftop terrace.

Don't Panic!

The first time I visited Rhodes, I flew to Athens' then airport, Ellinikon International, before swapping terminals to catch the domestic service to the island. The connecting flight was an evening one and we did the short transfer to the west terminal, checked in our luggage and boarded the plane. Although my Greek was not too bad, the hurriedly delivered message over the PA system as we prepared to taxi to the runway passed me by.

Suddenly we were surrounded by fellow passengers shouting and screaming, and cabin crew wrestling to reopen the aircraft doors. The only people still sitting in our seats, I enquired what was happening. Amid the panic, we were somewhat alarmed to be told there was a bomb on board!

Even before the aircraft steps had been attached to the fuselage flight attendants, who had prematurely released the doors, had to restrain passengers from leaping onto the runway. With some order restored we filed off the plane and back into the departure lounge. There we began the long wait for the situation to be resolved. A passenger, who claimed to do the trip regularly, assured us that this was a regular occurrence and that we would not be going anywhere that night. With which he took himself off to find a hotel.

With nowhere else to go, we waited with the other passengers, until we were told to reclaim our baggage that had been unloaded onto the runway. Standing over the pile of cases on the tarmac were four armed guards. Claiming our luggage we dragged it back to the terminal and, after what seemed like hours, were asked to check it in again. Sitting on the runway was one solitary bag. Uniformed men were surrounding it with sandbags.

Back on the plane we prepared for take off and taxied to the end of the runway. The engines suddenly increased their volume, ready to catapult the aircraft skywards. Suddenly they were throttled back and the pilot appeared from the cockpit and walked through the plane.

I asked the passing stewardess what was wrong, '*tipota*' she replied with a shrug, 'nothing'. Then she explained the pilot needed to use the toilet prior to take off. Fortunately we are not nervous fliers, but that experience certainly put our constitutions to the test. I sometimes wonder if the passenger who had checked himself into a hotel found himself with no luggage the next morning.

Old Kamiros – A City from a Golden Age

Lulled by the bay of Lindos, staying would have been easy. An early morning walk to the ancient Temple of Athena, followed by a languid lunch at anchor in the cockpit of our little sloop had taken their toll. The columns atop the acropolis now floated in the burnished mid-afternoon sky as we awoke from our siesta, staring up from the warm pine planking of the deck. Our state was of such somnolence that, like Homer's Lotus Eaters, we were loath to leave. But Odysseus-like, our skipper was a hard task-master and a quick dip shook out the last vestiges of the siesta.

While at anchor we hoisted the main bringing us bow into the gentlest zephyr. As the grapnel struck the surface, we broke the foresail, spinning the bow out of the wind until, balanced by the sheeted main, we headed out hard by the peninsula we had scaled just hours earlier. The tiny entrance to the bay named after St Paul slipped past to starboard in the blink of an eye. The apostle is said to have visited here en route to Patara, in what is now Turkey, on his third Missionary journey.

As our boat bends to the wind its timber creaking, she settles into a southerly course. Our plan is to sail through the night to make the 70-odd nautical mile passage to Kamiros, another of the ancient triumvirate of Rhodian cities, and make landfall by morning. The wind had filled in during the afternoon and settled into a comfortable Force 3 caressing the water just enough to provide the occasional ruffle of spray as we slapped seawards on a long starboard tack.

The sails cleated, the slightest of tweaks to the tiller kept a comfortable list to leeward as we settled to enjoy the last few hours before sunset. I had been to Lindos on several occasions, but had not visited Kamiros before, the nearest I had got was the excellent Art Deco fish taverna on the beach below where the ancient city lies. I make no apologies for this as the food and welcome at this bustling restaurant on one of the few sandy strips of shoreline on the west coast is enough to divert anyone's attention. Whole chargrilled sea bream, seasoned with crystalline sea salt, doused in lemon, garlic and olive oil sauce is a memory I will have to put aside if we are to achieve our aim this time.

Our hope was to circumnavigate half the island, turning north again around the Cape of Prasonissi, skirting the west coast past Cape Armenistis. Here the waist of the island narrows as if tightly belted as we set the last lay line for our destination. Unlike Lindos the burghers of Kamiros were not seafaring men, making their living off the land away from the coast. As such there is no suitable harbour and we had to pray that the weather would hold, as it was our intention to anchor off and make the shore in our inflatable tender.

The signs were good and the May weather more stable than it can be in the parched months of midsummer where the ebb and flow of the barometer can whisk up precocious winds at the drop of a hat. As the sun made its descent behind Rhodes to our west, a sliver of moon shared the half-light until the orange globe was snuffed out beyond the island coast and a riot of stars came out to play in the night sky.

We stow the main and crank the reluctant engine to life as the wind follows the sun into hiding. As a chill takes to the air, we reach for our thermal tops. With no need to rely on the gimbals to find the equilibrium for a brew, we spark the stove under a kafebriko of sugar and Greek coffee and serve up four small cups to take the edge off the cold, before toasting the night in ouzo as we forge forward alone, our wake leaving the only scar across the star-strewn panoply.

We decide to take two, four-hour watches, starting at 9 o'clock. I still don't turn in until 10, reluctant to let this evening go. Bleary eyed at 1.00am emerging from the forepeak to take the helm, the low thudding of the engine breaking the very stillness of the night which made its use necessary. A kaleidoscope of stars shines out of a universe of sky and sea that wrapped itself around our world. This is a night where nothing breaks that glorious monotony of the invisible black horizon where sea meets sky. My watch goes by in the twinkling of a shooting star and it is time to go below to catch some sleep before morning.

Only one hour into my slumber and a shaft of light breaks through the porthole, coaxing us awake. We arise to join the others on deck and are welcomed with yoghurt, nuts and honey, almond pie and freshly-squeezed sweetened lemon juice with ice.

The sun is rising from the heart of the Knight's Castle of Monolithos high upon its promontory to our east, like a ball fused with white heat fired from some glorious celestial cannon. From the sea the fortress looks even more imposing than it does from on shore. The stubs of the broken teeth of its battlements viewed from here do not detract from my imaginings of its heyday when the black standard bearing the Maltese cross fluttered from its ramparts. I daydream about the erstwhile Knights of St John who became the Knights Hospitaller and have a sudden realisation that their pennant is that which is now used by St John Ambulance back at home. This had not occurred to me before, but both the name and the healing connection surely could not be coincidence. A little research confirms that the modern day organization does indeed have roots in the Hospitaller Order of Jerusalem, Rhodes and Malta.

As we cross Kerameni Bay the castle towers some 800 feet above us perched on the enormous crag of *Monopetra*, which means 'single rock'. We are in the shadow of a stronghold that has stood here since 1476 AD when the Knights felt the need to reinforce the outposts of their island empire by building on top of defences already installed high on the hillside in Byzantine times. As we sail north this bastion is reluctant to let us go, and holds its diminishing realm in grasp for some time as we skirt the densely-pined forest on this hilly coastline.

As the sun begins to impose itself, enough breeze rises for us to break out the sails and coast along on a comfortable reach across a gently rolling sea, little troubled by the fledgling wind. Rounding Cape Armenistis, Monolithos is at last shaken from view and in the distance, off our port bow, we can see the islands of Chalki, Alimnia and their acolytes. Once a centre for sponge fishing, Chalki's three hundred or so inhabitants now rely on income from tourists seeking a secluded break to eek out a living, and boat trips there can be found from Rhodes Town and less regularly on various craft departing the west coast. Further away still I believe I can see the outline of Symi, shimmering on the horizon, but this may just be a mirage as it is some miles off. Thankfully the sea retains its benevolent state as we approach our destination. We will anchor some 50 yards offshore and make landfall by dinghy, leaving our skipper onboard in case the wind should rise or our anchor drag.

As soon as we reach shore and drag the inflatable up the beach we are heralded by the friendly hawkeyed waiter from the taverna, and resist the temptation to accept his invitation of some refreshment before we begin our ascent. Promising to take him up on his offer upon our return, we head inland and upwards.

From the coast the ancient site of Kamiros is only around half a mile uphill. Being the middle of the day, the hot air laced with pine resin dries the throat as we catch our breath. I am surprised how quiet the site is as we approach, for it is situated in the most beautiful of spots and is magnificent in the extent of its completeness. On the way our conversation is of how much of Rhodes' addictive charm lies in its compactness, in how much variety of architecture and landscape is crammed into this accessible island, which could comfortably be driven around in a day. The white, dust-brown and reds of the settlement seem to echo these thoughts, its self-containment giving a sense of completeness in the mind's eye, which belies the fact that the city was abandoned more than two millennia ago. The ancient city has been described as the Greek Pompeii, but the comparison does not bear scrutiny. It would seem that the relinquished town was not destroyed by natural disaster. Although it had fallen victim to earthquakes in 226 BC and 142 BC, it was the natural gravitational pull of Rhodes City itself, the town that Kamiros had been instrumental in founding in 408 BC, which was ultimately responsible for its demise.

It is clear as we pass through the entrance into what was the commercial district that this town was not built by a warring tribe. The defences are so absent, that rumours that its people, having been subject to pirate attack, may have hastened their fleeing to the safety of the new capital might be true. But it is here that the first significant settlement on the island is thought to have been built. The Dorians can lay claim to this, but lower down the slopes towards the sea is evidence that the Mycenaeans had first inhabited the area centuries earlier.

Indeed it was the discovery of an ancient grave amongst the reforested area of hillside running down to the sea, which led to the uncovering of an Achaean necropolis near the village of Kalovarda. This alerted archaeologists to the site's possibilities in the mid 19th Century. But it was the Italians who must be credited with much of the excavation work that we can see today, bringing an archaeological rigour, which defined the boundaries of the site before their systematic revealing of its entirety. That it was abandoned and ultimately forgotten until then is probably the reason that the city still retains so much of its integrity. It has a conformity to its origins that has not been sullied by layers of generational building.

Looking across the three-tiered site, I get the sense that there are few places that are so in tune with their environment. A small lizard scurries across the fountain square as I look south up the levels of this man-made amphitheatre cut into the hillside. The columns of the Temple of Athena Kamiros rise up from the apogee, dominating the lower levels of the settlement.

Against a backdrop of pine trees growing from the sparse, white rock the Doric columns watch over an army of cicadas sounding out their perpetual paradiddle. I am in the heart of the community space of the town, where people would congregate in the partly-shaded areas to pass the time and argue politics. In those days the square would have been graced with statues to the gods and goddesses, now long gone, only their inscribed marble plinths remaining.

Back down the hill is an area of stone altars laid out in ranks. Each bearing the inscription to a god to whom an appropriate, sometimes grizzly, sacrifice might be made. The largest is to the sun god, Helios. Others to lesser deities show the polytheistic nature of the original inhabitants, with tabernacles to the likes of Hestia, the goddess of Home and Agathos Daimon the God of Good Luck also in evidence. From the *agora* or market area of the town, with its small temple to Apollo abutting the fountain square, the central thoroughfare rises up through the houses of the citizens towards the acropolis.

A warren of alleyways, some barely wide enough to accommodate a laden mule, form a filigree of dusty paths to the east of the city where potters used to labour making *pithoi* to store the wine and oil on which the city based its wealth. Unlike the citizens of Lindos to the east, the wealthy burghers of Kamiros had not made their money by seafaring or piracy but by the more peaceful pursuit of living off the land. The lack of fortifications exemplifies their peaceful existence, and when they came together with Lindos and Ialyssos to form the political union which saw the pragmatic creation of the new city of Rhodes, it is clear that they had much to gain from having access to its seaports through which they could open up new markets for their goods. The tiny harbour of Mylantia directly below was too small, and carried too shallow a draught for any ship of significance. It is more likely that, prior to the creation of Rhodes Town under their patronage, they hauled their wares by hoof the eight or so miles to the south, and the small but deeper water jetty of the port which lies in what is now the village of Kamiros Skala.

Reaching the top of the climb we sit down on the parched earth that opens out onto a plateau. Remains of walls, columns and plinths stand in memoriam to a time when this was the huge colonnaded avenue of the stoa stretching across the whole summit of the acropolis itself, laid out in homage to the crowning temple of Athena Kamiros which stood behind. This is where the merchants would do their trading out of shop fronts and their deals in offices with the local farmers, securing their finest produce to hawk to citizens in the hinterland.

A giant cistern dating from the 6th Century BC lies to our right, with steps leading down into its bowels. This is one of two such storage reservoirs that supplied the city with water, the other being just off the Fountain Square below. Lawrence Durrell had talked of hearing the gurgling of water running below when he visited in 1947 and even went underground to explore the water conduits with Paddy Leigh Fermor and Xan Fielding, but I can hear nothing. We have to open our plastic bottles to secure a drink, and quench our thirst with mineral water.

Using these moments to take stock, it is hard to imagine a more perfect place to live and do business, what is left of the crowning temple gives a clue, but does not do justice, to what it looked like. Shaken to its foundations by the earthquake of 226 BC, what we see now is the remains of walls from the temple that replaced the Doric incarnation of the house of worship, which had collapsed. But as you look back down over the stoa, northwards over the ancient city and west across the sea below, it is hard for your imagination not to come to the rescue and fill in the architectural gaps which nature has rubbed out of the picture. If ever there might have been a golden age of

Hellenistic Greece, the remains of this wonderful town and the images it conjures up epitomize it. Why its inhabitants ever deserted such a spot remains a mystery. But thank whatever gods those citizens may have worshipped that they did, otherwise we would not have this boundless treasure left to us.

A welcome sea breeze is starting to come in off the sea, filling in where the hot air ascends from the parched ground. Back at sea level, we return in the dinghy to collect our skipper who is sure enough of the anchor now to risk coming ashore for some food at the beachside Taverna Old Kamiros. Needing something to pick us up after the night sail and climb, we order a shared plate bursting with golden *kalamari*, deep red king prawns, mussels glistening in a wine and butter emulsion and shiny-eyed bream adorned with wedges of lemon and bejeweled with large crystals of sea salt. Bread, salad and a harsh wine chilled to just off freezing to knock the edge off it completed the leisurely feast which we ate staring out at our sloop drifting, her head following the shifting wind, riding to anchor in the bay.

Fish for Lunch

Young George cast off the stern line from the outer harbour wall at Kolimbia where *Maria* was moored and scuttled forward to man the winch that Captain Lefteris set in motion from the cockpit. Whether ironic or a nickname from many years ago which had stuck, Young George, although probably nearing 70 years of age, was certainly very sprightly. No sooner had he stowed the anchor and the gangplank than he set about baiting hooks on the trolling lines with shrimps. Clear of our mooring, Lefteris gave the twin outdrives their head as they thrust us southwards, traversing the long beach of the bay. Sunshades were up as enthusiastic sun worshippers made an early start with their devotions. It was apparent that Helios would not disappoint today as not a cloud showed its face as we settled in to our passage on a sea as smooth as baize.

Lefteris throttled back and the boat dropped down off her plane to allow Young George to let out the lines astern, one to port and one to starboard, one armed with spinners the other baited hooks. He then turned his attention to the rods, which stood in holders on the guardrails, adjusting the ledgers and baiting the hooks before returning them to their sheaths.

At the end of the long bay the shoreline grew more rocky and indented with tiny inlets like secret bathing spots for sea nymphs. With the echo sounder bleeping and Captain Lefteris focused on his sonar fish finder screen, the weather couldn't have been more perfect for me, but Lefteris muttered something about it being too hot and sunny for the fish. Not to be deterred Young George heaved the anchor overboard before lowering some plastic buckets over the side to fill them in anticipation of our forthcoming catch. Lefteris told us that if we got a bite we must shout 'fish' so George could come and disgorge our prey in case it was too dangerous to handle, like a *skorpidi* or scorpion fish.

The trolling lines were reeled back aboard, and George set to rebaiting the barren hooks. I could feel almost imperceptible bites on my hook but every time I struck, the line returned empty. Judging by the number of times I had to replace the shrimps on my hook, something had been nibbling. After twenty or so minutes, none of the rods had caught anything, so losing patience Lefteris decided to try elsewhere.

We secured our hooks on the bail bars of our reels and holstered our rods and set off further south. To starboard a sweeping bay opened up, and even from out at sea I could detect the extent of its perfection. Flat and stretching way inland, the burnished sand only interrupted by the occasional shade-giving rock around the periphery, it appeared to only bear the beach paraphernalia so essential to modern tourism at its northern end. The rest of the beach was deserted. Young George told me this was Tsambika and I noted it down, with the intention of returning. I would have liked to have beached the tender there and then and taken the path up the mighty cone-shaped hill that overlooks the bay. George assured me that the effort to climb the 307 steps, which complete the path to a tiny monastery, was worth it, not least for the magnificent view. He also related a confused anecdote about an icon, which was too much for my limited language skills to comprehend. I looked the story up later and discovered that the chapel was erected on the site of a miracle. It sits nearly 1,000 ft in the air looking down on the bay we had been crossing, and houses a particularly splendid icon of the annunciation which, rumour has it, was miraculously transported here from its original home in Cyprus.

The legend goes that some centuries ago, what is now known as the icon of Panagia Tsambika used to reside in a monastery some 240 miles to the south east on Cyprus. One night a shepherd, out with his flock on the hillside the other side of the valley, noticed a light shining from the mountain. Ignoring this phenomenon for two nights, on the third his curiosity got the better of him and he decided to investigate.

Frightened of the unknown, he corralled a group of villagers who strapped on their arms and followed him up the mountain towards the source of the mystery. Following the light they emerged at the summit, to find a lone cypress tree, in its branches rested an illuminated icon of the Virgin Mary. Incredulous, the shepherd and his entourage removed the icon from the tree and returned with it to the village, but the icon was not to be denied its favoured spot at the summit of the mountain and mysteriously made its own way back to the tree. Three times this happened before the villagers succumbed to the wishes of the Panagia, and built a chapel to house the icon. The mountain on which she now resides is named after the word *tsamba*, which meant 'spark' in the local Rhodian dialect.

The Cypriots were not best pleased that their icon had been relocated, and they tracked it down and tried to remove it three times, smuggling it back to its native shores. They even burned the back of the icon to identify it, but each time the painting returned to where it hangs today, the charred markings clear for all to see.

The miraculous homing instinct of the insistent icon is not its only mystical quality. During the period of Ottoman rule, the wife of a local Turkish Pasha found herself unable to conceive. Putting her faith in the miraculous icon she prayed to the Virgin and did penance by eating the wick from the vigil light, which burned by its side. She duly became pregnant, although her husband was loathe to accept the intervention of the icon. That was until the baby was born, when the child emerged into the world holding the wick from the lamp that his mother had swallowed. Since then the monastery has had the reputation of helping women to get pregnant, and on its feast day in September they often climb the steps to the monastery barefoot or even on their knees, in obeisance to the Panagia and to ask for her to favour them. Only in Rhodes will you hear the name Tsambika for a girl or Tsambikos for a boy, the children named after the beneficence of the miraculous icon that undoubtedly feels this to be the place she truly belongs.

Lefteris still had the bit between his teeth and was determined to track down the elusive fish, as though failure would somehow have reflected on his manhood. We ploughed our furrow of wash southward further across the bay, passing a small beach with tiny open boats moored just offshore lying beneath a village further up the limestone cliffs. Consulting the chart, I identified this as Stegna.

As we left the tiny resort astern, Young George leaped into action as though some unseen instinct had alerted him to some fish taking interest in his trolling lines. He reeled in, and sure enough the hooks were alive with a modest, lustrous catch of chub mackerel and what looked like small bream among others, maybe mullet or wrasse. Lefteris was all smiles and headed for a small bay in which we anchored and cast out our rods. This time the success from the trolls was repeated and we felt bites on our lines almost every time we raised the bait from the seabed.

Soon the buckets were brimming with a myriad of fish and we were ready for a cooling swim. As we dived off the stern of the boat, the crew set up a simple barbeque on the beach. The dispatched fish were gutted and had their skin slashed with a knife before being dusted in seasoned flour and dropped into a pan of hot oil. In another pan rough-chopped garlic and rosemary were cooked in some butter before red wine and red wine vinegar were added and the whole sauce reduced.

The fish and the sauce were served with bread and salad with salty feta in lustrous green olive oil. The dish is a makeshift version of *psari savoro*, which can be found in any number of restaurants throughout Greece, the fish made to use it as variable as the exact nature and proportions of the recipe. As an experience, this serving was the best I have tasted.

We were to return to Tsambika sooner than anticipated but, I have to admit, not at first to visit the icon of the Virgin. That same day travelling back from Kolimbia to Lindos along the coast road we felt in need of some refreshment, particularly in the form of ice cream. Just past the road for Tsambika beach we turned off at a sign advertising the Panorama Taverna. What a find! We would not usually have stopped at a restaurant beside a main road but, set back from the traffic, this hidden enclave with its tables laid out beneath a pergola entwined with a mature vine, is the perfect spot to sit and enjoy whatever takes your fancy.

Overlooking the rocky hillside that slips away to Tsambika beach, with the sea we had so recently been fishing in the distance, we indulged our whim with a wonderful bowl full of ice cream and fresh fruit. Since then we have returned many times to dine there and have never been disappointed. In the evenings as the sun goes down under the twinkling lights nestling in the vines above, with the smells of the herbs used to brush the delicious fish and meat cooked over the coals on the outside barbecue, here is a secret most tourists do not know about but many Greeks do, as it is frequently full.

Anthony Quinn Bay

The sunset in Rhodes is like no other I have seen. From a burst of fiery orange it starts to sink behind the hills over the town turning them from brown to black. The medieval fortress and Turkish minarets hang on as best they can to the last minutes of light reflecting yellow, green then blue before becoming shadows silhouetted against a sky rapidly losing definition.

The strong afternoon sea breeze had dropped away to a mere whisper as we coasted out of Mandraki, the moon adequately supplementing our navigation lights. The gentle ripple of the wash of tiny caiques leaving harbour for a night's fishing barely made any impression on our equilibrium as we swung the helm over and headed south along the coast.

Ten minutes out even the faintest of zephyrs had deserted us and we cranked *Birba's* motor until it roared into life, propelling us at a stately five knots along Rhodes' east coast. By the trailing log we had travelled 10 miles when, through the beam of our handheld spotlight, we found our destination and turned towards shore.

As we headed into the coastline it opened up into a bay surrounded on all sides by the dark shadows of the wooded hills. I went forward to lean off the bow with a torch and Dean, on the helm, kept one eye on the echo sounder as we felt our way in over the rock-strewn shallows.

We threw an anchor out astern and I dived into the still warm water and swam a bow-line ashore making fast around a rock on the beach. With the engine turned off the silence was suddenly deafening. We had reached our destination of Anthony Quinn Bay.

Hard to get to by day in those days, at nighttime it was deserted. Named after the Mexican-American so beloved of Greeks for his portrayal of Alexis Zorba in the 1964 Michael Cacoyannis directed film of *Zorba the Greek*, the actor bought the land surrounding the bay after falling in love with the spot when he was filming *The Guns of Navarone* here. It was Anthony Quinn who was responsible for driving a road through to the bay. Before he purchased the land it was only accessible by sea or rough mountain tracks.

That he fell in love with it is hardly surprising. Sitting on the coachroof of Dean and Jo's boat in overwhelming silence with the stars giving a perfect show against a sky unpolluted by any other surrounding light it is difficult not to reflect on our place in the scheme of things.

Even though Quinn died in 2001 there is still controversy surrounding the ownership of the land which was seized back by the Greek government in the 1990s despite being sold to the actor for a nominal sum in recognition of his work in promoting tourism on the island and opening an international centre for artists and filmmakers there. The dispute is still continuing, with none other than US Secretary of State Hilary Clinton taking up the cause on her visits to Greece for bilateral talks in 2011.

For us back in 1986 we knew nothing of this but spent one of the most spellbinding nights on deck under the stars. As dawn broke the hidden cove revealed another side of its glory. The rising sun shone straight into the bay, some of its early rays bouncing off the surface of the water while others pierced down illuminating the submerged rocks below. Surrounding the beach, pine trees run in places down the hillsides right to the sea, their roots bathed by the lapping water.

We breakfasted on fresh peaches, yoghurt, walnuts and honey before casting off, weighing anchor and setting sail for home with a gently rising south easterly breeze chivvying us along from over the starboard quarter.

I have returned to the bay several times since that magical evening, the new road making access there all too easy. It retains its beauty like an aging film star might cling to her looks, yet the work done has to an extent obscured the natural beauty that lies beneath. Although it no longer remains secluded, it is still well worth a visit, particularly for the snorkelling.

Petaloudes – The Valley of the Butterflies

I was in some doubts as to whether or not to write about Petaloudes, better known as the Valley of the Butterflies. But, as details about it are hard to escape on Rhodes, it would be obtuse of me not to include this appealing, fertile ravine that would be unextraordinary, were it not for the butterflies that reside there. My reluctance is born of the fact that the population of butterflies that give this haven its name has in recent years been in decline.

Some 15 miles to the south west of Rhodes Town, lying in the shadow of Mount Psinthos is this unique refuge. Strictly speaking, the millions of 'butterflies' that migrate here for the summer months are a type of tiger moth that goes by the name of *callimorpha quadripunctaria himalaiensis*. Their rather grand Latin moniker alludes to where the moth was first identified, in the contrasting environment of the Himalayas. The reference to 'four' relates to the markings on the wing of the moth, which resembles that number expressed as a Roman numeral.

When at rest, the moths look an unspectacular grey colour as they carpet the trees that line the banks of the River Pelecanos, which burbles its way through falls and pools. However, when disturbed they arise like a huge iridescent magic carpet of yellow and black with a glimpse of red as they ghost overhead. Herein lies the danger for the moths as they retain minimal body fat, which they require just to survive. Repeated attempts by some visitors to see them fly, scaring them by clapping and shouting, has caused the premature death of thousands of moths. Fortunately warning signs appear to be improving matters and the decline has been halted in what is, after all, a protected nature park.

The small but insistent river provides a perfect micro-climate for both moths and humans. The latter are attracted to this little piece of paradise by the spectacle of the moths themselves; the former by the cool and humid air exuded as the river splashes from fall to pool beneath the shade of the prolific storax trees. These Oriental sweetgum exude a smell of resin that is attractive to the moths, as well as local church communities who use it for incense. Wooden bridges weave across the river and, in the early months of summer, purple blasts of colour ring out from the bell-like campanulas bravely clinging to the rocky terrain. The walk is leisurely, and it is well worth crossing the road at the top of the valley and walking on for another quarter of an hour or so to the tiny monastery of Panagia Kalopetra.

The story goes that the church was built by a Greek prince, Alexander Ypsilantis. In 1784 the Turks had usurped him from his kingdom of Vlachia, in what is now Romania. Banished to a life on Rhodes, he lived as the abbot of this foundation. Looking back it is easy to empathise with the words of celebrated local poet Theofanis Bogiannos when he writes: 'There isn't any place in Greece like this, so beautiful, so blessed with greenery, colour, such winged souls, so many human souls, and cool, singing cicadas, so much joy on peoples faces' – and the view back down the valley is one to savour.

Cape Prasonissi – A Lunar Landscape

As it is my intention to travel south, away from the tourist hordes, I decide to take the opportunity to go by motorbike. I would not usually advocate motorcycling in the Greek Islands, but the sense of freedom it precipitates is hard to resist so I hope you'll indulge my hypocrisy. I had been assured that the road to Cape Prasonissi was good and, in May, before the height of the surfing season, relatively quiet. It is not strange that Rhodes Town, with its many attractions commands such a gravitational pull on visitors, holding them in a triangle that has Lindos and Monolithos at its base and the capital at its apex. There is a feeling of wilful liberty about countering the tide and driving south out of Lindos along a road that flirts with both sea and land. Along here lie hidden coves and unspoilt beaches; tiny villages tucked away to the west of the road; and isolated villas, shuttered down awaiting a visit from their rich Athenian owners in August. Some houses are still awaiting completion, the stumps of reinforcing rods protruding through the flat roofs.

As I approach the south of the island, the road swings inland, cutting off its most southerly tip as it heads towards the Aegean coast on the west of the island. Along this road lies the sleepy village of Katavia. It has the feel of an outpost, lying indolent on a border to nowhere, and indeed it is the most southerly village on the island. Surrounded by flat arable land, its 500 or so residents make a good living off the plain it inhabits. Some houses here have long been deserted; others show evidence of a former grandeur. The village at one time would have been home to many more people and the Knights of

Rhodes turned it into a redoubt. The Hospitallers added fortifications to defend the local farmers from the tyranny of pirate bands who raided along the secluded coasts of the south, where the Aegean Sea returns to meet its mother the Mediterranean.

I stop at a kafeneon to quench my thirst. Along with my Greek coffee and water, the woman who serves me, dressed in widow's weeds, brings a small carafe of raki and a plate of mezzes, small fish, stuffed vine leaves, bread and olives. On leaving, my offers to pay for anything but the coffee are waved away as I take my leave to head for the cape.

The road is an extraordinary switchback ride through a unique landscape that has an almost lunar feel. I can see some way behind and beyond as I weave the five or so miles coastwards through this rock-strewn wilderness. I am totally alone save for the occasional swallow riding the low-level thermals thrown up by the shallow hills. Out of this limestone desert, the aroma of sage, thyme and rosemary confirm the existence of life and, every now and then, I glimpse delicate orchid-like flowers timidly peeking from behind rocks or in the sparse shade of a stunted holm oak.

Topping a small hill, Prasonissi lies below, and what a sight it is. To the west surf is rolling in, but to the east the sea is calm. *Prasonissi* means 'green island', and compared to the scrub-like phrygana surrounding the magnificent beach beneath me the name seems appropriate enough. At the moment Prasonissi is not really an island as it is joined to mainland Rhodes by a sandy isthmus which keeps the roaring Aegean from the serene Mediterranean. But during the winter months, when colder weather and increased precipitation causes an increase in the water level, this rocky promontory embraces its full status as an island. Parking up near a surf shop, I set off across the narrow, sandy causeway out to the island. A track climbs south across this deserted peninsula leading at its extremity to a lone lighthouse, guiding sailors around this rugged cape.

A few windsurfers and kite-surfers have taken to the waves in the western bay, exhibiting an extraordinary mastery of the conditions. It is understandable how, in high summer, this spot is a Mecca for water sports' enthusiasts, although this has come at some price to the environment. The caretta caretta, or loggerhead turtle, has a favoured breeding ground some five miles to the north near Cape Germata and used to come south to lay its eggs in the soft sand of the beach here. A combination of the vast numbers of tourists in the summer and the compacting of the sand by vehicles being driven on the beach has, sadly, made sightings of the turtle in the area something of a rarity recently.

I return to the beach and take the opportunity for a swim in the sheltered bay, the water is still refreshingly cool, not having yet warmed up from months of summer sunshine which, by August, can make it like swimming in soup. The sunsets here are supposed to be the best on the island, and I can certainly believe it, but today I cannot stay.

Asklipio – A Perfect Picnic

Just walking our picnic up to the car, which has to be parked outside the town of Lindos as there is no access for vehicles there, had taken its toll. The planned lie-in and late start meant the sun was already giving off a 90-degree heat and our picnic lunch was far heavier than we had intended.

We had only met the local shopkeeper, Poppy, a few days previously, but on learning we were taking the short trip to Asklipio to see what we had been told were some of the most complete works of iconography on the island and to picnic near the castle ruins, she had arrived bearing gifts of water melon, cheese pies wrapped up in a tea towel, a Tupperware box stuffed with delicious honey cakes, a loaf of bread and a chunk of hard sheep's milk cheese. If that wasn't enough, she also pressed us to take a half-gallon plastic container of honey-coloured wine!

All this, together with our more modest ham and salad baguettes, yoghurts and bottles of water were crammed into the boot of our tiny hire car before setting off southwards along the coast road. About 10 miles into our journey in the rather upmarket, but sterile looking resort of Kiotari, we follow a sign telling us to turn right and head inland as we start our ascent to the small mountain village where we hoped to picnic.

Tensing itself against the gradient and relaxing by turns, our car mades its way through pine forests and olive groves growing on the remarkably lush hillsides before we arrived at the outskirts of this remote village. Shaped like an amphitheatre, the small traditional white houses clustered around a square dominated by the magnificent Church of the Dormition of the Virgin or *Koimisis tis Theotokos*, all giving audience to the castle ruins which look down on them from the mountain top.

Outside the church, beside its terracotta-tiled barrelled roofs and domes, stands a detached bell tower, like a four-tiered wedding cake topped with a cross. Built in 1060 AD, this Byzantine church took the traditional cruciform shape before being later supplemented by two more modern apses to the south and north, which were added in the 18th Century to accommodate more worshippers.

The door was locked, but we were directed to a nearby house where an elderly retainer was more than pleased to open up for us. While the outside of this beautiful church exhibits a cool, clean, golden façade, the inside reveals some of the most extraordinary, colourful frescoes I have ever been lucky enough to see. We had been told that the paintings here were the equal of those in the wonderful 14th-century Church of the Holy Virgin, which nestles in the alleyways of Lindos near the main square. The paintings there by the Symian master, Gregory, are stunning, but what was revealed on opening the door here was more than comparable. Light dapples the pebble-set *chochlakia* floor as it forces its way through the small windows illuminating and casting shadow in turn on the frescoes with which almost every surface seems ablaze.

Looking up inside the central dome, a massive chandelier stares back. The walls tell stories from the Testaments, beginning with The Creation through to the life of Christ, and the Dormition of Mary. The narrative expressed fills the interstices of the church with a vibrant reminder to the faithful that God is everywhere, even reminding the pious that the Last Judgement will, some day, come. I am no expert on ecclesiastical painting but, whatever one's religion, it would be difficult not to be moved by the passion expressed by the artists who created these murals.

Throughout the Orthodox world a fast is held for the first fortnight in August in preparation for the feast for Theotokos, quite literally the bearer of God, or the Virgin Mary, to whom this church is dedicated, on the 15 August. I am struggling to find the names of the artists who worked here, indeed there is conflicting evidence as to the period from which the paintings date, guesses range from the 15th to the 17th Century AD. Whoever and whenever, a beautiful legacy has been bequeathed here.

Next door to the church are two tiny museums, one displaying more religious artifacts, the other a folk museum. Situated in the church's old olive press, this houses a wealth of agricultural equipment that has been used on the hills hereabouts over the centuries.

Returning to the car to retrieve our feast, we set off up the small road that leads to the castle ruins. Built by the Knights in the 15th Century AD, it is now little more than a ruin. At best a shell, two circular towers can still be discerned, but the serrated walls no longer hold fear for any would-be invaders. Inside, the castle is overgrown with wild grasses and herbs, and evidence of it being an occasional impromptu corral for grazing beasts. Sitting on this spectacular outcrop, we picnicked looking down on the church we had just visited and out to the distant sea across hills where the rocks were punctuated with holm oak and wild herbs, the sun cajoling them to give off their fragrance. The occasional small chapel sat comfortably on the sparse, lazy landscape, which lay devoid of any sound as we ate and drank too much, unhurriedly enjoying the panorama spread out below.

Myths and Legends of Rhodes

Rhodes appears more liberal in the distribution of its historical bounty than many of the other islands, which frequently set great store by the myths and legends prevalent in their ancient legacies. Although Rhodes shares its historical inheritance more equitably than other parts of Greece, its mythological endowment is not to be ignored. If legends pertaining to Rhodes are thin on the ground compared to other islands, those they have are big hitters and demand our attention.

The famous Colossus of Rhodes was the sculptural manifestation of Helios, the sun god born of the Titan Hyperion and his sister Theia. His story has been told many times and gained slight nuances of detail over time. One interpretation is this... Adorned with the sun as a shining halo, Helios arose each morning from a swamp in the east and drove his golden chariot pulled by nine, pure white, winged steeds who breathed fire as they galloped across the skies every day, before plummeting into the watery world of the Hesperides, over the western horizon. Here, adrift on the azure sea, was a ship aboard which his family waited for him. Safely aboard, the ship would sail overnight, ready for the sun god to reappear in the east at dawn the next day.

His reliability in providing people with life-giving light meant he was absent when the Gods divided up the world into the domains over which they were each to preside. Angry at his omission, Helios sought out Zeus to complain, and was awarded an island which was just being born from the waves. He named it after a nymph with whom he was in love. Although in many areas of Greece Helios's identity became inseparable from the cult of Apollo, on the island he named he was still held as a supreme divinity, celebrated by the ill-fated bronze statue fashioned by Chares, a task which drove the Lindian master sculptor to bankruptcy and eventual suicide.

No less tragic a fate was the destiny of Helen of Troy who also met her demise on Rhodes. Celebrated for her beauty, Helen's hand in marriage was sought by many suitors throughout the eastern Mediterranean. Each was made to swear to Helen's father, the canny Tyndareus, that they would come to the aid of the man who won her heart if ever he was in need. After three years of marriage to Menelaus the Mycenaean king of Sparta, a visit to her husband's court by Paris, the son of Priam the ruler of Troy, led to the favour being called in.

Abusing his hospitality, a besotted Paris abducted his host's wife and carried her off to Troy. Keeping their oaths, all the princes of Greece formed an alliance to put right this slight and, under the command of Menelaus' brother, Agamemnon, sailed to besiege Troy. Led by the mighty Hector, the Trojans held out for 10 years before they were undone by Greek cunning. Hidden inside a vast wooden horse a contingent of Greek warriors was pulled inside the walls of Troy by Trojan soldiers. Having breached their previously impregnable defences, the Greeks threw open the gates to the city from the inside and their armies poured in, killing and enslaving citizens and torching buildings. The 'face that launched a thousand ships' was reunited with her husband, but the conflict had created many victims and lived on in the memory of many who saw Helen as being responsible for the lives sacrificed to her cause.

On the death of her husband, she was driven out of Sparta by two sons of Menelaus', legends differ as to whether or not they were her own offspring. Seeking refuge on Rhodes, she sought the protection of the queen, Polyxo. But her duplicitous friend bore a grudge against Helen as her husband, Tlepolemus, had lost his life fighting in the Trojan War. She commanded her servants to exact revenge, and one day, while Helen was bathing, she was seized and hanged from a tree. In Rhodes she is known as Helen Dendritis, which means Helen of the Tree. A sanctuary was built on the island in her name, but where this was I cannot find out, I suspect its location has been lost in the sands of time, but on the island the most beautiful woman who ever lived is still venerated.

Siege City – Ancient Ialyssos

Spread out beneath me as I stand on this hilltop is the whole of the north of Rhodes and its acolyte islands. At the edge of the summit lie the precariously placed remains of a fortress, finished off by allied bombing in the Second World War. Byzantine in origin, it is easy to see why the Knights further fortified this castle before succumbing to the forces of Suleiman the Magnificent, who in turn used it as a base to mount his siege of Rhodes Town. This ultimately put paid to the Knight's supremacy here.

From the nearby monastery that they had built on the site of an earlier 5th-century Christian basilica, the Knights made off with a priceless artifact, the Icon of the Virgin from the Church of Our Lady. That they set so much store in retaining the icon when they scuttled from the island, gives some indication of its value. Unfortunately, we are never likely to see it as, when the French seized Malta in 1798, the then Grand Master of the Knights, Ferdinand von Hompesch, sent the icon to the Czar of Russia for safekeeping. It was never returned, and following the Russian Revolution it was moved to Yugoslavia and has never been seen since. Originally stolen by the crusading Knights from Jerusalem, the tragedy of the icon's subsequent loss is in no small part due to the belief that it was the work of the apostle St Luke.

But the history of ancient Ialyssos is rooted far further back in time. Considering this, it is surprising that the site is something of a hidden gem. Certainly this is the case when compared to the other towns of Lindos and Kamiros which, together with Ialyssos, made up the ancient power base of Rhodes.

Indeed the site is so undersold that on my first visit to the island it passed me by entirely. I have to admit that I only decided to visit it at all on the spur of the moment, finding myself at a loose end after a rather than quicker than anticipated visit to the disappointing aquarium in Rhodes Town.

I suppose I shouldn't have been surprised that the *Enydreio* was oversold in the leaflet left under our car windscreen, and I am assured that it does do marvellous conservation work. Perhaps I have just been spoiled by the wow factor presented at other aquariums I have visited, but this left me underwhelmed. The building is impressive enough, an art deco edifice built in the 1930s by the Italians on the seafront at Ammos Point right on the northern tip of the island.

The aquarium itself is in the basement, and a person with an average attention span and without a severe mobility problem could be in an out within 40 minutes. Suffice to say; emerging into the daylight, something was required to lift the mood.

We headed off on a voyage of discovery travelling south along the west coast. This side of the island was noticeably windier than the east coast, which probably accounts for the occasional disused windmill that still stands between the massive hotels that line the coast road. The hill of Monte Smith goes almost unnoticed as we pass behind its unassuming back, its face looking the other way surveying the grandeur of Rhodes Town. This somewhat unlikely named acropolis was previously known as the Hill of Agios Stefanos until, during the 1802 war against the incumbent Turks, a British Admiral, Sir Sydney Smith, set up a lookout post here, and left his name as a memento.

Fewer than two miles outside the city walls, this 350-foot hill was the religious focus when the town was first created by the *synoecism* of the three city states in the 5th Century BC. Some columns of the 3rd-century BC Temple of Pythian Apollo stand as a reminder of its former glory, re-erected by the Italians. Lower down on the south side a more complete restoration has been done to a 2nd-century BC stadium and theatre, both of which I am pleased to say are still used for concerts and the staging of plays. A trip up to the summit is worthwhile just for the stunning panorama of the city and if you can make the climb just before nightfall, the sunset is inspirational.

Resisting the temptation to revisit the summit and take in the inexhaustible panorama of Rhodes Town we struck on, the crescent-shaped bay of Trianda unfurling in front of our eyes. The waves roll in here endlessly, breaking onto the broad sweep of the bay, making this village a hot-spot for windsurfers during the summer months. Among the modern tourist trappings can be found a reminder of Trianda's historic past. A row of houses by the roadside hides a mosque with its appended graveyard, giving a clue to a relatively recent event in the history of the village.

Known as Kritika, this small enclave was built in 1898 for Turkish refugees escaping from Crete when it became an independent state under the governance of Prince George of Greece. They were not the first settlers here by any means. The legacy of Trianda can be traced back to the Bronze Age, long before its prominence was usurped by the hill of Ialyssos where I am now standing. Like so many places in Greece, this is a land of legend, but in this case the story is more recent, being medieval in origin rather than of Ancient Greece. There is talk here of dragons, and the sources are impressive.

It was the German poet, philosopher and dramatist Friedrich von Schiller who popularised the myth. A great friend and contemporary of Goethe, his 1785 poem *Ode to Joy* became the basis for the rousing Fourth Movement of Beethoven's *Ninth Symphony*. From such an unimpeachable source comes the 1799 ballad *The Fight with the Dragon*, a poem which tells the story of the Knight Francisco Deodato de Gozon of the Hospitallers who slayed the Dragon of Malpasso on a nearby hillside.

If Schiller was to revel in this story, he was not the only scholar to relate it. More than a century earlier, another German, the famed Renaissance man Athanasius Kircher, recounted the myth in his weighty work *Mundus Subterraneus* between 1664 and 1668. In the chapter *De Draconibus*, Kircher references Bosius's *History of the Cult of St John of Jerusalem* telling the story of how a monster terrorised the local area, emerging from his quarry to consume young maidens.

So many knights had died trying to kill the dragon that the Grand Master proclaimed that on pain of death should any knight make any further chivalrous attempts to rid the island of its scourge. From Gascony, the warrior knight Francisco felt the shame of allowing this behemoth to wreak havoc with the island's young women keenly. He vowed to defy his master and confront the beast.

Meticulously the noble youth plotted his assault on the hereto-invincible leviathan, undaunted by its axe-like teeth, bulging eyes and blazing breath. He made a hideout in the surrounding hills, from where he spent days observing the monstrous beast as it part flew, part galloped after its hapless prey for whom any escape was impossible. The Knight then commanded his squire, foot soldiers and servants to construct him an exact facsimile of the dragon from paper and hemp which could be operated from the inside by his men in a macabre simulation of the evil demon.

He trained his horse and two huge brutes of hunting dogs to attack the monster without fear. When he had prepared himself and his animals he pulled on his best armour and, lance in hand and sword sheathed, he set out for the dragon's lair. His entourage were also armed with swords and medicine and secreted themselves in the surrounding rocks.

At the small local church, Francisco pledged himself to his order, and to God and set out for the dragon's cave. Sensing some easy prey the monster charged the Knight, but his horse stood its ground, and the dogs harried and tore at the monster's flesh and chewed off its genitals before the Knight impaled it on his lance.

With his scaly armour breached, the dragon, weakened through loss of blood, made one last frantic challenge to the now dismounted Knight. Rearing up on his hind legs he slashed at him with his giant claws until Francisco eyed his target and struck at the underside of the beast's neck. Split asunder and in his death throes the dragon launched his full weight at the noble youth, crushing him.

Running to their master, his servants revived him with water from a stream until he could mount his steed again and ride triumphant back to Rhodes Town. The reaction there was not all that he had anticipated and, instead of gratitude, the Grand Master had him thrown into jail for defying his cowardly edict and to stamp his authority over his disparate knights. But as word spread of the young man's bravery, public opinion turned, and the Grand Master was forced to bend to its will.

Released from his dingy cell, all his honours were restored, and such was his reputation that he was elected as the successor to the Grand Master, a position Francisco Deodato de Gozon of Gascony held between 1346 and 1353. The presence of the dragon reigned even longer as its skull is said to have been nailed above the d'Amboise Gate in the Old Town right up until 1837, in case anyone might doubt the truth of the story.

To get to the acropolis of ancient Ialyssos the road leaves Trianda sinuously invading the surrounding forest of pine which crowds the lower reaches of Mount Philerimos. Emerging into the light at the summit the site is somewhat incongruous, and for the purist perhaps there has been too much restoration.

So be it, but the Monastery of Our Lady of Philerimos, rebuilt by the Italians in the early part of the last century, stands as a fitting reproduction of the church originally built by the Knights, which itself stands on the threshold of the foundation of the 3rd-century BC Temple of Athena. The Knights built over a basilica, which had been consecrated by a 13th-century monk from the Holy Land who was named Philerimos, or 'friend to the wilderness' after whom the mountain was latterly named.

Prior to this the Mycenaean Greeks knew it as Achaia. More recently the Greek philosopher Strabo recalled it as Ochyroma (fortress), during the period Rhodes was part of the Roman Empire in the 1st Century BC. As well as a fortification, this valuable piece of high ground was also designated a place of worship.

Even the Temple of Athena is not the inaugural place of devotion to have graced this table-top limestone peak. Beneath it lies a Phoenician temple, and who knows whether this was the first holy shrine to stand on the hilltop. Taking the tree-lined avenue near the entrance to the site and walking westwards past Italian relief images of stations of the cross, this Calvary leads to a huge concrete crucifix, which must be at least 50 ft in height, every inch of it a blot on this wonderful landscape. This, however, is but a shadow of the former cross built by the Italians, which stood approaching some 100 ft but was destroyed during the Second World War by Allied bombs. Despite the brutality of the sculpting of this stark cruciform, the views that can be seen from the platforms accessed via a staircase inside leading out to the ends of the cross's arms are breathtaking.

To visit here now is to enjoy a peace that has so often belied this beautiful hill where knights, dragons and the Ottomans all staked their claim, and where the axis powers of Italy and Germany scuffled after falling out following the Italian surrender to the Allies in September 1943. There is much to see here for those interested in ancient archaeology and dreamers alike as the layers of history unfold, showing glimpses of themselves through the parched, scarred white limestone.

Profitis Ilias – Little Italy

If the Italians sought to recreate the courtly era of the Knights through their reconstruction and renovation work on Rhodes, they also left one inconsistent legacy that smacks more of homesickness than glories past. Profitis Ilias is a forested peak, the third highest on the island and named after the prophet Elijah. At just over 2,600 feet tall it is worth the drive to the top for the view alone. We approached it from the east coast road as we were staying in Lindos at the time, but it is actually closer to the western shoreline and taking the road for Salakos from Kalavarda, just a few miles south of the airport is another option.

Heading north along the coast through Archangelos, we took a left turn headed for Archipolis in the village of Kolimbia. If the architecture here appears a little different and the planning rather more regular than the organic growth seen elsewhere around the island, that is because Kolimbia was part of the Italian fascist obsession with order.

Originally named San Benedetto, Kolimbia was built as an experiment as a model village to house Italian settlers in the 1930s. It is reminiscent of the reclaimed Pontine Marshes south of Rome, where Mussolini built his agrarian utopia for 2,000 loyal fascist families, usurping the indigenous poor who had previously lived there. It is of interest to stop and take it in, if only to be grateful that history prevented the extension of a madman's fantasies.

A more pleasing vista, but also the work of the Italians, lies inland of this 'model village'. Among a valley where plane trees and pines serve notice to the fertility of the soil is *Epta Piges* or Seven Springs. This tranquil retreat served both as a recreational getaway for the agricultural workers from Kolimbia and its environs, and also for the more practical purpose of being a supply of water for irrigation.

As its name suggests, hidden in this woodland sanctuary seven springs bubble up, feeding a small manmade lake via a narrow tunnel which it is possible to splash your way through in the dark. The walk takes the best part of 10 minutes, wading through almost a foot of fast-running water in places and is not for the claustrophobic, but for those who take on the challenge it is supposed to banish all future fears. Emerging out the other end beside the beautiful lake feeding a waterfall with its cool blue-green water is a feast for the soul.

It is possible to avoid the tunnel by climbing above the entrance, crossing the road and following a footpath. In May it was not too busy, and we marked it down for the future as a perfect picnic spot if you don't mind sharing your lunch with the magnificent peacocks, which proudly strut their stuff around the tranquil waters of the lake. It is rumoured that the springs are everlasting and have never dried up, even in the hottest days of summer, but some dispel this myth claiming to have been there when the springs ran dry. When we went they were abundant enough for me to believe in their immortality, either way they certainly enrich the spirit. Reluctantly leaving this magical enclave behind, we retraced our route back to the road that headed for Archipolis and the summit of Profitis Ilias.

Along this road is Elousa, a ghostly village that is haunted by memories of its seizure from the Greeks by the Italians who wanted the surrounding agricultural land to feed their growing emigrant population. Named Campochiaro, or 'bright fields' by the Italians, the name held a certain irony for the dispossessed Rhodians who, despite the not unpleasing nature of the Italianate architecture, have not been in any hurry to repossess their birthright.

If the influence of the Italian occupiers is overbearing around Elousa, just a mile and a half along the road, climbing upwards, is a tiny chapel so quintessentially Greek it stirs the emotions. At one with its surroundings this church, built in a cruciform shape, measures no more than 30 ft from apse to apse. Built in the 14th Century, and extended and embellished by successive generations, it is beautiful in its symmetry; the only deviation from this conformity a small bell tower over the west portal. A dome tops off this little gem of a chapel completing its visage with a simplicity that must have baffled those promoters of the fascist cause who plied their trade in these parts some 500 years later.

This is the Church of Agios Nikolaos Fountoukli, or St Nicholas of the Hazelnut. Not unlike the simple delicacy after which it is named, inside the shell lies a delicious delight. Frescoes dating from the 15th Century clamour for attention in all their faded glory. In the small space, I did not feel claustrophobic, but almost as though I was walking amongst the apostles and saints as they told their religious stories through these iconic representations.

Outside the church again, despite the blistering heat, it is easy to see what attracted the Italians to this part of the island. It reminds me of a south Tyrolean landscape, and it must have been with this in mind that they set about pruning and chopping the cedars and pines to create parkland that was reminiscent of the Italian Alps. Had they not been so intent on manicuring the landscape, what is revealed as we approach the summit of Profitis Elias would be more surprising. Two large balconied chalets with dormered windows and pitched roofs emerge in a clearing among the trees. The Italians originally built these chalets as a hotel retreat for the settlers here, and any resemblance to the buildings of their Alpine homeland was entirely meant. They called this resort Villeggiatura, meaning holiday, the name being only a little less imaginative than the design of the buildings themselves. The only acknowledgement to the local environment was the names of the hotels, one being called *Elafos* meaning stag, the other *Elafina* meaning doe, the symbols of the island as represented by the bronze statues on the pillars either side of the entrance to Mandraki Harbour in Rhodes Town.

When I last visited, the Elafos had been restored after years of neglect and hinted at something approaching its former glories with its 20 rooms and several suites, but the Elafina still stood in a state of neglect. Rumour has it that it, too, is to be restored, but in the current climate whether this will happen is a matter of conjecture. Don't get me wrong, this is a beautiful spot, and a visit can enhance the understanding of the mindset of the Italian settlers back in the first half of the 19th Century. I suppose my gripe is with the cultural imperialism, in Rhodes Town their architecture at least is restoration or pastiche, here it is totally out of character, but nevertheless charming in its way.

Close by the hotels is the church of Profitis Ilias itself, but it is not possible to reach the summit of the mountain as military shacks and communications aerials litter the fenced-off peak. But walking the rough tracks through the woods around the church and hotels, it is still possible to enjoy the cooler air at this higher altitude, which promotes the growth of some spectacular displays of pink-tinged cyclamen and the white-petalled, clove-scented peonies with their golden hearts. These are the cousins of the Clusius' peony, which grow high on the slopes of the White Mountains in Crete, but here the host island is more benevolent, shaded, greener and cooler, more temperate in disposition. It is amongst this carpet of flowers, rather than beside the disconsonant chalets, that this spot reveals its true beauty. If the story told through the architecture left behind by the Italians fascinates, it is the primal, ingenerate landscape that captivates.

Symi

To Symi by Sea

Birba edged her nose out of Mandraki Harbour and tensed, then pushed on ahead as the breeze and slight swell took hold of her. At the helm, my friend, Dean, rounded up to a reach and pulled in the sheet. The small yacht took up the strain and heeled slightly to leeward, then comfortably set course for Symi.

As the medieval walls of Rhodes Old Town slipped away astern, we settled into the cockpit for the 25-mile voyage. Conditions were perfect as we let out the trailing log. We were making about five knots over a sea reflecting a light so perfect no picture could ever do it justice.

Not having been out of harbour for a week, *Birba's* hull took up water where the sun-dried wood felt the sea again as her gunwhales dipped towards its surface. A pump every half-hour took care of the bilges, and any cold water sprayed on our faces and legs was a welcome respite from the midday sun relentlessly bouncing off the sea.

Panormitis Bay is as close to idyllic as it gets. Entering through its narrow mouth the natural harbour opened up, revealing a sheltered, enclosed cove. We dropped anchor 50 yards offshore and, through the crystal clear water, watched it settle into the seabed below. The sun had increased in strength, reflecting with eye-blinking intensity off the white-painted buildings ashore and the burnished metallic blue surface of the sea.

The stillness was palpable, only broken by the stop-start choruses of the cicadas ashore. The smell of the salt left on deck as the water evaporated blended with the aroma of thyme that laced the air. Pine trees grew up out of the parched rock which forms a backdrop to the village at the forefront of which, right on the seafront, lies the famous monastery.

This Greek Orthodox monastery dominates the village and is the second largest in the Dodecanese. At its heart is the tallest baroque bell tower in the world that overlooks the rest of the retreat, which was rebuilt in Venetian style in the 18th Century. These days Panormitis is a tourist boat destination either from Rhodes or Symi Town in the north of the island. It is well worth a visit by any means, but if you can make the journey by local bus or are lucky enough to approach on your own boat outside peak hours the tranquility is overwhelming.

We unlashed the inflatable tender from deck, launched it and rowed ashore. Mooring on the front near a taverna, we walked to the monastery. Through the gates we entered a haven of peace, the black and white paved courtyard dotted with potted trees and exotic plants.

Entering the church, the shaded cool provides some respite from the searing heat. The walls of the church are covered with iconography; the most spectacular being the glinting, silver-leafed representation of Archangel Michael of Panormitis to whom the monastery is dedicated. The angel is the island's patron saint and considered the protector of all sailors who go to sea across the Dodecanese.

Tradition has it that the archangel will grant favours if promised something in return. Failure to honour that due results in the angry angel performing obstructive miracles until it is fulfilled. Many a devout tour boat's captain will vouch for the efficacy of this by recounting how they have been unable to start their engines and leave the bay until requesting over the PA system that all their passengers keep any promises they might have made to Michael!

Outside the church but still within the walls of the monastery are two museums. One is an exhibition of religious artifacts and the other folk art. A memorial also stands to three monks and two teachers who were executed by

German forces in 1944 for operating a radio to help British forces and Greek partisans in their resistance against the occupying power.

Back aboard, we find ourselves alone in the bay as the sun goes down, not a ripple disturbs the mercurial water until we break the spell, diving through its surface for an evening swim.

Return to Symi

It had been some 28 years since I had last visited Symi, and my memory of that trip had made me determined to return. Sometimes it takes courage to revisit a place after such a time, especially when it has engraved such a perfect picture in the mind's eye. On that last visit we had been lucky enough to visit the island on our own terms. We had sailed there aboard a beautiful classic carvel-built Bermudan sloop owned by some friends who lived aboard in Mandraki Harbour. This time afforded no such luxury; we had to seek passage aboard one of the many tourist boats that now sailed from that same harbour. An easy task you'd have thought, and so did we. We strolled along the bustling quay, passing the fishing boats, bareboat charter hires and polished gin palaces to the moorings where a mish-mash of craft lay at rest, stern on to the sea wall, in serene contrast to their crews touting for business from passing trade.

We stopped astern of one such boat, a sturdy caique with planked, caulked decks and varnished topsides and the ubiquitous white hull with blue trimmings. Its crew hosed down the decks and carried crates of Coke and beer aboard to the rhythm of Lady Gaga playing through the wheelhouse sound system. A man sitting at a folding table, under an umbrella advertising Alpha beer, stopped flicking his worry beads to assure us his was the best boat, at the best price for Symi the next day, just as we wanted.

The price was good, and lower than expected, but that was not unusual in our experience on the island in these cash-strapped times. The next day was a Sunday, yet our new friend was insistent that we arrive at the jetty no later than 8.00am and ask for him, and him alone, 'only ask for Michaelis' he regaled us. 'And don't be late', he insisted with an unusual emphasis on punctuality. I assured him we'd be there, and he wrote us out a receipt as I parted with the cash.

At the time we were staying in Lindos, and thought an hour for the journey to Rhodes Town the next day would be plenty of time, and it would have been, had I learned to master the alarm on my mobile phone. We were left with a mad dash through the breaking dawn avoiding early starters weaving their way to work on bikes. We had no problem parking at that time and arrived on the quay with minutes to spare. Michaelis had not materialised, so we sat down on a bench to wait. Time ticked on, and for someone who had been so insistent that we were punctual, Michaelis was a little tardy.

After waiting twenty minutes, the cabin door on the caique moored next to us opened. Yawning, a crewmember emerged on deck, putting a cup of coffee down on the cockpit table and stretching. He appeared to have the demeanour of a man who was going nowhere soon, so I asked him what time we were leaving for Symi. I think I knew the answer before he replied. It was Sunday and his boat was not going anywhere today. I asked which boat was going and he said he didn't know, and what's more had never heard of Michaelis who had been selling tickets for the trip beside his boat.

At that moment a screeching of tyres announced the arrival of said Michaelis. He leaped out of the most decrepit, tiny, car I had ever seen and started berating me for talking to the man on the boat. The fact he was half an hour late and that no boat was going to our island destination seemed to escape him.

'You must come with me', he said, bundling us into the back seat through the driver's door, the only one apparently that opened. He let the clutch out and the car jumped forward – and stalled. He turned the key and we caught the last deathly gasp of a dying battery. 'This has never happened before', he shouted, although I was surprised the car had not been consigned to the scrap heap some decades ago. He jumped out onto the quay and summoned the crewmember from the caique, along with a couple of passing pedestrians, and inveigled them to push. Michaelis released the clutch with aplomb, for a novice, and the car spluttered into life.

As if afraid to take his foot off the gas, he ploughed through red lights as we sped south along the coast road. 'Today we go from the big ship harbour,' he informed us as we left picturesque Mandraki where our car was parked behind, travelling past the ancient city walls on our right to the more industrial setting of the town's outskirts.

We turned through some gates onto a dusty path in a boatyard where cruisers, yachts, fishing boats and other sundry craft stood beached on trailers, blocked up or propped in various stages of disrepair awaiting the attentions of the boatyard staff.

Through another set of gates we entered an empty car park beside a quay to which was moored a lone, workmanlike, if a little lacklustre, vessel, *Proteus*. We were deposited with undue haste some yards from the craft, which puffed and panted as it idled on its isolated mooring. 'This is your boat', shouted Michaelis, as he sped off leaving us bemused. I had a bad feeling about this; the day was not shaping up to be a sun-kissed voyage on a small traditional craft to revisit the island of our dreams. Undeterred, I approached the stern of the boat where crew in white uniforms sat on bollards smoking.

It didn't take long to realize that *Proteus* was a car ferry. Such workhorses plied their way between the islands, carrying people, vehicles, food and other cargo, which was the lifeblood of the smaller communities. I proffered my tatty receipt to one of the crew, who smiled knowingly and told me I had to go to a small kiosk on the other side of the quay to exchange it for tickets. I did as I was told and traipsed across to the kiosk, which was closed. A notice declared it would open at 10.00 o'clock. Returning to the ship I asked what time they set sail and was told 11.00 o'clock. They left dock later as it was a Sunday.

Proteus was well-named after an ancient God of the oceans, who Homer described as 'The Old Man of the Sea'. Our ship was certainly old, with rusty tears dropping from eyes beneath which hung two hefty anchors. But the boat revealed itself to be truly protean, and our voyage turned out to be all the better for being that of the everyday Greek who visited Symi.

One of the crew took pity on us. He invited us to sit on board until the ticket booth opened, and put out seats for us at the small impromptu café they had set out to the side of the car deck. Here, among boxes of tomatoes, crates of water and shrink-wrapped toilet rolls, their urn bubbled away and we were given coffee and a plate of sweet white grapes to sustain us. At 10.00 o'clock one of our new friends insisted on going and collecting our tickets, and on his return we were ushered upstairs to the saloon of the ship, with its comfortable chairs and tables, a bar selling drinks and snacks and multiple TV sets all tuned in to an animated post-election debate.

As the time ticked on towards 11.00 o'clock the room started to fill up. A party of children with teachers on a day trip to the Monastery of the Archangel Michael at Panormitis Bay; an elderly couple with a minute Chihuahua, its head poking out of a Burberry handbag; workers on a pilgrimage with men looking uncomfortable in Sunday suits, their wives in large-patterned floral frocks; an eccentric, chanting lists of English football teams as he searched bins for discarded food before being given a meal by the galley staff; a cross section of Greek life was aboard and we were the only foreigners.

The thudding of the engines grew louder and the deck floor began to vibrate as the lines were cast off and we headed out to sea. As soon as we edged out of the harbour mouth the swell took hold of the vessel, rhythmically pitching and twisting us as we progressed towards the northern cape of the island, before steering a northwesterly course leaving Rhodes behind.

Proteus felt at home in this significant swell but, as the cloud came lower and the sky darkened bringing with it more than a hint of a breeze, I began to be thankful we were aboard this Trojan vessel. As the coast of Turkey loomed ahead the wind abated and the rain began to fall almost vertically from the sky.

Our approach to Panormitis was in sharp contrast to that which we had made all those years ago by yacht. The unrelenting rainfall made the bay look smaller, as we inched towards the jetty beneath the monastery. Crewmen shouted instructions at each other to make themselves heard over the reverse thrust of the ship's engines and the excited chatter of the schoolchildren.

Hawsers were heaved ashore and secured around hefty bollards as the ship's ramp was lowered and we and the other passengers poured ashore. The monastery still retained an undoubted air of grandeur, but with the rain dripping down its walls and polishing the chessboard marble stones of the courtyard, it held us in a melancholy thrall.

Water dripped off the leaves of the potted chrysanthemums, off the brims of hats and hoods and down the backs of shirts. Unabated, the children ran hither and thither between the buildings, while the devout leafed through their guidebooks whispering to each other. We struggled to relive the memory of our first visit, inwardly disappointed that the weather did not allow this magnificent spot to give off its best.

If the rain had presented us with a clammy, uncomfortable feeling, and lacklustre picture for the eyes, it was compensated for by the aroma the soaking had released from the hills behind the monastery. Wild arugula, sage, thyme and selino made their presence felt as the rain subsided and the ground began to steam in the watery sunlight. The smell of herbs aroused the taste buds and we had to be strong to resist sitting down to eat, which we intended to do in Symi Town, our next port of call.

As *Proteus* edged out of the bay, leaving the small village behind, the sun began to dry us out and projected a beautiful rainbow arching from the sea over the monastery to the mountainside beyond. Making short work of burning off the mist and cloud, the sun re-established its dominance almost as sharply as it had previously been undermined. We settled down hugging the shore bound for Symi Town. Buffeting a slight swell we eased our way to the southern tip of the coastline before skirting around the small island of Sesklia, its stark landscape inhabited only by seabirds, including pink-footed shearwaters. At times seals languish here, but today they were hiding. This is part of the coast that made Symi famous and was the source of much of its wealth in the past.

The steep shelving rocks which dive into the sea were the ideal place for sponges to grow and the local population were second to none in their skill and bravery in harvesting these natural wonders. Since the time of Homer their renown had been widespread in the eastern Mediterranean and, apart from the direct riches diving for sponges brought to the island, it also endowed the people with a unique bargaining power, which they used to good effect when threatened by the expanding territorial ambitions of the Ottoman Empire in the 16th Century.

The pragmatic islanders sent representatives to the sultan, Suleiman the Magnificent. They proffered gifts of their best sponges and promises that, if allowed to trade freely in both sponges and in the fast and sturdy ships their craftsmen constructed, they could be of great use to the Turks – Suleiman assented. They enjoyed such privileges until 1830 when, after the islanders joined the struggle for Greek independence, their rights were curtailed. Prior to this the Symiots enjoyed freedoms unknown in the rest of occupied Greece. For the price of some nominal taxation and a yearly gift of the most extravagant sponges to the Harem of the Sultan's palace in Constantinople (Istanbul), the islanders were allowed to carry on trading much as normal. And trade they did. So much is obvious by the wealth exhibited in the wonderful architecture on display as we enter the protective arms of the natural harbour of Symi Town itself on the north-eastern coast.

The withdrawal of certain privileges by the Turks following the Symiots ill-fated alliance with other Greeks in the 1821 revolution was the beginning of the end for the wealthy sponge merchants and shipwrights. Much of the skill and bravery involved in diving for sponges was superseded with the invention of diving suits. Prior to this the fishermen used to dive naked, being aided to the seabed by a *skandalopetra*. As the '*petra*' in the name might suggest, this was a specially-shaped stone weighing around 30lbs, which was perforated to reduce water resistance. The stone would be tied to the diver with twine and by a rope to a boat on the surface. Holding on to the rock the fisherman would quickly descend to as deep as 100 feet below the surface where, for up to four minutes he would harvest sponges before cutting himself free from the stone and returning to the surface. The crew of the boat then hauled up his *skandalopetra*. The danger and skill involved made the sponges an expensive luxury, but the advent of more sophisticated sub aqua equipment meant that sponges rapidly became over fished and fishermen had to go deeper and deeper to find them. This in turn hastened the end of the trade. Many divers died due to their ignorance of the effect of water pressure on the human body and the resultant bends inflicted by resurfacing too quickly.

Honey, sand and terracotta pastel shades unveil themselves through the rain-rinsed skies as this gem of a town reveals itself, stepping backwards up the steep hills and making an amphitheatre around the long, narrow harbour. The buildings are mostly neo-classical, built in the 18th and early 19th Centuries, the heyday of Symi's trading, when their access to the vast Ottoman markets made merchants rich beyond imagination. The town's beauty is a legacy of a life no longer sustainable, and today the small local community survives mostly from the earnings from tourism.

Disembarking, our spirits lifted by the sunshine, it didn't take long to find a suitable taverna where plenty of Greeks were sitting down to tuck into their family Sunday lunch. I settled down to bread dipped in oil and vinegar with a black olive paste. This was followed by grilled mackerel, its tiger stripes burnished with lemon juice and crackling sea salt, served with a ramekin of mustard sauce glistening with the freshness of golden eggs, vinegar, mustard and butter and heavily scented with sage and thyme. The white wine was chilled to within an inch of its life. Served in a copper jug, echoing the steely edge of the wine itself, it cut through the oiliness of my fish as though every individual grape used in its making had been grown just for that moment. It would have been easy to idle away the remaining couple of hours just sitting there in that waterfront taverna, maybe eating an ice cream or indulging in another carafe of wine. But the narrow streets that led away from the harbour were beckoning and overcame any more sybaritic intentions we may have held. We paid our bill, and reluctantly brought ourselves up to ambling pace and headed away from the quayside.

The town is split into two areas – the low-lying port, Yialos, and the old town of Horio that looks down on it from the hills to the south. Just away from the bustling southwest corner of the harbourside is a flight of about 400 steps. These connect the low-lying commercial centre of Yialos with the older settlement of Horio, and replaced the older Kataraktis footpath, which runs up to the ancient acropolis. This was the preferred way up the hillside until the Kali Strata steps were laid in the 19th Century.

The houses that line the route are imposing. Some have seen better days, their flaky exteriors disguising their past grandeur. They stand testament to the halcyon days when the island's wealth from sponges, shipbuilding and wine production supported a lifestyle that was the envy of other islands in the Dodecanese. But the town's history can be traced back much further.

The island is said to be named after Syme who, according to the 2nd-century AD rhetorician, Athenaeus, was the daughter of Ialyssos the King of Rhodes and Dotis. The sea god, Glaucus, a fisherman who, if Ovid is to be believed, achieved deity by eating a magical herb, abducted the poor girl. He brought her to the deserted island, which then took her name. Glaucus himself was imbued with many of the skills that the island later became famous for, being one of the shipwrights who built Jason's ship, the *Argo*. As a god, he swam in the waters surrounding the island, ensuring safe passage for sailors and rescuing fishermen in distress.

Homer wrote that three ships sailed from Symi to join the Greek fleet at Troy and the island's king Nereus, who commanded these ships, perished in the campaign. The subsequent history of the island is inextricably linked to Rhodes itself, Symi being a satellite held by the comings and goings of the powers on the larger island. The Dorians, followed by the Romans, held sway here before the island became part of the Byzantine Empire.

The climb up the Kali Strata is steep and every step moves us further back in time. Small pathways feeling their ways between lime-washed and pastel-coloured homes, blue doors open and matching shutters closed in the afternoon sun. The Knights of St John built a castle on the top of the acropolis on the site of a Byzantine citadel, which had also taken advantage of this site with its magnificent views of the harbour.

The medieval fortress remained intact until the last century, when it was used as a munitions dump by the occupying German forces during the Second World War. When they realized the game was up, the retreating troops blew up their stashpile, destroying most of the castle, surrounding homes and the Church of the Assumption that was enclosed within the walls of the fortress. The remnants of the castle walls are all that is left, but a new church has risen on the hill to replace that destroyed by the Germans. Each Sunday as its bells ring, one of those that tolls serves as a reminder of those dark days, as it is forged from the nose of a massive German bomb.

Back on the north side of the harbour front, where *Proteus* was readying herself for departure, is a place that serves as a reminder of those times. What is now the Hotel Les Katarinettes was formerly the Kampsopoulou Mansion where, on the 8th of May 1945, the Germans made their formal surrender of the Dodecanese to the Allies. Nearby is a war memorial hewn out of the mountainside. Its inscription reads: 'On this day freedom whispered to me. "You twelve islands, no longer be downhearted."'

Sailing out through the headlands of the bay, we stood on deck enjoying the breeze created by the ship making its way south again. As evening draws in, the island will turn back in on itself, the population of little more than

2,000 reclaiming its tranquillity. We watched from the stern deck as Symi fell slowly under the shadow of the Turkish coast, and we headed back to Rhodes. A chilled sweet Samos Muscat wine from our cool bag made the perfect accompaniment to a pile of *loukoumades* coated in honey and dusted lightly with cinnamon to see us through until dinner time.

Corfu

Greece's Gentle Isle

If you are approaching this mystical isle from a European perspective, either philosophically or geographically, Corfu could be described as the gateway to Greece. I stepped through this portal somewhat late in the day and my recent discovery of this beautiful island left me not only tingling with the anticipation that discovering a new place can engender, but tinged with regret that I had not happened upon its splendours sooner.

Under Venetian rule for much of its recent history, the island only shed the 400-year law of the Italians when that Republic itself was dissolved after succumbing to the French forces of Napoleon in 1797. For four centuries the island had been seen as a gateway to the Adriatic and a bulwark against the marauding forces of the Ottoman Empire.

It says much about the Venetians and their skill in engineering a fortress that, Corfu, along with its Ionian neighbours of Zakynthos, Paxos and Kythira, is the only part of modern Greece never to be conquered by the Turks. That they landed and lay siege to the capital, Kerkyra, is not in doubt, but the mighty castle of the capital proved impregnable and on numerous occasions the invading forces were sent scuttling back to sea. Now the island has turned its face south, and can legitimately be described as the threshold to the Hellenic world.

As the Northern Cape of Agios Spyridonas approaches off the starboard bow of the Brindisi ferry, or far beneath the wings of your rapidly descending aircraft, something happens to the light; as if some celestial

switch has been flipped, changing everything. You know you have left the
rest of Europe behind and are now in Greece.

Corfu is one of Greece's enchanted triangle of islands which stand
sentinel to that country's archipelago, the numbers of which can be measured
in their thousands. It occupies that role on the north-west frontier, as Rhodes
does to the east and Crete to the south. But the island is not large. It is not
even the biggest in the Ionian chain, that distinction going to Kefalonia some
100 miles further south. But in stature it is a giant, punching way above its
weight in terms of its attraction as a destination and its historical and cultural
influence over modern Greece.

The creaking resonance of bass notes, the hawsers strain every sinew as
the winches reel our ship landwards, lending an accompaniment as
something new and vibrant opens up before us. Far astern lie the mannered
ways and manicured vistas of Italy as we are drawn, inch-by-inch, ashore to
the cheery confusion and careless landscapes that signal arrival at our port of
entry into Greece.

It is of little surprise that the town of Kerkyra, like the island itself, is a
gentle introduction to the Hellenic world, being the closest Greek landfall to
a country that held sway here for so long. That the Venetians contributed
their architecture, the French their cafés and the British their cricket and
ginger beer is undoubtable, but if life on Corfu seems less chaotic than that
on those islands further south and east, the dominant gene is still that of
Greece.

As the sun rises on the sleepy capital, the light reaches a level of
candescence that shines so keenly it divests everything of all but its essence.
It is as if every day you open your eyes for the first time and the world is
reborn.

As the shadows begin to stand erect and disappear under the full glare of
the rising sun, flaking pastel-coloured houses dressed in washing strung out
across narrow ways steeped in a promise of discoveries to come emerge.
Looking down upon this scene is the striking dome of the church of St

Spyridon, the final resting place of the island's patron saint who has stood protector of his charges since he arrived there in the 15th Century.

Almost one-third of the island's 100,000 plus population live in the capital, which shares the same name as the island itself. The name, Kerkyra, has its origins in ancient mythology and is derived from the name of a lover of the God of all the seas, Poseidon. So besotted was he with the beautiful nymph, Korkyra, that he abducted her. He whisked her off to an island love nest, that he named after her. And the name stuck.

Their union gave birth to an offspring whose name is also rooted in the classical canon. Through various linguistic to-ings and fro-ings between Greek and Latin, the child they named Phaiax lent his name to the whole population of the island in the form of Phaikes, which became Phaeacians. This transliteration allows Kerkyra to make a strong claim to be the mythical island of Phaeacia, the final place where Odysseus is washed up before arriving home in Ithaka following the shipwreck at the end of his protracted voyage in Homer's *The Odyssey*.

The sole survivor of his epic journey back to his kingdom from the Trojan War, a naked Odysseus threw himself on the mercy of Kerkyra's ruler, King Alkinoos, who, after hearing his story, commanded that he be delivered to Ithaka aboard one of the Phaeacians' magical ships. Navigated by thought alone, this sleek-prowed vessel ran faster than the wind to deposit our hero back in his homeland to the south. There is a certain irony in that, also according to legend, Poseidon was Odysseus' nemesis. On hearing of his escape, the sea god turned the ship that had carried Odysseus to Ithaka into stone.

Corfiots still argue with one another over which rock this ship might be. Some believe it lies just south of the capital, where the island of Pontikonisi, or Mouse Island, plays host to a tiny Byzantine chapel just offshore from the island's airport. Others argue for a rock suspended off the heart-shaped lagoons of Paleokastritsa on the island's north-west coast. Although the present monastery that inhabits this densely-wooded headland dates from the 18th Century, this heavenly place takes its name, which means the 'Virgin of the Old Castle', from much earlier; and before the advent of Christianity this is also mooted to have been the site of Alkinoos' capital. Take your pick as to which of these represents your petrified preference you are unlikely to be proven wrong…

After reintroducing ourselves to the pleasures of Kerkyra Town, we meander north along the coast road. It effortlessly winds its way in and out of olive groves, punctuated by the cypresses through which glimpses of the nearby Albanian coast are framed. The sun deserts us and the sea turns to mushroom soup, grey and grumbling as a wind-blown front, pregnant with rain, heaves in from the east.

We hunker down in Kaminaki, our isolated terrace opening straight onto a beach bookended by two tavernas, already closed for winter. As dark descends we sit under the protective veil of an arboured vine, heavy with grapes, the disturbed sea illuminated by forks of lightning over the Albanian mountains. The flickering citronella candles do little to discourage the mosquitoes seeking shelter from the storm. They target us as a tasty dish as we in turn tuck in to chicken cooked on the small patio barbecue under the shelter of the vine leaves.

A bank of pitching lights moving northwards signals the course of a ship braving the elements as it heads for Italy, like an island cast adrift on these raging waters. The occasional sound of music blown in on the gale gives reassurance that for this large vessel the conditions are nothing but routine as it shrugs aside the waves to head towards the more open waters of the Adriatic.

The storms here can be breathtaking. But the rain they bring is welcome. The climate is more temperate than the extreme conditions found on other islands further to the south and east. These regular downpours contribute to a benign landscape. The measured nature of the seasons is manifest in the self-contained temperament of the locals whose flamboyance is weighed in ounces rather than the pounds which balance the scales as we travel closer to Africa.

We awake to silence; the storm has blown itself out. Flinging open the shutters reveals the promise of the coming day. A fisherman casts his nets from a small caique anchored in the bay across a sea gently undulating with only a half-forgotten memory of the overnight storm.

The Ionian – 'Where the Blue Begins'

That most evocative of names – the Ionian – immediately conjures up images of islands sparkling like jewels on azure baize. No other country could put a claim on it but Greece. Its waters wash the shores of Albania as well as mainland Greece to the east and Italy to the west, but in every ripple of its being, in every swell, surge and crest of its deep blue soul, it is Greek to the very core.

Myths abound as to the origin of its baptism. Did the cow, Io, swim across its waters to find Zeus, be restored to human form and give birth to his offspring Epaphus and Keroessa? Or was the body of the unfortunate Ionius, mistakenly slain by Heracles, buried in its depths? Whatever the origin of its signature, the principal islands of the Heptanes (Seven Islands), as the Ionian archipelago is otherwise known, are all Greek through and through.

The main islands in the group are Kerkyra to the north stretching to Zakynthos in the south with Paxos, Lefkas, Ithaka and Kefalonia bridging the gap between them. But that, of course, is just six. The seventh Ionian island is Kythira, adrift off the southern tip of the Peloponnese, some 150 miles from its nearest relative, Zakynthos. It lies outside what most people would consider to be the natural boundaries of the Ionian, but who could begrudge it this association, which it has held since the early 13th Century? It was then that, like the other islands to the north, it became a protectorate of Venice after the fragmentation of the Byzantine Empire following the Fourth Crusade.

Since time began, it is the grumblings of the seabed at this deepest part of its mother Mediterranean that has been responsible for crafting these islands of barely comparable beauty, the result of tectonic plates grating in this alive and seismically-restless corner of Europe. If Lawrence Durrell's assertion that this is where 'the blue really begins' is true, I challenge anyone to see the join as you sail from the Adriatic into the Ionian as your ship travels south through the Strait of Otranto. It would be churlish, however, not to allow him that allusion, as the difference felt when crossing this imaginary border is almost palpable. For many it is around this mystical ley line that marks their first point of entry into Greece.

Like much of Greece, this strategically important archipelago has seen its fortunes mixed throughout the years. But as far back as their ancestry can be traced they are fundamentally Greek, with evidence of their settlement by Hellenic tribes going back to the second millennium BC. At times they might have seemed on the fringes of the Greek political ebb and flow, an insouciance that may be reflected in the relaxed nature of its people compared to elsewhere in Greece. But this must not be mistaken for complacency – when some of the largest tremors swept through Greek history, these islands were at the epicentre.

It was conflict between Kerkyra and the unwanted sovereign power of Corinth that encouraged an Athenian intervention that escalated into the Peloponnesian War in 434 BC. This was by no means the last time that the fate of these small islands was held in the palms of much greater powers. The ports around the Ionian Sea were already a casting off point for the fleets of the Macedonian Empire when Alexander made that coalition the most powerful in the world. Its winds drove his fleets north into the Balkans, south to Egypt and east into Persia and onwards to India, taking all before him. When he was laid to rest, embalmed in honey in a golden sarcophagus, the Ionian Sea continued at the centre of a Hellenic Empire, which survived in some form or another until falling prey to the expansionist ambitions of the Romans in 146 BC. Just short of four centuries later, as the Roman Empire was feeding on itself in the West, the Ionian seamlessly became integral to Byzantium as the Eastern Roman Empire, against all odds, disassociated itself with the mayhem that had seen its demise in its eponymous heartland some 500 miles away.

The fortunes of the Byzantine Empire waxed and waned but, throughout, the Ionian Islands were always seen as an attractive possession both strategically and as a place to settle. At times of weakness they fell prey to attacks from Saracens, pirates, Normans and numerous predatory Italian city states. By the beginning of the 13th Century it was the Venetians whose power was in the ascendancy, built on the wealth of their strong trading position and the ruthless governance of their rulers. When the Fourth Crusade proved to be the catalyst for the dissolution of a long-since crumbling Byzantine Empire, the Venetians stepped in to secure the islands of Corfu, Paxos and Kythira as vital staging ports along their trade routes to the Levant.

Over the next 300 years, the Venetians managed to acquire the other islands in the chain, much to the chagrin of the otherwise all-conquering Ottomans. The Turks, despite making regular sorties to the islands, never established a strong foothold on them for any length of time, with the exception of Lefkas, which succumbed in 1479 and was occupied for more than 200 years. Despite landing on Corfu on numerous occasions, the Turks were continually beaten back.

When the expansionist aims of Napoleon Bonaparte thwarted Venetian power by invading that city state in 1797 the French briefly took up ownership of the islands, only to be ousted by the Russian fleet and them placed under Russian-Ottoman protection and formed into the *Septinsular* Republic, the first time any part of Greece had had any form of control over their destiny since 1453. But it was not to last. Showing the tenacity of a small man with a big cause, Napoleon defeated the Russian army at Friedland and as part of the peace treaty the Ionian isles were handed back to France in 1807. This time the tenure lasted for barely two years as the rampant British fleet defeated the French at Zakynthos, capturing not only that island but also Kefalonia, Kythira and the following year Lefkas. Napoleon retained a foothold on the islands but when forced to abdicate in

1814, the game was up. Following his final defeat at Waterloo the next year, the Treaty of Paris put the islands under British protection.

Under British rule the islands became the United States of the Ionian, which had its own elected assembly that acted as advisors to the British High Commissioner. Its flag, which flew above government buildings, reflected the recent history of the islands with a golden Lion of St Mark clutching a bible on a blue background with the union flag in the top left-hand corner.

Following the Greek War of Independence and the creation of the new Kingdom of Greece there was increased pressure on Britain to allow the Ionian Islands *enosis* with the newfound nation. However, the Bavarian ruler King Otto, installed on the Greek throne, was seen as unsympathetic to Britain's interests in the Mediterranean and it was only following his deposition in 1862 that they succumbed to pressure and the islands were united with Greece two years later.

Like the flag that signalled the start of that journey to independence, the major foreign influences on the islands remain Venetian and British. This may account for the islands' popularity with tourists from Italy and Britain. The legacy of this turbulent history has been assimilated into a culture that, although unique to these parts, is still unmistakably Greek. This 'Greekness' is far stronger than any differences in culture, temperament, accent and even climate, and is what binds the nation of Greece together making the whole far stronger than any disparate elements.

Saints Jason and Sosipater – The First Evangelists

Even with autumn entrenched and the olive harvest nearly upon us, the sun was enough to make finding shelter within an unprepossessing taverna in a Venetian terrace near the old fortress a pleasant diversion. The tourist season almost played out, we settled for a long, lazy lunch until the heat of the day dispersed into the flaking pastel-coloured stucco of the buildings on the seafront.

The menu already dispensed with for winter, on offer was '*bakilarios scordalia*', a dish of sliced, dried cod brought back to life by soaking in milk before being dipped in breadcrumbs and fried in olive oil; accompanied by a traditional garlic sauce made of crushed boiled potatoes mixed with a copious supply of garlic and seasoned with lemon juice. A dry, amber verdea wine, its fruity flavour just restraining the almost overpowering oak, was maybe an unwise choice as the strength of the alcohol insinuated a wasted afternoon. With the sun still beckoning outside, a walk was the only way to rescue our day so we head south on foot.

Kerkyra Town and Rhodes Town both vie for the title of Greece's most beautiful island capital and both have their merits. Each of them is deservedly on the UNESCO world heritage list, but there the similarity ends. Their breeding lies in very different stock. Where Rhodes sports a chiselled, formidable Gothic façade, Kerkyra is honey soft and inviting.

But looks are deceptive: as many a proud Corfiot will tell you, it was the fortress of their town which was never breached by the Ottomans, whereas the Knights of Rhodes finally succumbed to the forces of Suleiman the Magnificent in 1522. Fifteen years later Suleiman tried his luck with Corfu, this time trusting the privateer Barbarossa and a force of some 25,000 to deliver him the island. The ruling Venetians trusted to their defences but cruelly barred the locals from inside the city walls. Over twelve days of pillage, the majority of the population were either slaughtered or captured and sold into slavery. But the old fortress held firm and the exhausted Ottoman army, running out of munitions and supplies and struck down with illness, retreated from the smouldering island and slunk back to Constantinople.

It was this attack that led the Venetians to rebuild the *Palaio Frourio* (old fort), which had been there since the Byzantine rule of the 6th Century, and this is the fort we now largely see today. They also decided to supplement their defences with the *Neo Frourio* (New Fort) to the west of the Campiello, as the Venetian old town is known, which they began building in 1572.

Leaving the labyrinthine alleys of the Campiello behind, we followed Dimokritas, the coast road, south. The street brushed up against barely-troubled waters breathing gently to our left, the earlier sea breeze abating as the land began to cool. We were skirting Garitsa Bay, which sweeps leisurely southwards away from the ancient town towards a pier on a headland where a reconstructed windmill stands, in Greek *anemomylos*, which lends its name to this suburb. This being the part of the town most exposed to the prevailing winds, it was the site where flour for the city used to be milled. Just inland from the beach, where locals cool off with a late afternoon swim and the road takes a turn south again towards Mon Repos, stands the church of Agios Iasonas kai Sosipatros, named after the two saints who brought Christianity to the island around 40 AD.

Disciples of St Paul, these bishops from Asia Minor spread the word hereabouts, while Paul evangelized in Rhodes and Crete. The story goes that the saints themselves had a chapel built which they dedicated to Saint Stephen, the first martyr, whose stoning to death was witnessed by Paul before his own conversion to Christianity. That Agios Stefanos is venerated on Corfu is undoubtedly the case as there are two coastal villages named after him, one in the north west and the other the north east of the island.

The church built to honour Saints Jason and Sosipater was built on the site of an earlier chapel, probably in the 11th Century AD. Byzantine in origin, it remains the only example of such architecture on the island. The church is built in the shape of a cross with a stained glass dome adorning the central intersection. The walls outside betray its Byzantine origins as the top half of the building is an example of cloisonné masonry work, a technique found in much of the architecture of Constantinople at the time.

The stones used for the building are surrounded by a course of bricks, framing the large blocks believed to have been reclaimed from the ruins of Kerkyra Town, which had fallen victim to the Norman adventurer knight Robert Guiscard in 1082 and again in 1085 – when he also conquered Kefalonia, where the small seaside village of Fiscardo is named after him.

The church's relationship with the capital of the Byzantine Empire does not end there. In 1453, when a besieged Constantinople finally succumbed to the Ottoman forces of Sultan Mehmed II, marking the end of the Eastern Roman Empire which had held sway for more than 11 centuries, the wife of the brother of the deposed Emperor Constantine XI sought refuge in the church whilst fleeing the advancing Turkish forces.

To the left hand side of the entrance to the church stands the belfry, inside which hang two cast bells, their ropes anchored to the outer wall of the tower. Passing through the entrance there are two icons representing the saints to whom the church is dedicated.

The bishops were not universally welcomed onto the island, and the island's ruler, Kerkylinus, threw Jason and Sosipater into prison. Incarcerated, they still managed to further anger the king by converting seven prisoners to Christianity. He promptly executed the prisoners by boiling them in pitch before turning his attentions to torturing the apostles.

His daughter, the princess Kerkyra, on witnessing the suffering of the bishops, converted to Christianity and gave all her wealth away to the island's poor. For this act of altruism, her father rewarded her by slinging her into jail and, after that failed to force her to renounce her faith, burned the prison down. The girl survived, and on seeing this miracle yet more of the people converted to Christianity.

Enraged, Kerkylinus ordered that his daughter be tied to a tree and face a firing squad of archers. On witnessing her fate, the faithful fled to a nearby island. The ruthless king, however, met his just deserts when, in pursuit of the refugees, his boat capsized, killing all hands. The successor to Kerkylinus himself converted to Christianity and was baptized into the faith as Sebastian. It is widely held that both bishops were now free to spread the word of God and lived to an old age, although there is a persistent rumour that Sosipater was martyred by being burned to death inside a brass bull.

The icons either side of the two stone pillars framing the aisle are credited to the 17th-century artist Emmanuel Tzanes. A member of the

Cretan School of iconography, he stopped on the island en route to Venice, where he was to produce his greatest work.

A huge chandelier is suspended high up from the dome whose eight stained-glass windows shed light upon the font beneath, and on the brightly-coloured Baroque chancel screen, which was painted in the 18th Century. This is a lovely place and is a rare reminder of Corfu's Byzantine past. From here on in, much of the island's splendour is revealed through its Venetian, British and French influences. Unlike the bustling church of the island's patron St Spyridon, in the heart of the Campiello, here is a haven of tranquillity. We were alone inside the church, and on emerging back onto the little plateia outside it too was deserted. A plane taking off from the airport broke the reverie and brought our thoughts back to the present. We will head this way again to visit the estate of Mon Repos, but that can wait for another day.

Where the Olives Fall

It is no surprise to anyone who has visited Greece before that the olive is a fundamental part of Corfiot culture. What may be more surprising to those visiting Corfu for the first time is the density of the crop and the vast acreage it covers. Again there is a Venetian influence at play here.

As in the rest of Greece the olive has been indigenous to these lands since prehistoric times, probably imported from Minoan Crete or from further afield in the Levant. Homer mentions olive groves in the Kingdom of Alkinoos, but originally the value of the oil was principally as a body moisturiser and a fuel for oil lamps. Gradually its value for culinary and medicinal purposes became clear, but during the Roman and Byzantine periods it was still only produced for local domestic consumption.

The Venetians however were canny. Although their principle reason for occupying the island was strategic, they knew a good thing when they saw it, recognising the profit that might be had from this humble crop, which took so easily to the conditions on the island. They tried cajoling and educating the local population into planting more trees, but eventually it was bribery that did the trick. Offering landowners a payment of 3.6 drachmas for every tree planted, it was not long before every spare yard of land was turned over to olive production, and little has changed. Estimates vary, but today there are believed to be between three and four million trees on the island – the bulk of which hark back to the Venetian era. Unlike elsewhere in Greece the trees are not pruned and are allowed to mature, making their presence even more dominant on the landscape. Similarly the fruit are not beaten or picked from the trees but are left until they fall to the ground when their oil content has reached a maximum. Nets are spread beneath the trees to collect the dark purple olives, which are picked up between November and April.

A Different Climate?

On disembarking the plane at Kerkyra airport in Corfu the differences between here and other Greek islands become immediately clear. There is a sense of order and calm. People queue; they obey no smoking signs; the level of noise is considerably lower.

Outside the terminal, the traffic is less chaotic. Tour buses are lined up in neat rows. Taxis single-park and the hooting of motor horns, although not totally absent, seems far from compulsory. These first impressions give a taste of the way the island differs in spirit from those further to the south and reflects the mellow temperament of its people and the gentle nature of its landscape.

It is possible that these differences can be attributed to the Ionian climate being less extreme than that of other island groups. Or could it be that Corfu's historical heritage, although turbulent, was more sympathetic?

Although it is pleasingly hot in the summer months, rain is not unknown, and throughout the rest of the year the temperate climate creates a fertile environment for trees, flowers, fruit and vegetables to flourish.

The pervasive olive trees and grape vines grow alongside figs, oranges, pomegranates, bananas, loquats and kumquats. Cypresses trees rise up straight and tall, above a carpet of myrtle, juniper, kermes, holm oak shrubs and prickly pear. Known in Greek as the 'fingers of God' (*daktiyla tou Theou*), nothing characterizes the Corfiot countryside more than the cypresses. They have been revered for their straightness of growth, which over the centuries have made them invaluable in the building of houses and boats. In spring the countryside can be mistaken for an English country garden, with carpets of poppies, bluebells and tulips covering the woodland floor.

More than anything, it is the Venetian influences, mostly in architecture and culture, which set Corfu apart from other islands further south and east. In Kerkyra's old town the buildings are predominantly Italianate in style. Unlike the Turkish occupation of other parts of Greece, Venetian rule was not resisted and the Italians were assimilated into Corfiot society. An example of this was the growth of the appreciation of opera. In what is now Corfu City Hall, the Teatro di San Giacomo, operas were performed between 1733 and 1893 and many famous musicians travelled from Italy to perform there.

Further evidence of cultural imperialism is to be found on the *Kato Plateia* (lower square) where there is a cricket pitch, a legacy from Corfu's time as a British protectorate. Matches are still played there, although the proximity of the many cars parked makes this somewhat hazardous and the main cricket square has been relocated to the outskirts of the city near Kontokali Marina.

The history of the game on the island goes back to 1823 when a match was organized between the Royal Navy and the army garrison stationed there. Within a couple of years two local sides had formed to challenge the British at their own game. And cricket has stuck to this day. To my knowledge, Corfu is the only place in Greece it is played and is a popular venue for touring club sides from the UK.

Of Gorgons and Kings – Mon Repos

In French *Mon Repos* means 'my resting place'. It can so easily bring to mind bed and breakfast joints in Eastbourne or seafront houses in Grange over Sands. Hereabouts, however, it is one of the most popular tourist attractions on Corfu. Not least, I suspect, because it was the birthplace of the Duke of Edinburgh.

The summer 'palace' was not built with this name in mind and was only given the dubious moniker when the house fell into the hands of the Greek monarch, King George I, following the withdrawal of the British from Corfu and the island's subsequent union with a fledgling Greece in 1864. Here on the Kanoni Peninsula, little more than an hour's stroll from the centre of the island's capital, this shaded estate lies on the land between the airport and the sea and, for me at least, holds more interest than being merely the birthplace of the Queen's consort.

The villa Mon Repos is grand enough, but not as big as the recent storm it created between the deposed Greek royal family and the Greek government over its ownership. As a royal summer residence, the villa had lain derelict in the years after the Greek King Constantine II and his family fled the country, following their failed attempt to overthrow the military dictatorship of the Colonels in 1967. A referendum in 1974 supporting the Greek Republic and the abolition of the monarchy left the house unoccupied until it was subsequently restored to its present state by the municipality of the island.

The former monarch took his claim to the house to the European Court of Human Rights. The judiciary took the pragmatic course of finding that the house should stay in the ownership of the Greek people, but that they must pay compensation of just one per cent of its true value to the deposed royal family. The villa was restored and reopened in time for Prime Minister Andreas Papandreou to host the European Summit during Greece's presidency of the Union in 1994. This neo-classical Georgian building with its faux Byzantine rotunda now houses artifacts from various archaeological digs that have taken place in the beautiful parkland which surrounds the house, the site of the ancient city of Kerkyra, known as Paleopolis (old city).

Its light and airy rooms are furnished in Regency style, reminiscent of when the house was first built, between 1826 and 1831, as the residence of the British High Commissioner of the time, Sir Frederick Adam. It was here he lived with his Corfiot wife, Nina Palatianou, before he became Governor of Madras in 1832. A fellow army officer, the architect Sir George Whitmore, designed the villa. He had also been responsible for the far grander, and more ostentatious, Palace of St Michael and St George for the former British High Commissioner of the Ionian, Sir Thomas Maitland. This building now houses the Museum of Oriental Art and stands at the end of the Spianada in Kerkyra Town.

The ruling British were only able to avail themselves of the pleasures of this beautiful house for a short period of time as Corfu, only having become a crown protectorate in 1815, was ceded back to Greece in the *enosis* of 1864. Briefly during that period, in 1859, the future Prime Minister of Britain, William Gladstone, was in residence as High Commissioner before being recalled to parliament for his second stint as Chancellor of the Exchequer.

On the first floor of the building is an exhibition of the history of Corfu Town, but it is from outside, away from the classical order of this elegant villa, that the story of that legacy truly reveals itself. Sweeping down to the sea, the well-tended 250 acres of parkland and gardens is home to more than 2,000 species of plant, many of them rare. Most of this horticultural spectacle is a result of gifts given when royalty was in residence. But the earth itself has given up other secrets, revealing Corfu's more distant past.

The Kanoni Peninsula is fertile in terms of revealing glimpses of Paleopolis, the city thought to have been the island's capital from the 8th Century BC to the 6th Century AD. Perhaps it is this fecundity of heritage that has led to any amount of confusion between various ruins in many of the guidebooks on the area.

Part of the ancient city lies within the Mon Repos estate. The Venetians did their best to eliminate all traces of a temple dedicated to Hera, demolished by the Romans around 30 BC, the original incarnation of which was built around the year 600 BC, by carting the stone away to use as hardcore in their fortification of the new city of Kerkyra to the north. The footprint of this temple still exists and, for those with a fertile imagination, can still entrance.

But it is the remains of another temple, which lies nearby, outside the grounds of the estate, which is perhaps of most significance. To find out why, I recommend a visit to the town's archaeological museum before visiting the site. The Temple of Artemis is considered to be the first exclusively stone-built temple in the Doric style in the world. However, it is what crowned the giant limestone Doric columns of the temple that most captures the imagination, and pieces from this triangular pediment are the prize exhibits of the museum.

At nearly 60 ft long and 10 ft tall at its apex, this sizeable restored fragment of what used to be the western side of the temple is considered to be one of the most important pieces of Greek architecture ever discovered. The museum is small, but well worth a visit and is situated to the south of Kerkyra just off the coast road on Vraila Armeni Street.

When the temple was built as a sanctuary in 580 BC, the gods of ancient Greece called the shots. Of the myths and legends passed down either orally or through the written word, it is easy to fall into the trap of viewing the giant frieze as a familiar interpretation of the myth of Medusa, maybe as expressed by Hesiod or other later tellings of the tale. But look again, and remember, we are in Greece and these myths are as slippery as the serpents that emanate from the Gorgon's hair and around her waist.

Yes, she is Medusa: easily identified as such by the full relief sculpture of her child, Chrysaos, to her right, and beside the lion to her left as we face the Gorgon, the imprint of where her other son, Pegasus, would have flown. Remnants of the winged horse, however, remain undiscovered.

This Medusa is very much alive. Her children were not born as a result of her decapitation by Perseus. One can only presume that it is the capacity of Medusa to turn all who stare upon her to stone that inspired the stonemasons to award her pride of place above the west façade. Here she is the protector of the temple and the wider Corfiot society. In the left corner lies the body of a dead enemy behind the Trojan king Priam, a symbol of Greek power over their enemies. To the right of Medusa, the god Zeus wounds the King of the Giants, Porphyrion, with a bolt of lightning, symbolic of the power of Greek deities. Although the Gorgon was protector of the temple, her look is one of malevolence. Her stance, the trunk and head facing those wishing to enter and the legs in profile running away are reminiscent of something that to the contemporary visitor is even more sinister, a swastika.

Today the Gorgon looks scary enough, but traces of colour found on the sculpture hint at the fearsome bright hues sported by the figure before time eroded her looks to their present grey façade. A blood-red tongue would have poked out between the sharpened, ivory white, fang-like teeth, as the green-eyed monster held any who approached in the jet black stare of her piercing pupils. Green snakes slither in her hair, sending a shiver through any soul who would have come here to worship.

The temple, which played host to this frightening custodian, was indeed worth protecting. It is understood that the architecture of this Doric temple with its eight columns that supported the pediments to the front and back of the building, is echoed in the more recent Parthenon in Athens and undoubtedly influenced the façade of London's British Museum.

Opposite the impressive gates to the present-day estate of Mon Repos are the remains of the church of Agia Kerkyra. In its original incarnation, this chapel dates back to the 5th Century AD, although it has suffered demolition at the hands of any number of barbarians over the years. A belfry and the remains of its wall lying open to a cloudless sky are all that is left after repeated bombing during the Second World War.

Alongside the church is the road that winds down to the even more sparse remains of the Temple of Artemis. For those of us who have faced up to the fierce Medusa in the museum, it is hard to shake off her stare and the site has a haunting quality at odds with the tranquillity of its surroundings. French soldiers under the command of the governor Francois-Xavier Donzelot originally discovered the site as they dug in to defend against the siege of the British in 1809 during the Napoleonic Wars. But it was the Prussian King and last German Emperor, Kaiser Wilhelm II, after taking up residence at the nearby Achilleon Palace, who was instrumental in the excavations that retrieved the remnants of the Gorgon.

Perhaps the Kaiser's obsession with this horrific figure was prescient. As he occupied himself with its recovery, the world hurtled towards the most horrific war in its history. For now the soil has given up its demons, and what is left lies at peace with its surroundings at this crossroads of the old and the new Kerkyra – to the east what remains of Paleopolis, to the west the runway of the international airport reaching out across Lake Halkiopoulo.

Kerkyra – A Confident Capital

Kerkyra, or Corfu Town, is alluring. Compelling and authentic, it manages to contain the inevitable influences of tourism which result from it being a major stop-off point for cruise ships and ferries from Brindisi in Italy and from all over Greece. I had been warned in advance about the traffic but, undaunted, headed for the city in torrential rain one Monday morning.

I should have taken notice of the advice and set off earlier. Cars were nose to tail as we approached town and, when we got there, the car parks were full. Exasperated by one of the most frustrating one-way systems I have ever encountered, eventually realizing it was impossible to drive to the other side of town along the coast road, I gave up and parked half a mile or so from the centre, braved the rain and walked.

Even the continued downpour was not enough to dampen the spirits. In my experience Kerkyra is unique in Greece and has a totally different feel to towns elsewhere. Passing the New Fort that dominates the north-eastern part of town, I noticed the Venetian Lion of St Mark carved into the wall below the Greek flag at the entrance – evidence that the *Neo Frourio* was, in fact, quite old, having been built by the Italian rulers in 1576.

I stopped to dry out, taking shelter under the awning of a cafe. Trade was brisk as suited businessmen held meetings and made noisy telephone calls over cups of cappuccino, and laughing students clutching files and books shared pizzas. I ordered an Americano and watched the world go by.

A break in the clouds signalled an easing off of the rain and a watery sunlight at last penetrated, brightening the face of the town. I paid the bill and left to take advantage of the dry weather. Heading back to the sea front, I kept the water's edge on my left. The old town essentially lies between the new and old fortresses and stretches inland from there.

Taking a right turn I entered another world – a maze of alleys, passageways and small squares. Tall pastel-coloured buildings still retaining their classical Venetian beauty, despite their peeling mortar, glowed warmly in the weak autumn sunlight. Above my head women chattered as they took advantage of the break in the weather to hang washing on lines suspended between the balconies of houses.

This is the Campiello, which is now a World Heritage site and it is easy to see why. Stone steps transported me from one hidden delight to another; small gardens and hidden tavernas and kafenions emerged at every turn. Although the old Venetian quarter of the town is compact, there is too much to take in all at once. Just wandering wherever my fancy took me, I emerged from the narrow streets into the open space of the Spianada.

In front of me was an expansive green with cultivated flowerbeds in glorious bloom, to my right the paved, colonnaded terrace of the Liston filled with busy open-air cafes. If it has the feel of Paris, this is because the Liston was built in 1807 by the French. It is a pastiche of the Rue de Rivoli and is the most lasting legacy of the period in the early 19th Century when Corfu was briefly under French control.

I was now looking out from the Esplanade across the large park, which is an unlikely venue for cricket matches. I caught sight of the waterfront again, dominated by the magnificent Old Fort standing on the promontory. I made my way towards it, crossing a small garden dedicated to the writers Lawrence and Gerald Durrell. Separated from the town by a narrow moat, the fortress can now be entered across a concrete bridge where there once stood a wooden structure that could be removed in case of an attack.

Like the *Neo Frourio*, the *Palaio Frourio* is also Venetian, but constructed on an earlier Byzantine site. Much of the current fortification was built following the failed attempt by the Turks to seize the island in 1537. Although they were repelled, the Venetians thought it best to reinforce their stronghold at the 'gateway to the Adriatic' and the fort was completed in the late 1580s.

Just as numerous pirates and the might of the Turks had been seen off, I too was driven back from the gates of the castle, but unlike earlier would-be invaders, I rather meekly retreated thanks to a lightning flash and clap of thunder followed by the downpour they precipitated.

A Drive Up Mount Pantokrator

As mountains go, Corfu's highest peak, Pantokrator, is congenial, but don't let this detract from the pleasure that can be derived by journeying to the summit. Its name loosely means almighty, and is frequently used to refer to Christ. It stands at 2,955 ft, and you can drive almost to the top – like so much about Corfu, it is not extreme. Indeed the journey holds as much of the pleasure of this trip as the extraordinary view from the summit.

On so many of the Greek islands, just venturing off the main road will transport you into a different world. Following the coast road northwards out of Kerkyra through the slightly-faded Ipsos, segueing into the unspectacular Pirgi, the road then begins to climb from sea level.

Taking a left turn for Spartylas, we started our ascent of the mountain. The road has an adequate surface but twists and turns around a series of sharp, blind bends as it rises steeply through the olive groves.

The road is at its narrowest as it passes through the small villages en route. Through Spartylas, the road straightens and ascends more gently, traversing wooded mountainside to the right, levelling out to flatter farmland on the left. The olive nets here appear to be kept down all year and beside the road the brilliant red of poppies, yellow broom and deep purple campanula create a sea of spring colour.

In Sgourades we stopped at a roadside taverna where two locals played *tavli*, a Greek form of backgammon, watched over by three other friends drinking milky white ouzo and eating nuts. We ordered an *ampelofasoula* salad to share.

The green beans, olives and tomatoes complimented the freshness of the morning air as we lingered, enjoying the isolation before setting off for the next village of Strynylas and the last bit of the climb to the top. Just through the village there is a turning signposted to the mountain. The road leaves the olive groves behind as it edges through stunted trees and shrubs on the boulder-littered hillside, softened by a blanket of wild flowers.

We parked the car at the roadside just shy of the summit to walk the final few hundred yards up the narrow road. At the top the view was breathtaking as we looked down across the undulating green hills to the north of the island, right out across the indigo sea to the mountains of northern Greece and Albania.

I have been assured that, on a clear day, you can even see Italy more than 80 miles away to the east, but it was not to be. Incredibly there were only a few other carloads of tourists taking in the view, although the small cafe indicated that more visit in the summer months.

There is a pretty little monastery at the top, which has a 19th-century facade but was originally built in the 17th Century. This in turn was constructed on the site of an earlier church dating back to 1347. In stark contrast to the monastery dedicated to Christ the Almighty is a large telecommunications mast that dominates the summit.

Looking down the mountain to the north, the small village of Ano Perithia (Old Perithia) can be made out. This is the oldest surviving village on Corfu, records of it go back to the 14th Century and its villagers were responsible for building the original mountaintop church. Now largely deserted, this small settlement has four tavernas serving the needs of the energetic who want to do the trip to the summit on foot. Recently three of the old cottages have been sympathetically restored into bed and breakfast accommodation and there are welcome signs that this old community is coming back to life.

We drove down again, arriving back in Strynylas where we turned right going down the mountain, this time towards the north coast and the town of Archavi before rejoining the coast road home to Agios Stefanos.

Paleokastritsa – Corfu's 'Most Beautiful Spot'

Furling the jib as our small boat navigated the entrance to Paleokastritsa, it immediately became apparent that it lived up to all I had heard about it. Our anchor dropped some three fathoms through water so clear we could witness the flukes nestling into the silver sand of the seabed.

The surrounding hills are dressed in olive groves. Cypresses towering over the verdant blanket that drapes itself all the way down to the sea pierce orchards of lemon trees. It is hard not to wax lyrical about Paleokastritsa; it wears its sobriquet as the 'most beautiful spot' on the island in a relaxed fashion but confident in the knowledge that few are likely to dispute this.

This magnificent crop of bays on the north-west coast is presided over by the serene Monastery of the Virgin Mary, or more literally the virgin of the ancient castle from where Paleokastritsa gets its name. In the middle of summer this spot can become a victim of its own beauty as hoards of tourists swarm all over Agios Spyridon and Alipo Bay. Away from these peak periods it is easier to appreciate these silvery beaches that clinch the emerald waters just as settings grasp stones in some priceless ring.

All around the hills are clad in lush forest before falling away into the sea with a flash of white cliff. If you're approaching by road, glimpses of the Ionian flicker enticingly through the trees before revealing the true refulgence of their bounty as you approach the shoreline. I have visited here before, but this time we have come at it from the sea, as most would have until the British High Commissioner of the island, Sir Frederick Adam, liked the spot so much in the 1820s he commanded that an access road be built across the hills. He bequeathed the island some beautiful buildings, including Mon Repos villa, but to my mind opening up this corner of the island so that people can experience its sublime natural setting is a greater legacy.

The popularity of this enchanted panorama is no passing fad. The ruling aristocracy during the period of British occupation would load their wicker picnic baskets into their traps and trot out of Kerkyra for rest and relaxation on the shaded hills and sun-baked beaches of the peninsula. Long before them, however, the advantages of this site had been recognized. This is alleged to have been the capital city of King Alkinoos, ruler of the Phaeacians, where much of Homer's *Odyssey* is related before the king avails Odysseus of a ship to deliver him home to Ithaka.

It is not difficult to believe that it was here that a naked Odysseus, clinging to the wreckage of his raft, was washed up and discovered by the Princess Nausicaa. Like Mouse Island off the remains of Paleopolis on the opposite coast, here the offshore rock of Kolovri lays claim to having been stopped in its tracks, the winged galleon petrified by an angry Poseidon for returning Odysseus home. Take your pick, both tiny islands have reasons to claim this link, but it's not difficult, lying here on the warm pine decking of our tiny sloop, to imagine being much closer to the land of the gods.

It's hard to rouse ourselves from the deck and take the inflatable tender ashore, but not as hard as the climb up to the monastery high upon the western headland overlooking Liapades Bay. Leaving our anchorage we take the beach road traversing the headland, which divides our landing place from another, smaller cove where the path rises steeply, zig-zagging its way upwards. It takes twenty minutes to climb to the summit at a snail's pace, but on arrival we are pleased we made the effort. Every second of our walk was worth the exertion as we enter the monastery, which has stood here since the 13th Century.

Its present incarnation is more recent, having been built over the remains of the earlier retreat in the 18th Century. The lower part of the grounds are beautiful gardens with stone arches and the bowed branches of trees forming a splendid arboreal canopy to the pathway which leads upwards to stone steps ascending to the monastery itself. A patchwork of beige, sand and cream stones pave a courtyard resplendent in blooming bougainvillea, geraniums and lemon trees.

The late afternoon sun projects a hint of purple, red and orange hues upon the whitewashed walls of the buildings. This is a working monastery and eight monks are still in residence, attending to their devotions, ministering to the local community, pressing olives to make oil to sell in the gift shop and running tours around this popular tourist spot.

From the terrace the view is spectacular enough for even the most secular amongst us to consider the possibilities of a life of piety, and the tiny church at the heart of the monastery embellishes the sumptuousness of its location with man-made masterpieces. Inside the walls are ablaze with frescoes and icons, the wealth of which belies the small size of the church. A giant chandelier illuminates the lectern and saints and apostles look down from the walls. Above a doorway in the southern wall is perhaps the most famous of the works to grace the chapel, a painting of the Last Judgement.

Above all, a Tree of Life carving spreads its branches, casting a celestial shadow over us. In Eastern Orthodox religions the tree is symbolic of a link between its appearance in the Garden of Eden in the Old Testament and the cross on which Christ was crucified in the New Testament. Whatever it signifies, to those who gaze towards the ceiling of this exquisite little church, it could be said that the chiselling and hewing of such timber on display here is as close to a modern day Garden of Eden as one could get.

Outside, a cat sleeps atop a stone-capped, whitewashed wall in the shadow of the honey-coloured belfry, its three bells waiting patiently to call the monks to prayer. A butterfly swoops around a *pithos* cascading scarlet blooms as a tourist throws a coin into the well and makes a wish that some day they will return.

There is a museum that exhibits a further impressive display of Byzantine and more modern icons, the most striking of which is a representation of the *Dormition of the Virgin*, celebrating the falling asleep of Mary before her body is reunited with her soul in heaven in the assumption.

We step back outside; the sun is casting a haze as, blinking, we gaze northwest but cannot catch a glimpse of the precipitous castle of Angelokastro that, chameleon-like, has blended with its mountain setting. But that is for another day. It is getting late and we have plans for the evening. A barbeque screwed down to the guardrails and stanchions waits to be lit. It stands ready to cook red mullet, herbed with fennel, sage and basil, seasoned with oil and lemon juice, salt and pepper and loosely wrapped in foil parcels to steam in their own juices while we prepare a fresh salad on deck and drink a chilled rosé wine as subtle and refreshing as the breeze that catches the water of our sheltered anchorage.

With barely a ripple on the water and refreshed by our meal we decide to make use of the remaining hour or so of daylight and explore further along the coastline. With the larger outboard firmly mounted to the stern of our inflatable tender we head out of the protective arms of the little harbour and skirt the coast.

The visages of the rocks hereabouts are pockmarked with caves and grottos waiting to be explored. Several we could, in these calm conditions, navigate right inside and snorkel around the edges among the myriad-coloured fish, the shoals of which seem to stretch forever vertically down the cliff walls to the centre of the earth. The water is cold here, starved of the strength of the sun, and without a wetsuit 10 minutes swimming is enough. But even back aboard our tiny boat the caves display a many-varied palette as the evening light descends.

At the portals of these grottos, the cliffs turn from grey to shadowy black and, as they plunge into the chilling depths, the dark blue of the ocean is transformed to the deep red of a well-aged wine. We stay slightly too long and, as the sun slips away, we have to rely on our memory and a powerful torch from the stash bag to feel our way back to our anchorage and a nightcap aboard. On the hills surrounding the bay, solitary lights exhibit a chimerical display, mimicking the stars, which on this clearest of nights are putting on a show besides which all others pale into insignificance.

Awaking with the dawn, I untie the tender and row ashore, the oars making the only ripples on a sea of grey, polished granite. We need some cheese and spinach pies for breakfast, bread to make packed lunches and some chocolate donuts, simply because I remember the bakers here make the best I have ever tasted. Today we are catching the first bus out of Paleokastritsa and heading for Makrades, from where we will take the little under two-mile hike to Angelokastro.

Fuelled up for the day, we head ashore again in time to board the coach that takes the steep, winding road out of the village in its stride. The sun has not long been up but already the heat through the plate glass windows of the bus makes clear its intentions for the day. After we reach the top of the hill the bus passes through the tiny village of Lakones. Those few who reside here must count their blessings every day because it is hard to know which way to turn to best take in the sublime views of the west coast.

Looking back down on Paleokastritsa we imagine we can see our boat nestling among others in the bay and we can definitely see the monastery to which we had climbed the day before. Ahead can be made out today's destination with enough clarity of definition to whet the appetite. In the distance the fortress of Angelokastro stands proud on a stark, rocky promontory, so at ease with its place in the world it looks as though it was birthed from the rocks that surround it, rather than the sweated lifting, winching and sculpting of man.

From here the journey is quick. In no time we emerge in the small village of Makrades, ready to embark on our trek. The disproportionate number of tavernas and ouzeries already going about the business of opening, and the street stalls selling all manner of goods from embroidery to pottery and oil, hint at the volume of tourist trade which passes here. I am pleased for our early start and disembarking at a junction signed to Krini we set out straight away towards the castle.

Our destination lies at the highest point along the whole of the west coast. The castle stands nearly 1,000 ft above the sea lanes it surveys, which made it one of the crucial bastions for the defence of the island, along with strongholds in Gardiki in the south, Kassiopi further to the north and the later forts of Kerkyra Town itself. From its lofty position, beacons could be seen across the island warning of attack by enemy forces and privateers.

Finding our way is easy, reaching our destination not so effortless. From a car park beneath the castle, rugged steps hewn out of the rock steeply ascend in a scabrous fashion until, breathless, the modern-day assailant passes through the narrow entrance to the inner keep. This is the first bulwark protecting the nucleus of the sanctum, which lies above.

It is thought that due to its imperious position, heady enough to view approaches from the Adriatic to the north, that there has been some form of fortress here since at least the 11th Century AD. It is also likely, considering the many advantages bestowed on this spot by nature, that it had been an acropolis for many years previously.

Evidence uncovered during an archaeological dig in the final year of the last century uncovered stone slabs that have been confirmed as dating from the Byzantine era. What is certain is that by 1272 the castle was extant. It had been requisitioned by Giordano di San Felice, the leader of the Angevin forces who took over the island in 1267 as part of his ruler Charles I of Sicily's (later of Naples) ultimately thwarted ambition to reform the Latin

Empire of Constantinople. This lofty aerie stayed in the hands of these maverick relatives of the Plantagenets until it slipped through the fingers of the house of Anjou, whose weak rule allowed the island to place itself under the protectorate of the powerful Venetian empire in 1386, the forces of which took the castle by siege that same year.

That the present bastion was built under the auspices of the Komnenos dynasty, whose short-lived tenure on the island began in 1214 after they wrested control of Corfu from the Venetians is in little doubt. Some claim the castle is so called after Angelo Komneni himself, the first Despot of Epirus. It is altogether more likely, however, that it was named after the Archangel Michael as, in the first written reference to its existence in 1272, Angelokastro is mentioned as the 'Castrum Sancti Angeli', which in Latin means the 'Castle of the Anointed Angel'.

I have to admit to being not great with heights. Staring down the vertical rocks on the seaward side of the fortress it is easy to see how, after the Venetians first took possession of it in 1386, it was never wrested from their grasp by force despite the repeated attempts of the Ottoman Empire's marauding troops. It was not for want of trying.

The Venetians on the other hand were determined that the Ottoman Empire, which had enveloped much of the rest of Greece, would not get a toehold into the rest of Europe. Weaponry and men were lavished upon the island to bolster it against any such eventuality and the line was drawn here at the southern reaches of the Adriatic.

Alongside the Venetian castles in Kerkyra, the Byzantine sites of Gardiki, Kassiopi and Angelokastro proved too much for the Turks and despite repeated attempts at siege in 1431, 1537, 1571, 1573 and 1716 they were repulsed on each occasion. Glorious victories as these might have been for the Venetian nobility and the armies that defended their wealth and property; these were paid for in the blood of the ordinary Corfiots. Those who lived outside of the castle keeps were sacrificed to the onslaught of the forces of successive Sultans as, on each occasion, they ran amuck at will outside the castle walls. The cost of keeping the 'door to Venice' slammed firmly shut has been estimated as being as much as 100,000 innocent people murdered or sold into slavery. The Turks finally got the message in 1716 when, buoyed up by having finally quelled resistance in the Peloponnese, their army of some 35,000 troops and auxiliaries boarded ship and set sail from the mainland across the short strait to the island. Although the force landed at Ipsos, the off-lying fleet were engaged by the Venetian navy and sunk, scuttled or scattered to the winds as their stranded forces lay siege to the island fortresses. On this occasion 3,000 locals picked up what arms they had to join the 5,000 Venetian troops and their mercenaries to repel the repeated forays made on the fortress walls. Time and again they came forward, for 22 days, until their supply chain finally snapped and they scampered from the island for the last time.

This great victory was celebrated by the composer Vivaldi in his oratorio of the same year entitled *Juditha Triumphans Devicta Holofernis Barbarie*. This barely disguised allegory is based upon the *Book of Judith*, a little known book of the *Bible* only included in the *Apocrypha* in the Protestant and Jewish tradition but as part of the Old Testament in Eastern Orthodoxy and the Catholic faiths.

A Jewish widow, Judith – the name itself meaning 'Jewess' – becomes impatient when her people loses its faith in God's ability to deliver their lands from the conquering Assyrians. She takes it on herself to enter the camp of the enemy commander Holofernes, whom she befriends. As the drunken general lies asleep one night Judith seizes his sword and decapitates him. She transports the head of the luckless invader back to her people as a symbol of their liberation as the Assyrians retreat from Israel.

But it was not a Venetian, or even a Corfiot, who masterminded Kerkyra's liberation from the Ottoman onslaught. It was a Prussian aristocrat and mercenary, Johann Matthias von der Schulenburg, who had previously taken much more than the shilling from each of the many kings across Europe whose battles he had fought for them. His final, unlikely victory saw him able to retire in some comfort to his adopted homeland of Venice and spend his hard-fought earnings on a substantial art collection. He is honoured on Corfu with a statue that stands nearby the Old Fort in Kerkyra Town.

High on his pedestal he stands dressed in the rather fanciful uniform of a Roman legionnaire. It is at this spot that every year a procession in honour of the island's co-saviour, St Spyridon, winds its way to the sea front and, emerging from the narrow streets of the town, stops and pays tribute to the man who ensured their island would never be enslaved by the Turks.

Moving away from the unstable cliff edge we stop to drink water and rest. The crenellated remains of battlements poke like grey, rotting teeth from the gums of the north-eastern fortress wall. The portal to the castle faces northward. The remains of the circular tower that protected it are still to be seen looking down over the barracks which housed the troops outside of the inner keep. A simple, tiny stone-built church erected here as recently as 1784 and dedicated to the Archangels Michael and Gabriel stands high upon the acropolis, outside of which are eerily fascinating graves cut out of the ancient rock into the shape of the humans they inter.

Back down in the lower keep we enter another tiny chapel; a cave dug out of the rock and dedicated to Saint Kyriaki. Beside the entrance is an opening to the sparse quarters that once housed religious hermits seeking solitude while, inside the tiny whitewashed interior of the church, a fresco of The Virgin and Baby protect a small stone altar on which stand more modern votive icons in frames and a simple cross.

Despite the heat outside, here it is cool and tranquil, a momentary relief. It is hard to imagine a life alone between these desolate walls; but emerging outside it is hard to imagine a place closer to heaven.

The descent is welcoming as we delve downwards into the sparse forest of shrub. The intermittent shade of the trees that cling to the rock protects us from the worst of the heat as we head towards the nearby village of Krini to eat our picnic.

Refreshed, it is still only midday and we decide to explore the coastline further north. We head back into Makrades to discuss our options over a cold Mythos. We agree to make for Peroulades at the north-western cape of the island to see the famous Canal d'Amour, taking in the other numerous coastal villages like Agios Georgios, Afionas and the island's second spot named Agios Stefanos.

Usually bus services on the island are good, but after a discussion with the owner of the taverna we come to the conclusion that such a trip would be a logistical nightmare. We decide to head back to the boat and pass the afternoon swimming, reading and sleeping in the sun and rent a car to make the trip the following day.

I was pleased we decided to make our first stop Sidari, a tourist resort in the north of the island. From here we would wind our way slowly back along the narrow roads which make darting sorties to the coast before heading inland to the olive groves which predominate the landscape here. I was also pleased it was not the height of the season, for just a glimpse of this resort could only hint at the dubious pleasures it might offer when operating at full capacity. Sidari's only saving graces were the sunshine and some flat, sandy beaches. The few families walking dejectedly from one souvenir shop to another, had plenty of time to rue their ill-advised holiday choice.

Hastily we head west out of town to find what we hope will be Sidari's one redeeming feature, the Canal d'Amour, and it does not disappoint. Leaving the car on a sandy car park we take a well-worn path across rocks, up and down steps until we arrived at a remarkable rock formation. Carved out by the erosion of sea stacks and collapsed arches, this unique series of coves and natural canals is extraordinary. Legend has it that, as the name suggests, any couple who swim together through these waters will end up getting married. At this time of year, when it is quiet, it is indeed a romantic spot. Here creamy limestone, topped in a covering of green shrub and exhibiting the strata of centuries of wear, plunges into the crystalline blue pools.

Climbing to the top of one of the hills, out to sea one can see Cape Drastis beyond which, a further five miles out, lie Diapontia Nisia (the Diapontia Islands), the most north-westerly part of Greece.

Othonoi, Erikoussa and Mathraki make up this small archipelago. The largest, Othonoi, is reputed to have been the nymph Calypso's island where she held Odysseus captive for seven years before reluctantly letting the object of her affections free, aboard the raft on which he was shipwrecked.

Boats to the islands set out from Sidari, and some of the other nearby coastal villages, and a ferry runs from Corfu Town. If you enjoy seclusion, these beautiful islands might just be for you. Accommodation is available on all three, but is limited, particularly on Erikoussa and Mathraki. Othonoi has the most facilities having some shops and tavernas and a medieval fort rising out of the olive groves and pine trees on an island hilltop.

Most trips, however, seem to go to Erikoussa and, although facilities are limited, it has beautiful sandy beaches stretching in an arc out from the tiny village of Porto. There is a yacht harbour on Othonoi and the islands have long been a haven for ships running from storms in the southern Adriatic or fishermen seeking shelter when seas cut up rough off Cape Drastis.

The islands have in the past been a refuge for brigands and pirates, the privateers making a living from sacking ships passing south from Venice and other Italian city states. But there is evidence that life here went back much further, and remnants of Stone-Age settlements have been uncovered on all three islands.

To the west of the Canal d'Amour we encounter the small village of Peroulades. This unassuming settlement could also have appropriated the magical coves we had just left behind. But, unlike its brash neighbour, Sidari, it would seem like this might be too much effort for this sleepy, faded village, the closest on the island to the dramatic white cliffs of Cape Drastis. It is a shame, as the natural beauty of that wave-worn coast has a more natural synergy with this somnolent olive farming community.

Some concessions have been made to supplement the meagre income from the olive groves but they appear half-hearted, the village content to bask in the traditions of the past. A few old men sit smoking and chewing the cud in the village square beside an ancient water pump as we feel our way along a road barely wide enough for our car. The buildings claustrophobically jostle each other as we bump along before a steep hill leaves them, and not long afterwards, the road, behind.

It soon becomes clear that, if we want to go further, we will have to abandon the car. It is well worth it as in less than a mile we emerge on top of the striking cliffs of the wind-buffeted cape. Today the sky is clear and we can see the Diapontia Isles lying at anchor on the horizon. The sense of seclusion is overwhelming. Looking back there is nothing but olive groves clinging to the limestone cliff tops and out to sea a lone ship holds course for Brindisi in Italy some 175 miles to the west.

Reunited with our car, we drive cautiously until we meet some tarmac and head to the village in search of sustenance. Turning right at a sign to Longas Beach we stop at a taverna. Steps descend steeply to a beach previously invisible, as the cliffs are so vertiginous. Deciding upon a swim we discover that the waters that lie in the shadow of these white cliffs are decidedly cooler than elsewhere and, although cleaning away the dust of the day, do not encourage us to linger, particularly with a taverna with such magnificent views so close at hand.

A traditional *pastisada* is on offer. This appropriate dish gives a nod to Corfu's past relationship with Venice and also acknowledges Italy's invisible presence somewhere over the horizon we now stare out on. Chicken is layered with pasta and a béchamel sauce in a style similar to a lasagne with a tomato sauce, cinnamon and paprika then added to mark it out as distinctly Corfiot. The whole dish is slowly baked in an oven. The chilled, earthy wine served up alongside it is deep red, its flavour perfectly balancing the sweetness of the tomatoes and spices. We are replete and the bread-wiped plates sparkle in the sun as evidence of the deliciousness of the meal.

Relaxed, we are ready for a leisurely drive along the coastal road back to our mooring at Paleokastritsa. It is slow, but far from leisurely. This road is a riot of bends as it in turn flirts with the coast and the mountains inland. This game of hide and seek goes on revealing breathtaking glimpses of the sea one moment, strobing into the lush hillside canopy of olive grove the next.

We had stayed before at Agios Stefanos on the other side of the island and were interested to visit its namesake on this north-western headland. Taking a diversion to this unremarkable but pleasant enough small settlement whose wide expanse of beach makes it understandable why this purpose-built resort was constructed here. To the north the white cliffs stretch away to Cape Drastis shimmering in the haze of the heat radiating off the sea. To the south is the small chapel dedicated to Saint Stephen after which the village is named.

Beyond is a small harbour. Fishing boats, their blue and white hulls moored amongst the tour boats, are a reminder of a more traditional existence that is still lived here by some. Looked at on its own merits, Agios Stefanos is a pleasant enough place to holiday. It is unfortunate that it is compared to so many places nearby that possess such exceptional natural attributes.

One of these is only a few miles away in distance, but its whole aura lies an eternity away. Afionas lies at the end of a track that pulls up abruptly just before it feels it might plunge, like Sappho, into the waves beneath. Out to sea lies the island of Gravis with its smaller acolyte, Sikia, astern in turn towing another rock like a petrified tender. We park up near the square where villagers sit as they have for centuries, under the shade of a huge olive tree. In the sunlight the classic belfry of the small village church of Agios Giannos displays itself as almost pink as it casts a shadow over a small memorial, a reminder of an incident that happened in 1996. This simple cream, marble statue stands in memory of Ektora Gialopsos. Ektora died in a Greek army helicopter far away on the eastern borders of Greek territory, believed to have been a victim of a Greek sovereignty dispute with their neighbours, Turkey.

A further manifestation of the animosity so frequently exhibited between these two countries, most visibly illustrated by the ongoing dispute over Cyprus, the Imia-Kardak incident showed just how raw the skin of these two nations is when they rub up against one another. Just four miles off the coast of Turkey, the tiny pair of uninhabited Dodecanese islands, known in Greece as Imia and in Turkey as Kardak, became the centre of a diplomatic incident when a ship flying the Turkish colours struck ground on the islands and required salvage.

The Turkish captain of the ship disputed the Greek authorities' right to salvage his vessel. The Turkish government then upped the ante by wading in saying they considered the islands to be Turkish territory. To most it seems clear that the 1947 Treaty of Paris, which ceded all the islands previously under Italian rule to Greece, that as part of the Dodecanese these were sovereign Greek territory. Whatever the rights and wrongs of the case, the legal ramifications are still rumbling on.

The mayor of the nearby Greek island of Kalymnos, along with a priest, landed on one of the islands and hoisted a Greek flag which failed to calm the situation and resulted in a grandstanding Turkish TV channel pulling a stunt and landing some of their own journalists to rip down the flag and replace it with a Turkish ensign. This tit-for-tat continued with the Greek navy getting involved and again raising the blue and white stripes of Greece on one of the tiny rocks.

Warships from both countries sailed for the islands to land expeditionary forces ashore on the rocks, the Greeks on the island to the east the Turks on its partner to the west, both in ignorance of the other's activities.

Whilst the two nations played political brinksmanship a reconnaissance helicopter was launched from a Greek frigate, and plummeted into the sea above the disputed islands. Some speculate that it was hit by Turkish fire that killed its crew of three, including Ektora. The severity of the disaster and the possibilities it precipitated were such that both sides covered up the incident for fear of the consequences and it required diplomatic intervention from Washington to draw the two parties back from the brink of war. The dispute, just one of many surrounding the borders between these two old enemies, is still unresolved. For many these incidents have been pushed back into the dark recesses of their political minds, but here in this tiny Corfiot village one of its victims will always be remembered.

Following the track past the church we head towards a narrow promontory that divides two bays and leads to the Cape of Arilla. Excavations have uncovered evidence that, as early as the third millennium BC, Neolithic man had settled here on this windy outcrop with its heady outlook north to the Diapontia islands and south to the bay of Agios Giorgios and the cape of Angelokastro far in the distance. On this exposed headland can be seen foundations from a more modern era, these remains date from around 500 BC.

For the visitor today there is a choice of two paths leading down either side of the promontory and giving the choice of descending to a sheltered beach depending on which way the wind is blowing. The beach in the tiny cove below Cape Arilla is intimate and inviting, but the spread of the wider vista which unfurls as I glance further around the whole expanse of the bay to Cape Falakron is majestic and calls out for us to move on to Agios Giorgios, one of the pearls of the north-west coast.

The road tries to shake us off, determined to discourage the casual visitor as it twists and turns, navigating a spectacular headland before coming to rest where a valley, looking for all the world as though cut out of the rock by a river of olive trees, reaches the sea.

Not to be mistaken for another holiday resort of the same name near Lake Korrision in the low-lying flatlands of the south of the island, this village manages to cater for the needs of a loyal group of tourists who return time and again to enjoy the relaxed pace of life and the pleasures its unrivalled beach has to offer in the shade of these wooded hills. About three miles of fine shingle and sand stretch out in either direction from the village, which hugs the coast road. Umbrellas and sunbeds are dotted around the beach, children build sandcastles and swim or take advantage of the many watersports' facilities. The beach still retains a sense of serenity, large enough to happily absorb all those who come to enjoy it. We decide to take a walk along the shoreline as the sun starts to go down and the bay falls asleep, its hidden depths slumbering under a black satin sheet.

At the end of the beach where the wooded hills plunge into the water a sprinkling of alert cypresses look down at their own image, fleetingly recorded in that mercuried mirror. As we return along the beach it has emptied out, some couples lingering to catch the sunset, others returning home to their pensions and hotels to wash the salt away or eat in one of the many traditional tavernas. We return to the car to slowly navigate the darkened road which helps keep the secret of this beautiful little spot, as we head the few miles south to where our boat lies at anchor in Paleokastritsa bay.

A Slippery Encounter

Lake Korission was almost deserted. Not only had we escaped any tourists; we also appeared to have outrun the bad weather we'd been experiencing throughout the last few days, leaving it behind to the north and west. The autumn sun had dried the country roads and, driving down off the mountains onto the plains of south-east Corfu, I almost ran over a snake basking on the tarmac.

It was the longest snake I have ever encountered in the wild. As it whipped off in front of the car wheels I estimated it to be over five ft long. By the parallel black stripes running the length of its brown body, I later identified it as a four lined snake. Although it looked more dangerous than it actually is, I was still pleased to be in the car.

My theory is that you never know with snakes. When you encounter them, there is scarcely time to refer to your little book of local wildlife to see if they pose a threat! If it is any consolation to visitors to Corfu, the only dangerous species of snake on the island is the nose-horned viper.

Considerably smaller than the snake I encountered, it still slithers along at a not inconsiderable two-and-a-half ft. It also has an impressive strike distance, although I'm assured it won't attack unless provoked. As its venom is enough to kill small mammals, birds and lizards, if bitten it is recommended that you get medical help as soon as possible. Although unusual, without an antidote death has been known to result from a bite from what is Europe's most dangerous snake.

Through a landscape of nurseries growing plants both outside and under plastic we drove on. Horses grazed in the fields, their tales swishing at the infestation of insects that filled the damp air as it warmed in the autumn sun. Here, right at the northern inland shore of the lake we stopped at a solitary taverna. Seated by the entrance, an elderly woman with a 20-foot-long pole marshalled the chickens and ducks that were running free among the tables and chairs.

A mother cat and her kittens soon congregated beneath our table as we sat down. Another woman, the poultry minder's daughter I presumed, emerged from the farm gate to the side of the taverna to greet us and take our order. We were the only visitors she had had that day and seemed happy to talk, and was tolerant and encouraging of my halting Greek. We ordered some grilled fish, bread and water to set us up for a walk by the lake.

We were on the inland side of the expanse of water that, strictly speaking, is a lagoon rather than a lake. Created out of marshland by the Venetians, its eastern shore is separated from the sea by a wide beach, which is a popular spot during the tourist season.

The inland shore of the lagoon was more secluded as we walked through a landscape scattered with juniper alongside the waving reeds growing at the water's edge. Besides the mosquitoes taking a light snack from our arms and legs other wildlife abounded. Apparently more than 120 species of birds have been recorded here.

Now a wildlife sanctuary, the Venetians dug a channel through from the sea to make a saltwater lagoon in order to farm fish – and fish trapping is still practiced here. This large, flatland area is a stark contrast to the part of the island we are more used to further north. It has its own unique beauty. The vistas are endless, stretching out to an imagined horizon somewhere between the sea and sky in the space that separates Italy from where we now stand; another country no further than a night's boat journey, but a lifetime away by almost any other measure. Although the Venetian influence is stronger here on Corfu than elsewhere in Greece the differences between the two cultures are still greater than the similarities.

Then we headed back north east to the rugged terrain with which we are more familiar and a view towards the mountains of Albania and mainland Greece that hold this sparkling island in their natural gravitational forces.

Agni Bay – A Political Scandal

From our balcony in Agios Stefanos we look down on this idyllic small bay and out seawards to the narrow channel that separates Corfu from Albania, to which we are so close you can almost hear it breathe. As I throw open the shutters, the village is coming to life. The van delivering bread to the local shop arrives, the sleepy owner of Taverna Cocheli cranks down his awnings, and the faint pinging of halyards on metal masts announces the yachts at anchor are preparing for sea.

Tucked away beneath the olive-shrouded hills on the north-east coast of Corfu, this is a place for idle contemplation. The pace of life is slow enough to relax the mind but with enough to occupy it should you choose.

The stroll of some 50 yards to the mini-market to buy bread for breakfast can take some time. The chef from Cocheli's stops to pass the time of day, as does Yanis, the owner of the boat-hire business. Then the friendly elderly lady in the grocer's flatters me, complimenting my Greek before teasing me by hiding the price of my purchases on the till display to test my counting prowess. Four free oranges are proffered with my shopping before I retrace my steps, stopping this time to sympathize with Yanis' assistant, Georgos, at having to bail out his boats after last night's spectacular storm.

Today we will go nowhere; we will eat a breakfast of freshly-baked bread with honey and the oranges from the grocers, then take time to sit and read on the balcony or just watch the boats come and go as swallows fly into our apartment then swoop down to their numerous nests in the rafters of the tavernas and bars which line the waterfront.

As the sun rises high in the sky and the cats stretch out, too content to search for scraps, we will walk the length of the village to the Eucalyptus Taverna. There we will sit at a table on the beach for a salad and perhaps sardines and a glass of wine before returning for siesta.

A beautiful secluded bay just south of Agios Stefanos, Agni can only be reached by a steep narrow road that tapers off to a single track before becoming a dead end at the beach – or by boat. It is here we are heading for dinner. Three tavernas, all excellent, a snack bar and a boat hire business are the extent of activity on the seashore and several wooden jetties allow space for visiting boats to moor. If its slight inaccessibility gives Agni a certain exclusivity, an event in the summer of 2008 launched it onto the front pages of every national newspaper in the UK.

It was here in Taverna Agni that British Labour Peer Peter Mandleson and the then Tory Shadow Chancellor of the Exchequer, George Osbourne, famously shared a seafood lunch. Over the marinaded anchovies things were reportedly said by both parties that proved to be political dynamite, and became common currency in parliament during the dying days of the Labour administration of Gordon Brown.

Whatever the rights and wrongs of this particular political storm in a teacup, the proprietors of Taverna Agni and the other establishments on this quiet little bay in north-east Corfu must have been rubbing their hands at the sort of publicity which money just can't buy.

Even more impressive than the cachet of the restaurant having been at the centre of a scandal is their speedboat taxi service. A phone call and a few euros provides us with a spectacular sunset high-speed ride from Agios Stefanos to the jetty outside the taverna and a captivating return through a starlit night alive with red fireflies, and blue-green phosphorescence illuminating the coal-black sea around our bow wave.

A Magical Mystery Tour

All we could see of the cars in front were their tail lights. The rain was too much for the windscreen wipers. They flailed to little avail as we crawled through the outskirts of Kerkyra Town. It just kept falling, sheeting out from a black midday sky. Rain like I have never encountered in Greece.

Where was that coast road south? An inability to see any signposts and the need to keep vigilant to avoid errant motor scooters darting out from between double-parked cars meant that we just had to play follow my leader.

Somewhere near the airport the traffic cleared, unlike the weather. The rain showed no sign of abating as we left the town behind. Winding our way south into the hills, the car pushed upwards against the gradient and the water streaming down over the road's potholed surface.

Driving steadily, taking each turn as it came late into view, we drove on. With little to do outside the car and not knowing where we were, we decided to just go where the road would take us. As this was uphill, it was certainly not to the coast.

The deserted road narrowed, taking sharp turns through the wooded hillsides. Then, out of nowhere, we came upon a cluster of parked cars. We still could not see any road signs through the torrential rain, so I followed the herd and parked up.

People getting out of their cars hurriedly opened umbrellas, which proceeded to blow inside out in the wind. Others pulled coats over their heads and ran towards a grand entrance in a tall, stone wall. We also made a dash for it, following the other visitors.

It turned out we were in the village of Gastouri, six miles south of Kerkyra Town, although the drive in the rain had taken a lot longer than the distance would indicate. At the entrance, where we paid our admission fee, we learned that we were at the Achilleion Palace, named after the legendary Greek hero Achilles.

It was too wet to linger long in the gardens but, despite the weather, it was still apparent just how beautiful a setting it was. The layout of the grounds is very formal and surrounds the rather incongruous architecture of the palace itself.

An impressive statue of a recumbent Achilles lies at the heart of the gardens. He stands out among the numerous paeans to the hero and other Greek gods and goddesses that adorn the palace grounds.

Called *Dying Achilles* the statue was the work of German sculptor Ernst Herter and depicts the hero in his final moments. Gazing towards the heavens, his face is lined with pain as he tries to remove Paris' arrow from his heel. Heroic in death, he wears a simple cloth and warrior's helmet as he looks to the gods above for help.

A romantic neo-classical homage to the Trojan War, the Achilleion was built in 1890 as a summer palace for the grieving Empress Elizabeth of Austria. Inconsolable since the death of her only son, Prince Rudolph, in the infamous Mayerling tragedy of the previous year, the distraught philhellene sought refuge in this extraordinary palace built high in the hills looking down over the Ionian.

The escapist style of the architecture, art and sculpture reflects well the palace's purpose as a bolthole from the reality of the Empress' life. This itself was to end tragically in 1898 when she was assassinated by an Italian anarchist in Geneva.

In 1907, nearly a decade after Elizabeth's death, the palace was bought by Kaiser Wilhelm II. During the turbulent years before the First World War he used it as both a holiday home and as a meeting place for political leaders to discuss the rapidly deteriorating state of world affairs.

The German Emperor loved only one thing more than holidaying in Corfu, and that was himself. He had a bridge built, named after him, that went from the lower gardens of the palace to the beach. Kaiser's Bridge spanned the coast road heading south out of Kerkyra Town, and its remains can still be seen when driving this route.

The grandson of Queen Victoria, Wilhelm visited his palace right up until the outbreak of the First Word War. His other significant contribution to the site was his commissioning of the tall bronze statue of Achilles that faces north toward Kerkyra.

In contrast to Herter's earlier work, this depiction of the warrior by the German artist Johannes Gotz is more formal and intricate. It portrays Achilles in full fighting regalia, an adversary to be feared by all. Although not such a human treatment of Achilles, framed by the surrounding palm trees it is an imposing presence on the garden's landscape.

Inside the palace is an elegant staircase rising out of the main hall. On its wall is one enormous painting of Achilles mounted on his chariot, dragging the body of Hector behind him. Other paintings of lesser magnitude celebrating the great warrior and other Greek legends line the walls of this impressive, but largely inauthentic, building.

With the rain still coming down in droves, we headed back to the car. Following the rivulets running downhill we drove in the opposite direction from previously. Minutes later we found the elusive coast road and headed further south. On our left the Ionian had worked itself up into a rage. Where the road came up against the sea wall, spray was hurled in sheets over the car as rogue waves crashed against the shore.

After several miles we came across the small tourist resort of Benitses. Many of the shops, bars and tavernas had closed early. Although not the end of their tourist season, the unseasonal weather that refused to go away had forced them to pull down the shutters and lock up for winter. The town was deserted apart from a couple of tavernas opposite the small harbour. We chose one and sat out of the rain, cozily cocooned inside the canopied area looking seaward through the tightly zipped-down plastic windows.

It was no day to be at sea. A solitary yacht, reefed down so it was carrying a handkerchief of a mainsail, heeled alarmingly as it reached south along the coast heading for the safety of the harbour. Over moussaka and salad, from the comfort of the restaurant, we watched as the small boat made its layline for the harbour entrance.

Small figures busied themselves on deck to stow what was left of the mainsail as it was lowered and the foresail roller reefed. Under engine, the craft looked uncomfortable as it wallowed in the large seas pushing it towards the harbour wall. And then it was in, the yacht recovering its equilibrium as it reached the calm of the sheltered waters and headed for its mooring.

The following year I returned to Benitses in springtime. The rest of the island had awoken from its winter torpor and was in full bloom. Businesses were starting to see an upturn in trade for the summer. But Benitses proved a sorry sight; with graffitied grills still firmly shut down on shops and car-hire businesses, and faded shutters still padlocked on the small pensions that lined the coast road. Small groups of lost-looking tourists waited at bus stops or drank beers in the isolation of the terraces of the larger hotels. It looked like a place that had given up. A victim of the financial difficulties or somewhere that had just had its time, I don't know.

An Inspirational World

Turning off a roller-coaster road running north, we descend steeply through olive groves, pine trees and the ever-present cypresses. The sea glistens tantalizingly below through gaps in the trees. We also catch glimpses of a small village set aside the tiny bay, clinging to the bottom of the rocks beside a secluded beach. As the road flattens, it narrows to squeeze between the houses and tavernas. Perched right on the sea front is the White House, once the home of the author Lawrence Durrell and his first wife Nancy.

We are in Kalami, so typical of the picturesque isolated Corfiot settlements on the north east coast. But Kalami's association with the Durrell family has marked it out as a destination, due to its connection with Corfu's adopted sons, Lawrence and his brother, Gerald. Both men did much to bring the delights of this small island to the attention of the world by writing of their time spent living here in the years immediately preceding the Second World War.

Following the death of their father in 1928, Lawrence persuaded his mother to move the family away from the bleakness of England to Corfu in 1935. They lived on the island until the onset of war when the rest of Lawrence's family returned to the UK. He and Nancy remained until 1940 when Greece fell to the Germans, and they escaped to Egypt via Crete.

It was in Egypt, the setting for his masterpiece *The Alexandria Quartet*, that Lawrence penned his affectionate account of life in Corfu, *Prospero's Cell*. Published in 1945, it was the first of a number of books the novelist was to write about Greece; with his account of *Rhodes, Reflections on a Marine Venus*, coming out in 1953; followed by *Bitter Lemons*, which documents the time he spent teaching English on the island of Cyprus, printed in 1957. Lawrence's all-encompassing *The Greek Islands* came out twenty-one years later in 1978.

If Lawrence's books are considered to have the most literary merit, for many people it is the work of his brother, the zoologist Gerald, which best evokes the island. His popular book *My Family and Other Animals* tells the story of his idyllic childhood growing up with his family on Corfu. The book was filmed twice for television by the BBC; once in 1987 and again in 2005. Gerald's light, humorous, self-deprecating style was developed by his own admission in response to his need to make money to fund his passion for wildlife conservation.

Although both books are captivating accounts of island life, there are substantial fictional elements to both of them. Gerald makes no mention of

Lawrence being married and living with Nancy, whereas Lawrence hardly acknowledges the existence of his wider family.

Both brothers did, however, capture the spirit of this wonderful island, and have been posthumously rewarded by having a park named after them in Kerkyra Town. Bosketto Durrell is not only a fitting tribute to the brothers whose work did so much to encourage visitors to come to the island, it also, I am led to believe, houses the only public toilets on Corfu. Meanwhile, the White House is now a restaurant.

Corfu's Great Protector

On a walk around the old town of Kerkyra, the spire of the church of St Spyridon can be glimpsed around most corners. The tallest tower on the island, its red roof atop the stone bell tower stands in proud celebration of Corfu's patron saint. This magnificent church is a fitting tribute to the saint whom many Corfiots view as being their island's protector.

The church is the final resting place of St Spyridon who is attributed with a number of miracles that saved the people of the island. He has, they claim, protected them from famine and the plague and is also credited with inspiring the defence and subsequent repelling of the attempted Turkish invasion of the island in 1716.

The popular Greek name Spyros is prevalent on the island, being given to many sons of families in honour of the saint. On four occasions each year his body is taken from its resting place and solemnly paraded around Kerkyra Town. To the locals by far the most important of these occasions is on Easter Saturday when their saint is borne upright in his casket at the heart of Kerkyra's large procession.

Despite their devotion to him, Spyridon is an adopted son of the island, not having visited it until his body was brought here 1,200 years after his death. He was born in Cyprus, and worked as a shepherd before joining the church where he rose to become a bishop. Included in the evidence for his beatification was the claim that he turned a tile into its basic components of water, earth and fire, a miracle that reflected the holy trinity of God the Father, God the Son and God the Holy Ghost.

After his death, his body was moved on several occasions to escape the clutches of marauding invaders. A monk, Georgios Kalohairetis, finally brought him to Corfu in 1453 following the fall of Constantinople to the Turks. The body of the saint was passed through the family as an heirloom and a dowry and eventually found its present resting place after the private chapel in which it lay was demolished during the fortification of the Old Town.

As we stand outside, on the steps of the church sits a young lad selling candles. Inside is cool, a welcome sanctuary from the summer swelter. The saint's remains are interred in a silver sarcophagus beside the altar that lies beneath an imposing Renaissance ceiling depicting his life. Hanging from the wooden, painted ceiling are huge candelabras filling the air with the smell of molten wax, and incense burners too large to be swung by any hand of man.

A priest chants over the remains, as both the devout and tourists alike approach to kiss the tomb of the patron saint. Such obeisance is supposed to bestow protection on the faithful. A mobile phone rings and breaks the spell as an embarrassed tourist reaches into the pocket of her brightly-coloured shorts to silence the offending article. Another tourist tuts in disapproval as the woman hurries from the church, but the Greeks at prayer show no such admonition.

Back outside, the narrow street is lined with shops selling icons of the saint, and salad bowls, bongo drums, corkscrews and phalluses carved out of olive wood. Kumquat liqueurs are offered up for the visitor to try before they walk through the winding alleyways in the footsteps of Roger Moore and Carole Bouquet in the Bond film *For Your Eyes Only*, which was filmed here. The bells of the old church toll the hour of midday as we head to the Liston for a pre-lunch drink.

Kostas Georkakis – The Man Who Changed History

In an unassuming small square in the old town of Kerkyra, I come across a monument, a well-tended flowerbed in full bloom encircling the statue of a half-kneeling figure bedecked in jacket and tie. Here, surrounded by modern shops selling shoes and clothing, and café bars, this statue, at the time I write, is particularly poignant. Somewhere in my memory I had heard the story of a student who had sacrificed his life to let the world know of the plight of Greece under the fascist military junta, but until I stumbled upon this statue was not aware of the detail.

This quiet spot in the town is a fitting tribute to the normality this extraordinary young man gave his life to help establish. And in these dark days as Golden Dawn, the dubious benefactors of that evil oppression, fight to get a toehold in Greek politics, the story of this brave and principled man is well worth remembering.

Haltingly translating the plaque on the plinth of the statue, I am intrigued by his story and determined to find out more. I think the gist of it is:

'Kostas Georkakis, student, born Kerkyra 1948, died Genoa 1970. He burned himself to death in the Italian city of Genoa on the 19 September 1970 giving his life for the freedom and democracy of his homeland, Greece. "I can only think and act as a free individual."'

The son of a tailor from Corfu, Kostas lived in Kerkyra Town, close to where this statue stands today. Despite the family's meagre income, Kostas studied hard and won a place to further his education as an engineer in Genoa in Italy. His proud parents struggled to provide him with a small allowance, and Kostas was acutely aware of their sacrifice. Just four months after the colonels mounted their coup in 1967, Kostas left the family home to move to Italy.

A year later he became a member of deposed former Prime Minister George Papandreou's democratic Centre Unionist party and began to take an active interest in politics. Following the death of Papandreou whilst under the house arrest of the military dictatorship, Kostas became increasingly politicised, aware of the cruelty and hardships being suffered by the ordinary people in his homeland. Living abroad he was also conscious of the ignorance that existed outside Greece of the suffering of its people and the tyranny of the fascists. In 1970 an Italian magazine interviewed Kostas anonymously, and he expressed his views on the current situation and also exposed the activities of agents of the Junta who had infiltrated student bodies abroad.

He was right to be concerned about the activities of the dictatorship overseas and it was not long before those very same agents discovered his identity and began a campaign of persecution both against him and his family back at home.

He was beaten up on the streets of Genoa and he and his Italian fiancée were constantly harassed. The exemption students held from national service was withdrawn and the small financial allowance provided by his family to pay for his studies was intercepted and stolen. Powerless to escape the clutches of this evil regime and feeling guilty and afraid for his family, he set about drawing attention to the plight of his nation and made the ultimate sacrifice. In the middle of the night of the 19 September 1970 in Matteotti Square in Genoa, outside the Doges' Palace, his clothes doused in petrol, he set light to himself.

Hosing down the streets, the early morning cleaners rushed to extinguish the flames but he ran from them shouting, 'I did this for my country. Free Greece from the fascists. Long live free Greece!' By the time they caught him and the flames were extinguished it was too late and the inevitable happened, Kostas dying an agonizing death some 9 hours later.

This time the Junta were unable to stifle the attention Kostas' self sacrifice had turned on the regime, although it did not stop them from trying.

Some of the measures taken by the discredited dictatorship would have been laughable if not so sinister. Rumours that the Italian film director Gianni Serra was to make a film about Kostas' life sent the hapless colonels into a frenzy of undercover activities posing as buyers trying to snap up the rights so they would not fall into the hands of the BBC and the American networks.

But the genie was already well and truly out of the bottle, the right-wing dictatorship had already been dealt a significant blow. Following Kostas' death, opponents of the Junta mounted a vigil to prevent Greek agents from abducting his body. During his funeral cortège the internationally renowned Greek film star Melina Mercouri, who later went on to become Minister of Culture in the government of Andreas Papandreou, led a demonstration against the Junta.

In a press conference that followed a message of support for the demonstrators from Papandreou himself was read out. In the January of the following year, Kostas' body was secretly squirrelled out of Italy and, with only his family in attendance and under heavy guard from the authorities was buried in the cemetery in Kerkyra Town. In the square where he died in Genoa a plaque which bears the inscription *'La Grecia libera lo ricordera per sempre'*, 'He will be remembered forever by a free Greece'. I fervently hope over the coming months and years, as Greece is again threatened by supporters of the far right, that his sacrifice is remembered.

The End of the Road – Kavos

One of the best things about Kavos is that it is at the very southern tip of the island, thus sparing anyone who doesn't feel the need to explore here any reason to go near or pass through it. I feel I must mention this 'party town', as it is the holiday destination of choice for tens of thousands of tourists, mostly British, every year. If you find yourself having booked a holiday to Kavos and have never heard of it before, you have probably made a big mistake.

I have been criticised in my previous books for being too hard on places like Malia on Crete and Faliraki on Rhodes, interestingly always by people who run businesses there or who like to holiday in these hell holes. Intrinsically there is nothing wrong with Kavos, a long sandy beach providea great swimming and watersports facilities. Running parallel to the seafront is a dusty strip of bars, clubs and tavernas hugging this road to nowhere. For anyone who feels the need to investigate further, the morning is the time to come, as the streets are all but deserted while the village's temporary residents sleep off the excesses of the night before.

It is the favoured destination of any number of young adults, many of whom are holidaying alone for the first time seduced by the heady mix of cheap booze and sex. As far as that goes it is fair enough, but the fallout from over-consumption of alcohol is frequently messy and sometimes dangerous and the subsequent loss of inhibitions can cause offence to the local population.

It must be said that many of the people who live in the area are immune to such behaviour by now and see this annual influx of young, naïve tourists as the opportunity to make a fast buck. Whichever way you look at it, for the outsider looking in it is often not a pleasant spectacle. I have often wondered if by developing this resort at 'the end of the road' the Corfiot authorities have not been rather canny placing it out of sight and out of mind for the more discerning traveller whilst coining much needed revenue from those who enjoy the kind of holiday it provides. Any hint of Greek culture has been eroded here as English is the *lingua franca* spoken and clearly visible on signs and menus everywhere. The only nod to Greek food is *souvlaki*, which occasionally is available amongst the plethora of burger and fried chicken outlets.

The authorities have been careful not to allow high-rise building here, unlike in some other 'fun-loving' resorts around Greece. A swim away from the shore out to where the few remaining fishing boats are moored off the beach reveals a glimpse of what this village looked like before being caught in the grip of untrammelled hedonism and greed. It is not too late for Kavos to be put back together again if ever the will was there to do so.

Octopuses' Gardens

From the beach outside our house in Kaminaki I headed along a narrow coastal path that wound its way across the rocks that skirted the bay. A local, who fished every night, was setting his lines in the milky sea.

The wind disappeared as evening drew nearer, and the break in the rain gave me the rare opportunity to explore on foot. Out to sea a mist hovered only feet above the surface, leaving the coast of Albania a barely detectable outline in the distance.

As I took the gentle climb away from the beach, the path was slippery with mud. Houses and villas were dotted around the hillside, all in the vivid pastel shades of yellow, red, blue and terracotta so typical of Corfiot buildings. Flowers were still in bloom and the whole hillside was covered in dripping, verdant greenery pierced by tall cypresses.

I had been hoping to get to Prospero's Cell chapel and the underwater cave made famous by Lawrence Durrell in his book of the same name. As the path reached its highest point before descending into the next bay, I was confronted by a long beach strewn with seaweed brought ashore by the previous night's storm. A few hardy holidaymakers were making the most of the dry weather lying on sun loungers, whilst others, mostly children, played in the sea.

In front of me, built right on the water's edge, stood a yellow architectural monstrosity. The Nissaki Beach Hotel was not looking its best in the early-evening gloom, and was blocking my path. Not being dressed to swim around the headland, I sat on the sand to contemplate my options.

A spear fisherman emerged from the water, a tripod gun and fins in one hand and a dead octopus dangling from the other. I have eaten and enjoyed octopus, but have been put off it after going on one of the best trips I have experienced in the Ionian. It was not on Corfu, but Lefkas, the next major island to the south. Out of the port of Nidri we went out on a small caique owned by a marine biologist who was researching the local environment and doing work to conserve the marine life, in particular the octopus.

A highly intelligent animal, octopus numbers are getting dangerously low around the shores of Greece due to over-fishing. The skipper and his team of researchers would move the creatures to safe havens, which no doubt didn't endear them to the local fishermen. It is not, however the spear hunters or even the traditional pot fishers who are causing the devastation, but the larger-scale operations.

Part of the problem is that, although intelligent, octopuses are quite easy to catch if fishing in the right area. They have been hunted since ancient times and the method of catching them has changed little in technique, only in scale.

Traditionally ceramic pots were lowered onto the seabed and left overnight. As octopuses like to hide in holes they take advantage of these ready-made hideouts and climb inside, only to be hauled to the surface by fishermen the next morning. Nowadays this method is replicated but using huge numbers of plastic pots in known local habitats, very quickly devastating the octopus population.

The sight of fishermen tenderizing their catch by bashing them on the quayside before hanging them out to dry from the rigging of their boats has been commonplace in Greece for centuries, and evidence of their fishing goes back to Minoan times. A carving excavated from the Palace of Knossos in Crete shows a fisherman carrying his catch. It would be a shame to see sustainable fishing have to come to an end because of the over-exploitation of these waters.

Octopuses really do have gardens; on the trip in question we went diving in a number of locations and saw several. They look like walled areas, which in fact are made up of the deposits of broken shells of crabs and shellfish that the octopus has eaten in his lair.

The biologist caught a live octopus and put it in a large aquarium aboard the boat for us to observe. Apparently they can learn tasks like taking corks out of bottles or remembering geometrical shapes, and they have been known to board small fishing boats and enter their holds to find crabs! Some years later I returned to Nidri, but the biologist had moved on. However, whilst in Fiskardo on Kefalonia recently I noticed a similar boat excursion advertised.

The light can rarely do wrong for me in Greece but that day on Corfu the gathering dusk held little promise and I decided to return back over the rocks to our own little bay. Tonight we could light a barbecue and sit out. Warmed by the glowing embers we would cook our food by the light of citronella candles, watching the disembodied rows of lights ghost through the mist-filled darkness as ships made their to-ings and fro-ings from Kerkyra Town to the south.

Ioannis Kapodistrias – A Voice for Unity

I have to admit that after having landed several times at Corfu's Ioannis Kapodistrias International, I was none the wiser as to who it was who had lent his name to the island's bustling airport. It was only when I stumbled across a statue of a man that bears the name, near Kerkyra's Old Fortress, that the cogs started turning and I became intrigued by who he might be. That I had not heard of him before is surprising as the full name of Athens' university is 'The National and Kapodistrian Unniversity of Athens', and in Corfu itself there is a Kapodistrias museum near Evropouli just a few miles to the west of Kerkyra Town.

On finding out more about Ioannis Kapodistrias, I felt somewhat ashamed of my ignorance as many people consider him the man responsible for ushering in the modern independent Greek state. More than that, this Corfiot-born diplomat gave his life in the service of his country when he was assassinated in 1831, aged just 55, in the then capital Nafplion, of that first Hellenic republic.

Born into a well-to-do family he was entitled a count, being a member of the Corfiot nobility listed in the *Libro d'Oro* a book of all those considered to be nobles by the ruling Venetians that had been instituted since 1572. His father, a prominent politician and artist, could trace his ancestry back to the gulf of Venice before the family moved to Corfu in the 13th Century.

His mother was also of noble stock, a countess whose family had found their way to Corfu in the face of the Ottoman invasion of their native Cyprus in the 16th Century.

A brilliant student, Ioannis studied the law and philosophy as well as medicine at Padua University in Italy before returning to his native Corfu aged just 21 to set up a medical practice. This was in 1797, the same year as the forces of Napoleon initiated the demise of the Venetian Empire, and Corfu was ceded to France. This was not to last, however, and just two years later, in 1799, Russia and the Ottomans, aghast at the danger posed by the forces of post-revolutionary France, took the islands from the French by force and set them up as an independent Ionian state known as the *Septinsular* Republic.

Being a brilliant man of noble birth, Kapodistrias was selected as one of the ministers of this fledgling state, and his sensitivity and legal and philosophical training made him a highly-respected politician. When democratic elections to the new Senate were implemented in 1802, Kapodistrias won a landslide victory to become chief minister.

Although the newly-appointed ministers were somewhat limited in their jurisdiction, Kapodistrias made his mark with radical changes to the health and education policies of the islands. But the political machinations of this troubled part of the world decreed that France's fortunes were again in the ascendancy and, in 1807, they duly retook the Ionian Islands and abolished the infant republic, replacing it with a governor, Francois-Xavier Donzelot.

Strangled at birth the new republic may have been, but Kapodistrias had caught the eye of Emperor Alexander I of Russia. He was recruited to the Russian diplomatic service in 1809 before becoming instrumental in securing independence for Switzerland in the face of the diplomatic shenanigans of the Austrians and French at the Congress of Vienna in 1815. Alexander I rewarded Ioannis by appointing him Russia's joint Foreign Minister.

His involvement on the world stage of international affairs had made him a consummate politician but Ioannis still remained true to his liberal and humanitarian principles. When the game was finally up for Napoleon Bonaparte, following his defeat at Waterloo, the Ionian Islands became a British protectorate. They installed Sir James Campbell as the first in a line of High Commissioners of the islands. Although the British had got their feet well and truly under the table in the island of his birth, Kapodistrias became more and more involved in the wider picture of a united Greece, and in 1822 he left the service of the Russian court and decamped to Geneva from where he dedicated himself to supporting the revolutionary Greek cause as they fought to overthrow their Ottoman rulers.

When, in 1827, the Peloponnese was liberated and a Greek National Assembly was formed to rule this tiny package of land and to further espouse the cause of Greek unity and independence, it was Kapodistrias to whom they turned. His ship sailed into the capital of the newly-formed Greek Republic, Nafplion, in the first week of the new year of 1828 to a welcome which all of Greece hoped would usher in a new era led by their first elected head of state.

It was the first time Kapodistrias had set foot on the mainland of the country he now governed. But, as is often the case with infant democracies, it was difficult to find a consensus. Although Kapodistrias held firm to his fervent belief that education and rights of the individual were paramount in establishing a successful democratic state, he struggled to quell the traditional conflicts that raged between factional dynasties in the region. This, coupled with continued hostilities with Ottoman forces around the edges of the state, made the task of government almost impossible. Fiercely independent and angry at their lack of inclusion in the new government, the powerful families of the Mani and Roumeli regions resisted the rule of Kapodistrias and refused to contribute the taxes imposed. They rebelled against the new regime and seized the Greek Navy's ships in Poros.

Kapodistrias found support from his old allies, the Russians, who sent a fleet to stand off Poros while a small force of Greek soldiers attacked the rebels from the land. The revolt was over, but the action was unpopular and several ships were destroyed.

Counter to his libertarian instincts, Kapodistrias felt forced to impose more draconian measures to keep control of the small republic and prevent further civil war from breaking out. In 1831 he took the decision to arrest the leader of the Mani, Petrobey Mavromichalis. This was a brave decision as the Mavromichalis family was the most powerful dynasty in the region and adhered to a code of family honour, which showed no respect to any who slighted them. Their revenge was swift. Ioannis Kapodistrias was assassinated by a knife in the stomach and a bullet to the head administered by Petrobey's son, Georgios, and his brother, Konstantis, on the steps of Nafplion's Church of St Spyridon.

Although not universally popular towards the end of his life, Kapodistrias was responsible for the many reforms that made giant strides in the health of the nation and also introduced its first currency. He is also credited with signing the armistice that ended the war with Turkey. This heralded the ambition for *enosis* for the Hellenic states and islands which eventually resulted in the current Greek state.

Kapodistrias also has something in common with the British buccaneer Sir Walter Raleigh. If rumour is to be believed, it was his ingenious plan to relieve poverty and starvation that led to the introduction of the potato to his country. That this story is as likely to be apocryphal as the one attributed to Raleigh himself is neither here nor there because now it has become part of Greek folklore. It is said that, being familiar with potatoes from his years spent living abroad, Ioannis was keen to introduce this nutritious, cheap and easy to grow tuber to his native land. He tried, but his initial attempts were met with indifference. Then the wily doctor stumbled on a plan, which played on the national psyche of his countrymen.

He ordered a large cargo of spuds to be shipped to the harbour of Nafplion. Here they were unloaded with as much brouhaha as possible before being surrounded by a heavily-armed guard. The perceived value of the unfamiliar vegetables was not wasted on the local population. Consequently they sought ingenious ways of diverting the guards' attention so the cargo could be stolen from under their noses. With orders to let the pilferers get away with their ill-gotten gains, the humble crop acquired an elevated status. Now perceived as desirable, potatoes have been planted in most of the local smallholdings from that day.

I'd like to think the story was true. Whatever the case, it is just one more thing for which the Corfiot people should be proud to honour their favourite son. He is buried next to the grave of his younger brother, Augustinos, who briefly succeeded him as Governor of Greece for all of six months, before the Great Powers, who had been aching to install a monarchy to the newly-formed state which they feared was sliding towards anarchy, imposed the Bavarian prince Otto on the throne in 1832.

They lay in the Monastery of Playtera, in Mandouki, a suburb of Kerkyra Town hard by the commercial port. This monastery is little visited, perhaps because it is off the beaten track. But it is only a short stroll out of the centre of town, and well worth a look. As you approach, the monastery cannot be missed as the red-roofed campanile of the building completed in 1866 soars some 100 ft, dominating the skyline.

The entrance to the basilica lies in a tranquil courtyard in the shade of the belfry. The darkness of the interior makes for a cool comparison with the heat and light dancing off the honey and white stucco of the exterior walls. A well where the monks drew their water is surrounded by tubs of plants and the occasional bifurcated palm tree, which has penetrated the undulating slabs of the flagstone flooring.

Little light filters into the church, but the walls are ablaze with colour. Vibrant icons, silver and gold ornaments, candelabra and chandeliers, white painted balustrades, and the raised pulpit on top of which stands, perched, an eagle lectern, golden wings outstretched, illuminate the dusky shade. Around the edges of the chapel, in twilit nooks and crannies, the headstones of those interred, including the Kapodistrias brothers, lie diffident. But it is the icons that are perhaps of most interest, for they include works by the celebrated artists Nikolaos Koutouzis and Nikolaos Kantounis. That these works exist at all is a miracle for which we should be grateful.

Fifty years after Chrisanthos Syropoulos, a monk from the more southerly island of Lefkas, founded the monastery in 1743, French troops under the colours of Napoleon occupied the island. This occupation was short lived. In the face of the onslaught of a combined Russian and Turkish siege they torched the building but, being French, their artistic sensibilities prevailed. The works of art and religious finery were cached away safely and returned to the church following its subsequent restoration in the second half of the 19th Century when the bell tower was added and the community was walled in.

Nikolaos Koutouzis came from Zakynthos, an island some 120 miles south. Not only was he a masterful painter, but a fine exponent of the arts of music and poetry. Like many artists of his day, he spent time in Venice and learned from the masters there. When he returned to his homeland, he was ordained into the priesthood in 1770.

Nikolaos Kantounis was also from Zakynthos, and also became a priest, he at the tender age of 19 years. Heavily influenced by Venetian painting, both artists' work in this small chapel in Corfu is less expansive than many of their better-known canvases that hang in the National Gallery in Athens or in the museums on their native island. They are nonetheless exquisite, and alone make a visit to this monastery worthwhile.

In addition to the University of Athens and the airport in Greece being named in his honour, the celebrated Cretan writer Nikos Kazantzakis wrote a play, the tragedy called *Kapodistria*, in Ioannis' honour. Just a few miles to the west of Kerkyra Town, on a hilltop in the small village of Evropouli is the Kapodistrias Museum and Centre for Kapodistrian Studies. In the very building that has been in the Kapodistrian family for generations and was used by the great man himself as a summer house is a curated collection celebrating his life and achievements. Maria Kapodistria, the great granddaughter of Ioannis' younger brother, George, bequeathed the house to the nation. Maria herself was a significant figure in Greek politics, being the first woman to become a mayor. She held office in Corfu between 1956 and 1959 and donated the house to the nation in 1979. It was opened as a museum two years later.

When the Rains Came

It started overnight. Autumn in Corfu came in with a bang that year taking no time to ingratiate itself as was its usual custom. Like an unwanted gate-crasher it rolled up at the party and wouldn't leave. Just a few hours earlier I'd been swimming, the weak October sun still giving all that could be expected of it.

We spent the evening outside on the terrace as day slipped into darkness and the night ferries from Kerkyra slid out of port to the south and sailed through the straits bound for Brindisi in Italy. The lightning came first, illuminating the Albanian mountains a few miles to the east. Then the downpour began.

Big drops of rain bounced vertically off the water, ushering in the hint of a breeze that before long grew, whipping up the waves which crashed on the beach in euphonious concert with the ever more frequent rumbles of thunder as the storm drew nearer. From under our arbour of vine, the view was spectacular.

We sat, enthralled by its beauty, the flickering citronella candles failing to halt the invasion of mosquitoes heading indoors encouraged by the damp atmosphere outside and the warmth and light inside. Unwilling to pass inland over the imposing figure of Mount Pantocrator, the storm circled throughout the night. Sometimes flattering to deceive by calming as it moved away, only to return minutes later with renewed vigour.

And so the weather was to remain. Still warm, but in a reversal of the customary bright days with some rainfall, the sun rarely penetrated, and the heavens felt no inhibition to open, sometimes leaving rainbows spanning from the lush green hillsides to the milky sea.

The Miracle of Kassiopi

I have taken to buying my fruit and veg from a small shack that sits on a run off on the road which travels north out of Kerkyra Town along the east coast. The displays outside are stunning in their colour and quality. The freshness of the produce is in no doubt as farmers frequently stop by to drop off their harvest straight from the earth. Today we are on our way to the small resort of Kassiopi on the north-east coast of Corfu, and stop off to buy some oranges, grapes and bananas for our picnic. The elderly lady who runs the business has fast become a friend and greets us with an offering of grapes and melon before we shop.

After choosing our fruit we move to the shady back of the shack to get it weighed and pay. As we do our friend scuttles through a gap in the wall carrying a plate, which she proffers, signalling that we should eat. A mound of shining amber-coloured jewels is pushed towards us. I try one. Sticky, the flavour is sweet and intense with a slight bitterness as you chew. I ask her what it is and she rounds the counter pulling me outside by the sleeve, where she picks up a kumquat from her magnificent display. I have drunk kumquat liqueur, which is ubiquitous on the island, but have never had it raw, or as a glacéd sweet.

Biting into the fresh fruit the flavour is extraordinary. The smooth, dimpled orange skin is sweet but the inner flesh is bitter, in a reversal of its fellow citrus fruit the orange. Here it is cherished, and Corfu is the only place in Europe where it is commercially grown and it has even been given Protected Designation of Origin status by the EU. But it is only a relatively recent addition to the island's agrarian repertoire. Despite being new on the scene, there are the inevitable discrepancies as to how it arrived here, although there is consensus that, along with the introduction of cricket, the British were responsible.

Originally from the Far East, its English name, derived from Cantonese, gives a clue as to its source and it is indeed to China where this small citrus fruit can be traced back, it is mentioned in writings dating back to the 12th Century. Prolific in the countries of south-east Asia, kumquats are hardy evergreens whose fruitfulness makes them an attractive cash crop across the region. The plant became familiar in Europe and subsequently in America after being brought back to London by horticulturalist Robert Fortune in 1846 and subsequently was established as part of the British Colonial plan to increase the commercial viability of Corfu's farming community during their brief control of the island in the first half of the 19th Century.

A more romantic, although less likely version of how the tree came to such prevalence on the island, is the story of Sidney Merlin. This Greek born son of a British diplomat won a gold medal in the shooting competition at the Athens Olympics of 1906 and went on to travel the world, returning to his estate in Corfu bringing with him a kumquat tree from Japan, that he planted there in the years between the world wars. He also had an estate on Crete which, in the face of the oncoming German invasion during World War Two, became the home of the Greek War Cabinet. When Crete finally succumbed to the German Forces with them practically on his doorstep, he and his family and household fled to Sfakia on the south-western coast and were evacuated by a British naval vessel.

Whichever story you chose to believe, the kumquat has become an unlikely part of Corfiot culture and cuisine. The liqueur of the ripe fruit macerated in vodka or other clear spirit is sold as a souvenir throughout the island. Marmalade is also made; alongside the sweet preserve we are now being offered.

Soaked in water, then dried in the sun the kumquats are immersed in a syrup of sugar, lemon juice and vanilla, which they greedily absorb before being stored in an air-tight jar for preservation. A spoon of this delicious treat is often given as a traditional show of hospitality to a guest, a simple offering showing generosity to strangers and friends alike.

With our picnic aboard we set off again, and in no time leave the flat, open beach of Ipsos behind us. At Pirgi the road climbs steeply and winds around the tree-lined cliffs that abut the deepest of blue seas glimpsed in flashes beneath us to our right. Despite being the main thoroughfare on this side of the island, the road is quiet enough for us to enjoy the spectacular views and the verdurous plant life that spring from every nook and cranny in the rock. Every meadow is laced with a full palette of colour and each shady orchard floor with a carpet woven in every imaginable hue. The road winds its way through tiny villages where it frequently narrows, only accommodating single file vehicles, and to our right tracks plunge seawards down impossibly steep gradients through the olive groves.

We pass turnings to our familiar stomping grounds of Agni, Kaminaki, Kalami and Agios Stefanos, determined not to be diverted from arriving at our ultimate destination of Kassiopi.

A resort town, Kassiopi is the largest along this north-east coast of hidden exclusive enclaves, and has a mixed reputation. Walking down the road that leads to the harbour, it is not difficult to see why. The needs of the tourist are at the forefront of the town's commercial imagination. Bars, clubs, souvenir shops and travel agents prevail, but have not snuffed out the welcoming atmosphere the town exudes. It would be cantankerous to complain about the recent arrival of these fun palaces as it is believed that the discredited Roman Emperor Nero passed this way and danced in front of the altar in the temple his forbears had built in honour of Jupiter here. The Roman incarnation of the Greek god Zeus, also sometimes known as Kassius, is thought to have lent its name to the town when it was established as a pivotal port of the Epirotic Empire.

The Romans were not the first to recognize the glories of this spot of great natural beauty. Its wooded hills and shingle bays are protected from the worst the sea can throw at them by the natural promontories which shelter the small harbour. More recently this was further protected from human invasion by a castle on the northern outcrop.

The Corinthians first developed the town, when Kerkyra became part of the Hellenic League in the 3rd Century BC. After this it regularly changed hands before Corfu was offered as a dowry by one of its conquerors, Agathocles, on the marriage of his daughter Lanassa to the King of the Epirotic Alliance. It was this king, Pyrrhus, who gave the town the name Kassiopi, which has stuck, even after the island succumbed to the Romans in 299 BC.

Nero was not alone in taking the voyage across the Adriatic to sample the delights of the town. The generals Tiberius and Mark Anthony also made landfall here, as did the philosopher Cicero and statesman Cato. The Romans, as far as we know, were the first to build a fortress looking down on the harbour. This fortress was further modernized during Byzantine times before the Angevins built another castle on the site sometime in the 13th Century which, alongside those fortifications in Gardiki and Angelokastro, turned the island into a redoubt. Weak rule from strong castles, however, was not enough to protect the island from a mounting wave of attacks from disparate groups of medieval pirates and fortune seekers. The weakened house of Anjou finally succumbed to the inevitable and, despite making a last stand in the castle of Kassiopi, surrendered themselves to the protection of the powerful Venetian state in 1386.

Standing at the gateway to the Adriatic, the strategic importance of their new acquisition did not pass the new rulers by. The Venetians knocked down the old fortress and built another even more formidable stronghold, and it is the remains of this castle that still sits upon the hill overlooking the harbour. Restoration work is ongoing, as archaeologists are painstakingly trying to reconstruct the old castle walls.

On the right-hand side of the town's main street as you walk towards the sea, set back from the road, is the church of the Blessed Virgin Kassopitra. A splash of purple wisteria half conceals the entrance to this chapel, which was built on top of the original temple to Jupiter Kassius. It was rededicated as a Christian church in the 5th Century before being razed to the ground by marauding Turkish troops during a failed attempt to invade the island in 1537.

The Venetian rulers rebuilt the church, but this new place of worship was unusual in that it had two altars, one for each of the prevailing Orthodox and Catholic faiths. Inside the church is an icon of the Blessed Virgin, which holds particular significance to those who have worshipped here as it has long been held to have miraculous powers. If St Spyridon had not such a firm hold on his role as the island's protector, this icon would be in with a good shout to take his place. Well before the body of the Cypriot bishop ended up on these shores, this icon had performed her great miracle and turned Kassiopi into a place of pilgrimage. The sick, distressed and impoverished would come to this small town to seek succour from this vision of the Virgin. It was in medieval times that the icon had performed the miracle that earned her this reputation.

It is said that a boy, Stephen, had been falsely accused of stealing flour and, under the rough justice of the times, had had his eyes put out. For several years the lad struggled with his disability and the injustice of his plight. Living off the charity of strangers, one night he sought refuge in the church and miraculously his sight was given back to him and he found himself staring upon a vision of the holy Virgin. His eyes had been brown before his blinding but now were a vibrant blue. Every 8 May there is a sacred day held to celebrate the miracle. The icon hangs veiled in a canopy of lace, surrounded by votive flowers, orange marigolds, white lilies and daisies and yellow roses. The Virgin is dressed in gold with a red robe and haloed in silver and lifts the tranquil gloom of the church which makes a welcome contrast to the bustling brashness of the town's main thoroughfare.

If the eponymous church appears incongruous among the tacky temples to tourism that surround it, take a walk to the seaward end of the street that opens up to the town's unlikely treasure of the seafront. Dotted with tavernas and kafenions, the harbour front is the perfect place to sit and watch fishing boats take to sea and tours set out on trips to the coast of Albania, a few miles to the east.

This spot wins us over. We sit savouring cold beer and ice cream as swallows flit in and out of the rafters above while we contemplate the steep walk to the castle that looks down on us from the headland. Maybe another day!

Paxos

Where Life Stands Still

Corfu's satellite island group of Paxi is the smallest cluster in the Ionian. It is made up of Paxos, its close neighbour Antipaxos and several smaller acolytes. Paxos lies just 30 miles shy of the southern tip of Corfu and little more than eight miles further than that from Kerkyra Town. In the summer months it can be reached by the Flying Dolphin hydrofoil service from the town's new port in little over one hour.

I have always had a sentimental attachment to travelling the Greek islands by ship, so we chose to travel this way, despite the passage taking almost four times as long and going via the mainland port of Igoumenitsa. Arriving at the dock I was somewhat smug at having made that decision as the wind blew in a darkening sky which, combined with an irritable grey sea, foretold of a lumpy crossing that was not to be entirely unexpected in mid October.

From the comfort of the saloon we listened as the comforting thud of the engines warmed up for the task ahead. Bow and stern lines were winched aboard as the ship edged away from the quay and turned its broad shoulders into the oncoming swell. Rolling comfortably like a habitual drunk finding his way home on autopilot, we left the shelter of the port behind. Spray from the churning sea competed with the lashing rain to obliterate all views from the salt-stained windows as we cosied ourselves inside to read, clasping cups of hot chocolate.

After docking at Igoumenitsa the rain stopped as quickly as it had begun and the sun re-established itself. Memory of the storm washed clean, the only reminder a sea still grumbling as we rode its galloping white horses south. Legend tells us that Poseidon created the island of Paxos. As the God of the Sea, he sought somewhere to escape from the pressures of his day-to-day duties. Striking the southern tip of Corfu with his trident, he sheared a rugged shard from the island and towed it south to create a refuge for himself and his wife, Amphitrite. To this day it remains a place of escape for many of the rich and famous, and the modern-day traveller here will still find a place to escape the pressures of everyday life.

As the ferry draws close to the island capital of Gaios, we stand at the guardrail. The scale of the tiny port makes clear the self-contained understatement of this fertile paradise. A few red-tiled tavernas sit across from the harbour road, beside and behind which a sprinkling of whitewashed houses and shops make their way up the gentle hillside. The village whispers its intention to keep the pace of its life so slow that sleeping might be considered an unnecessary exertion.

It is now afternoon and we have been on the go since early morning, so opt to have lunch at one of the quayside tavernas and watch the world go by before we seek some accommodation for the night. We had heard good things about the Genesis restaurant right on the front and, although at first wary of its up-market appearance, it does not disappoint. The *kleftico* is of a quality that I have never savoured before, the leg of lamb almost melting into the seasoning of rosemary, oregano and lemon with a cinnamon finish that takes the edge off the dry, chilled red wine that accompanies it.

Out to sea, the view of the island that protects this tiny port is splendid. A fortress built by the Venetians in the 15th Century stands on the tree-strewn island of St Nicholas, and the smaller islet of Panagia at its tip is home to a walled lighthouse and an ancient church. Its light still guides seafarers home and the islands themselves protect the channel from the worst ravages of the sea as, in times gone by, they had from unwanted invaders.

The Venetians were just one in a long line of those who had craved the virtues of this tiny Ionian haven. Its proximity to Corfu meant that, after its larger cousin had been appropriated by some passing power, it was never long before Paxos suffered a similar fate. The Phoenicians made it part of their homeland, although evidence suggests earlier settlement by prehistoric tribes. The Romans annexed it to their empire, which in turn ceded ownership to Byzantium as the axis of power swung eastwards.

The island became an outpost of the Venetian empire in the latter years of the 14th Century. A period of protection and stability of more than 400 years followed. The Italian rulers bequeathed upon the island the legacy of its dense counterpane of olive trees held in terraces by drystone walls exhibiting a formality that betrays their origin. Through these groves, hidden paths dustily infiltrate their ways to isolated villas and farmsteads. I do not have the figures to hand, but the density of the olive groves here must be one of the heaviest in the world. In places the only relief from their relentless coverage is the occasional pine tree or cypress perforating the canopy.

We found a comfortable room in a small hotel and a stroll around the 'capital' confirmed our hopes that there was little to do here, and we had several days in which to bathe in that delicious idleness which Paxos engenders. There are two other 'significant' settlements on this modest sanctuary which runs to just seven miles from Lakka on the northern tip to the cliffs and sea caves of the south where a bridge connects the island to Mogonisi with its views over to Kaltsonisi a stone's throw away. At its widest, the island's waist measures a slender three miles. Between the harbour village of Lakka and the capital, Gaios, on the east coast lies the somnolent community of Longos. Buses rattle down the dusty roads between these three centres, but the scale of the island and the leisurely pace of life encourages those with time to explore by foot.

As Venetian power waned under the ambition of the invading forces of Napoleon, the tiny island was taken by the bullying Franco-Turkish Alliance. This, in turn, brought it to the attention of the British who were at odds with the French general. In 1814 a stand-off by the British man of war *HMS Apollo* with her armoury trained on the capital and an expeditionary force of some 160 soldiers aboard ready to storm the beaches, led to the French surrendering their brief residency. The following year the Ionian Union was formed under a British Governor as the precursor to the whole of the Ionian Islands' *enosis* with the new Greek nation in 1864.

I have not visited yet, but Antipaxos, just to the south, can be reached by ferry from Gaios in the blink of an eye. It is hard to imagine, but life on this tiny square mile of land floating in the lee of our current location is lived at a pace hardly perceptible by any known measure. Not much more than 100 people inhabit this tiny rock but, in season, a handful of tavernas set up close to its near perfect sandy beaches. There are no hotels to be found here, although a few locals do rent out rooms.

This little island has a big reputation for the quality of its vineyards and the wine they produce. If the paradisiacal perfection of that panorama is reflected in the taste of its fruit, it is not difficult to understand why. If ever I was looking for a real retreat, Antipaxos would be somewhere near the top of my list to try. For my needs Paxos was doing just fine, and did not encourage me to move on anywhere, so we stay put, enjoying the simple pleasures of food and drink and swimming in the remote coves where the sea nibbles at Poseidon's island. Time slows down here and in the course of the couple of days spent strolling from beach to taverna and back our stay felt more like a week before it was time to return to Kerkyra Town.

Kefalonia

To Kefalonia by Boat

The July sun was just starting to signal its intent for the day ahead as we made an early morning start from the harbour at Vasiliki. When past the harbour wall, the skipper Georgos pushed the throttle forward and the rib inflatable rose up onto a plane, thrust out of the water by the enormous twin outboard motors mounted on the stern. The boat flattened out and skimmed effortlessly across the flat calm Ionian as Lefkas rapidly became an outline of cliffs on the horizon.

We were heading for Kefalonia, the largest of the Ionian archipelago, which lies just 10 nautical miles south of Lefkas. The breeze created as the rib flew forward was welcome and the odd bit of spray thrown up when the boat encountered wash from passing shipping helped neutralise the effect of an already scorching sun.

It takes the ferry from Vasiliki an hour and a half to travel the distance between the two islands but in these calm conditions, at full throttle in the rib, we made the passage in somewhat less than half an hour. We entered a deserted bay only accessible by boat where the cliffs rise vertically off the beach. No paths run here so we had it all to ourselves. The beach is in the shade of the backdrop of rocks but the water is still like a warm bath.

We anchored up and rolled backwards off the inflatable tubes to snorkel in the crystal clear water. I don't know whether it's the bay's relative isolation, or the shade provided by the vertiginous shoreline but the waters provide a haven for the most dazzling array of fish, a rainbow of colours shoaling across the rocks and golden sands beneath us.

I returned to the rib for some pellets, and dived down among the larger fish, holding out my hand. Remarkably unafraid they darted in to feed, grabbing the food before retreating to rejoin their shoal.

Climbing back into the boat, we lay in the sun to dry off before setting out to sea and around the headland at the northernmost tip of the island into the channel that separates it from its neighbour Ithaka. Going more slowly now, we could take in the stunning shoreline as we headed south.

The hilly landscape is a patchwork of olive groves and cypresses. A small car ferry crossed ahead, its wake causing the bow to momentarily slap up and down, sending more refreshing spray flying into our faces.

We turned inland following the course of the ship. Up on a hill is a tall, rectangular, grey stone lighthouse and below it, down the hillside, a much shorter, squat cylindrical structure. This, Georgos explained, is the old 16th-century Venetian lighthouse that was decommissioned when the taller, more visible tower replaced it in 1892. This is the light that still guides boats into the small harbour of Fiskardo that we were now entering.

To our right the ferry had moored bow first to its small quay and its crew were winching the ramp down for its cargo of cars and foot passengers from Lefkas to disembark. The rest of the small harbour is picture perfect. Multi-coloured fishing boats bob up and down on their moorings, nets glistening on the decks and red and yellow buoys tied to their rails. Among them, moored stern-in, are flotillas of sailing boats and privately-owned yachts and motorboats of all shapes and sizes.

Skirting the L-shaped harbour is a cluster of traditional 18th-century Venetian-built houses, tavernas, cafes and shops painted in a multitude of pastel shades, providing the backdrop to this busy village; fishermen, waiters and tourists all going about their business in the mid-morning sunshine. Rising up behind the waterfront houses, the surrounding hills are densely populated with rich forest, only broken by the occasional villa set in a clearing overlooking the straits.

We rafted up alongside a couple of other boats and took a stroll through the winding streets. We walked under the shade of numerous striped awnings and sprays of bougainvillea of every hue, which overflowed from the balconies above. Fiskardo is one of the more fortunate among the towns and villages on the island in that its buildings survived the terrible earthquakes of 1953 which caused so much devastation elsewhere.

In August of that year, four earthquakes hit Kefalonia. The largest, measuring 7.3 on the Richter scale, had its epicentre directly below the southern end of the island and destroyed the majority of buildings in the area. This, following the devastation wreaked on the island a decade earlier in the Second World War, means that many of the buildings are relatively modern.

The terrible history of Kefalonia during the war is well known, not least as a result of the English writer Louis de Bernieres' 1994 novel *Captain Corelli's Mandolin*. The book and the subsequent film released seven years later tell the tale of the developing love between Pelagia, the daughter of the local doctor, and Antonio Corelli, a captain with the occupying Italian forces.

This fictional story is set against the remarkable events that unfolded after the invasion of Greece by the Axis powers. Enemy forces that mostly comprised Italian personnel, along with a much smaller German contingent, occupied Kefalonia. Following Italy's armistice with the Allies in September 1943, the Italian forces sought to return home.

The German command, however, not wanting Italian weapons to fall into the hands of the islanders, demanded they be surrendered to them. Not trusting the Germans to let them go, the Italians refused to hand over their arms and dug in awaiting evacuation while the Germans sent reinforcements to the island.

The former allies were now at war with one another and the fighting came to a head with the siege of the capital, Argostoli. After brutal hand-to-hand fighting in the streets, the town fell to the German forces. Of the surviving Italian troops, around 5,000 were subsequently massacred as a reprisal by the Germans.

De Bernieres' book has in no small way added to the island's popularity as a tourist destination. The subsequent building of more facilities to accommodate and service that trade has been welcomed as a valuable source of income by most of the islanders. Fiskardo itself, however, has been spared much of such redevelopment. Planning regulations and conservation laws protect both its architectural heritage and the outstanding natural beauty of the surrounding hills.

We sat down at one of several quayside tavernas, to a plate loaded with seafood. Mullet, herring, mixed small fish and prawns grilled with herbs and sprinkled with olive oil and lemon juice were accompanied by bread, olives and a beer.

In contrast to the earlier passage, the return journey to Lefkas proved to be livelier. The afternoon wind rose noticeably as we left the shelter of the channel between Ithaka and Kefalonia and powered northwards into the open sea. The waves had turned into rollers and at high speed the rib would take off between crests, slamming down on landing before surging forward again to meet the next peak.

Going flat-out we got drenched and the salt spray stung as it hit and made the eyes sore. Wearing sunglasses for protection was not an option as they would be blown off in the wind or washed off by the bow waves. At lower speeds the boat would wallow and slam, jarring the back continuously. We opted for the high-speed option and just enjoyed the adrenaline rush. Georgos was a master of the conditions and his confidence made the whole experience exciting rather than terrifying.

The wash from passing ships had to be treated with more respect in these conditions and met bow on, so as not to risk capsizing. The wind-speed gauge was reading about 30 knots as we suddenly came into the lee of Lefkas and the sea conditions moderated as we approached the small harbour of Vasiliki. Hundreds of windsurfers were out just off the shallow sloping beach showing off their spectacular skills in the testing conditions. Soaked and exhilarated we climbed ashore, on the lookout for a cold drink to get rid of the taste of salt water.

Lefkas

Onassis's Island

Lefkas is a delight of an island that seems unnecessarily unsure of its credentials. Sandwiched between its better-known neighbours of Corfu to the north and Kefalonia to the south, it is something of a rough diamond. Driving along the unexceptional marshlands and onto the causeway approaching the swing bridge that connects Lefkas to mainland Greece, I ponder whether this is the key to the island's doubt about its true identity. Is it an island at all?

Greeks, more than any other nation, have a natural gravitational pull to their ancient past and it is true that the Corinthians only separated Lefkas from the mainland as recently as 650 BC. It was then that they cut the umbilical cord to the motherland by constructing the narrow canal, which the bridge now crosses.

It is, however, this very connection to the mainland that contributes to the island's ancient heritage. Locals believe that Lefkas is the mythical island of Ithaka (hotly disputed by the residents of the island that actually bears this name just to the south) that can be reached by foot in Homer's *The Odyssey*.

Be that as it may, although the island hides its light under a bushel, its charms have not gone unnoticed by the rich and famous. Most notable of these was the late Greek oligarch Aristotle Onassis. A statue of the tycoon stands proudly in the town of Nidri on the island's east coast. It looks seawards, out across the bay to Skorpios, the island retreat he bought from the Greek state in 1963.

Onassis is fondly remembered around these parts. He brought the island much-needed wealth, both personally and through his glamorous friends who visited and the tourist industry they engendered. His life is the stuff of legend. Born in Smyrna in Turkey in 1906 into a rich shipping family he was forced to leave, virtually penniless, following the persecution of the Greek population by the Ottoman Turks in 1923.

Ending up on the other side of the world in Buenos Aries, Argentina, the young entrepreneur quickly made a name for himself. He amassed a fortune out of the tobacco trade and shipping. The speed at which he became a millionaire would suggest that not all his business dealings were above board. Later in life he was quoted as saying that he would never trust anyone who would not accept a bribe!

The vast wealth he went on to accumulate bought him power, influence and women. His first marriage to Athina Livanos, the mother of his two children, Alexander and Christina, ended in 1960 when his wife caught him in bed with the opera diva Maria Callas. The affair finished when, in 1968, he married one of the most famous women in the world, Jaqueline Kennedy, the widow of the assassinated US President John F Kennedy.

That marriage was put under tremendous strain when Onassis' son, Alexander, tragically died in a plane crash at Athens' Ellinikon International Airport in 1973, aged just 24. It is said that his father never recovered from the heartbreak, and died two years later in France aged 69. He was buried alongside his beloved son's grave on Skorpios.

Skorpios, Meganissi and a number of other small islands are the destinations for a plethora of boat trips from Nidri. Although landing is not allowed on Skorpios, the boats go close in to the shore, some anchoring up so passengers can take a swim.

Lefkas derived its name from the Greek world *leukos*, meaning bright or brilliant white, the word used to describe the cliffs at the extreme south of the island. It is from these cliffs, so myth would have it, that the celebrated

Greek poet, Sappho, committed suicide, unable to bear the agony of her love for the ferryman Phaon.

Nidri, despite being the main tourist resort on the island, is a peaceful place. I also particularly like Vasiliki in the south. A small town characterized by its long, gently sloping beach, it is a Mecca for water sports enthusiasts, particularly windsurfers. Virtually every afternoon a strong wind blows across the bay, allowing the more experienced among the sailboarders to show off their prodigious sailing prowess.

In Vasiliki the pace of life is relaxed. The harbour is lined with a number of friendly tavernas that provide not only excellent food, but a grandstand view from which you can watch the antics of the yacht flotillas as they try to moor up for the night. Scrapings and collisions are commonplace and even the odd man overboard is not unheard of.

Bigger gin palaces also visit, with their professional crews in livery manoeuvring about the harbour with distain as diners crane their necks in case a celebrity might be spotted. Hours can be pleasurably soaked up here doing nothing but eating, drinking and watching the world go by; there is not much else to do here, something for which the visitor should be grateful.

Masters of the Sea

The sun had just risen as we launched our kayaks off the deserted beach. I shivered slightly as the first drops of water ran down the paddles and struck my arm. Heading south, the light bounced off the mercurial surface of the sea, its low trajectory making us squint and reach into our stuff bags for sunglasses. Nothing broke the surface except the rhythmic strokes of the four paddles in our two canoes, the whispering surge as we glided forward the only sound to interrupt the solitude.

Making an early start meant we could get some miles behind us before the sun rose high and slowed our pace. We reckoned that if we did not succumb to the temptation to stop off in every secluded bay, we could make the ten or so nautical miles to Sivota for a late morning breakfast.

With the lack of tide and flat calm the going was easy and we settled into a comfortable rhythm. The two kayaks left the slightest of wakes ruffling the surface of the bay. The route to Sivota from Vasiliki couldn't be simpler, just keep the land to port, first heading south to the headland then turn east, then north east until the well-camouflaged portal finally reveals itself, opening from its narrow entrance into a hidden, protected bay.

With visibility good and weather benign, the trip was everything we had hoped for. Each tiny headland rounded revealing another secret cove, many unreachable by land, giving a unique perspective on the southern coast of Lefkas. At our steady pace we reached Sivota by midday, pulling our canoes out at the slipway and settling into a seafront taverna for breakfast.

A little-known pearl of a place on the island, Sivota is situated down a winding road off the main route from Nidri to Vasiliki. On the wooded slopes surrounding the peaceful bay are pastel-coloured villas enjoying elevated views, the sun glinting on the gently swaying masts of the anchored yachts dotted around the bay. The few shops and businesses along the waterfront service the needs of visiting boats – provisioning, chandlers, brokerage and maintenance. It is the start point for some of the flotilla and bareboat charter companies and a stop-off for many others cruising the Ionian.

Refuelled with breakfast, refreshed by a snooze on the beach followed by a swim in the bay, we set off on the return journey. The breeze was just starting to rise, blowing over our port side as we left the shelter of the cove before, we hoped, pushing us from astern on the last part of our voyage home.

Leaving Sivota in our wake, we pushed on before finally approaching the headland where we would turn northwards. Keeping a metronomic rhythm, each of us remained in contented silence, lost in the experience. Then, not more than 50 yards in front of us, a fin broke the water, followed in quick succession by several more. It was difficult to count them as they would dive down and then reappear but there must have been more than ten.

Suddenly a dolphin leaped out of the water just in front of our bow. Its dark grey, almost black back, in stark contrast to its light underbelly, shimmered as the droplets of water it shrugged off hung in the air. Then another breached, its long snout identifying it as a bottlenose.

It was quite a size. I would say about eight feet long. We stopped paddling and watched this pod just play in the water around us. As we moved forwards they would swim slowly alongside. Ducking and diving they'd then get bored of our sedate pace and bolt ahead, leaping out of the water, before diving down only to emerge behind us in a very unequal game of chase.

I have seen dolphins many times around the islands, but this was the nearest I have been to these graceful creatures. In the canoes we got a sea-level view of their amazing athletic abilities and were more aware of their speed, size and power without once feeling threatened.

It is easy to see why the Greeks have revered these creatures since the earliest of times. The first scientific report on dolphins is recorded in *Historia Animalium* written by the Greek philosopher Aristotle in 350 BC. But well before then, these magnificent mammals appeared on coins, in jewellery and on frescoes and mosaics belonging to the Minoans. Stories about these sacred beasts were handed down through the generations even prior to this.

Legend has it that when the great Greek god of the sea Poseidon first saw and fell in love with Amphitrite, the embodiment of all sea creatures, she feared for her honour and fled to the seas at the other end of the earth. Smitten with love for her, Poseidon sent his loyal messenger the god of dolphins, Delphin, to seek her out and persuade her that the sea god's love was genuine so that Amphitrite would return and marry him. Delphin was true to his word and, as a reward, Poseidon set his image in stars in the form of the constellation Delphinius.

Because of their benevolent nature, and the part Delphin played in uniting the god of the oceans with the queen of the sea creatures, they are seen as good luck and protectors of all seafarers.

In the west wing of the palace at Knossos in Crete is the dolphin room, named after the brightly-coloured dolphin frieze that adorns the walls. This was reconstructed from thousands of pieces found scattered on the floor by archaeologists following Arthur Evans' excavations, the fresco having been shattered by the disaster that overcame the Minoan civilization in the second millennium BC. The vivid blues used in the paintings, although not strictly representational, do capture the spirit of these masters of the sea.

As we got to about a mile and a half offshore, the first of the hundreds of sailboards that ride the strong afternoon breezes from Vasiliki beach approached. With that, our companions dived one last time and left us.

Zakynthos

Zakynthos – Flower of the East

It would be hard to write about the Ionian Islands without the inclusion of Zakynthos, or Zante as it is known by its adopted Venetian name. From what I have seen of the island, it is worthy of more than I feel able to write about it. Unfortunately my experience of this third largest of the island group is limited to a day trip taken when visiting the Peloponnese, on the mainland, 13 miles to the east.

Said to look, from the air, like an arrowhead with its tip aimed at Kefalonia, its larger neighbour just nine miles northwards, until recently Zakynthos's reputation had belied its size as it hid behind the reputation of its more popular northerly cousins of Corfu and Kefalonia. The island's fortunes have, for most of its history, been shackled to those of these two islands but, recently, Zakynthos is starting to emerge from the shadows and become a popular destination in its own right.

Regular direct charter flights have brought an increasing prosperity from tourism supplementing the visitors who traditionally arrived by boat from Brindisi in Italy, Igoumenitsa and Kyllini on the Greek mainland or island hoppers from Kefalonia.

My boat set sail from the small port of Kyllini with all the practiced flourish of a ship that plies these waters every day, but for passengers like me with all the anticipation of sailing into the unknown. We pulled away from the dock at just after 8 o'clock on a morning packed with promise, and a sea smooth and glinting like spilt mercury. I was flying home from Preveza the next day so wanted to make the most of my trip by catching the first ferry out and the return packet at 7 p.m. That more people have experienced this island affectionately named '*Il fiore de Levante*' (Flower of the East) by the Venetians who once ruled here is down to the extending of the domestic airport in 1981 to take international flights, which have been increasing steadily in volume until nowadays they deposit more than half a million tourists here each year.

The clubs of the capital, also called Zakynthos, attract a younger crowd, but the beautiful beaches and traditional tavernas and laid back lifestyle also appeal to families. These modern-day travellers, if Homer is to be believed, are all following in the footsteps of the son of the legendary Trojan King Dardanos, named Zakynthos, who gave the island his name in the 16th Century BC. Archaeologists have unearthed artifacts that indicate that the Trojans were not the first settlers, with evidence pointing to human occupation of this spot since Neolithic times.

The founding father of the island is celebrated on the island's green flag that can sometimes be seen fluttering alongside the blue and white stripes of the motherland's ensign around the island. On the flag a representation of Prince Zakynthos sitting, outlined in gold, is captioned with the words of the 19th-century local poet Andreas Kalvos, '*theli areti ke tolmi I eleftheria*' ('to achieve freedom requires both virtue and courage'). The island was later to become part of King Odysseus' empire when the warrior conquered his more peaceable neighbours from his homeland of nearby Ithaka.

We had heard much about a beach only accessible by boat on the west coast of the island. Navagio beach was the last resting place of a ship, the *MV Panagiotis*, the washed up rusting hulk of which still lies unsalvaged on the pebble beach some yards from its natural environment of the turquoise waters of that bay. We had hired a high-speed inflatable rib to take us around the north coast of the island and down the western coast to Navagio and, minutes after setting foot on the island, we were heading back out of the entrance in the V-shaped harbour wall and setting a speedy course towards

Cape Skinari at the northern tip of the island. The sea looked inviting, but
still had an edge of chill as the spray from the bow wave brushed my cheeks.
Leaving the town astern, we skirted a coastline where groves of olive trees,
vineyards and orchards provided a backdrop to some spectacular sandy
beaches. We'd have loved to stop and I felt I was out of step with the pace of
life on the island, but time was short and I was determined to visit Navagio
and hopefully have time to experience the much-vaunted Blue Caves of the
Cape.

Less than half an hour after leaving port, the skipper throttled back and
the boat lowered itself down off the plane and edged towards some
extraordinary rock formations. The vicissitudes of the waters here had cut a
corridor of caves and arches out of the limestone cliffs beneath the lighthouse
that stands warning of their presence to passing shipping. The caves
themselves are spectacular, but it is beneath the water that they reveal their
true secret. Like some celestial kaleidoscope, the light conspires with lacunae
in the cliffs to sprinkle the sea in the magic dust of its own reflection and turn
everything that dives beneath its surface blue. The skipper anchors and hands
me a snorkel before rolling off the boat, down into the clear waters where he
glides, transformed into a chameleon of the sea. I too dive down into the cool
waters with shimmering rays of light penetrating deep below the surface like
spotlights illuminating colourful troupes of dancing fish. I must return here,
as it is one of the most spectacular places I have ever dived. Aware of our
tight schedule I return to the boat and we speed off to the pinnacle of the
Cape at Skinari. Still wet from my swim I pull on a T-shirt as we round the
headland, the wind causing a chill as it buttresses our rapid progress and
tickles the sea, which wriggles and slides beneath our speeding hull.

Although we left the town of Zakynthos early, our stop at the caves has
meant we do not have Shipwreck Bay to ourselves. A replica pirate galleon
has anchored off, its black and gold hull disgorging its ship's company of
temporary hearties. The romantic picture this tourist vessel paints is several

fathoms away from the rusting hulk of the pirate ship, which lays beached on the sands that brush along a sea of milky turquoise.

Its demise was as recent as 1983 when, suspected of carrying a cargo of illicit cigarettes and drink, the *MV Panagiotis* was pursued by a Greek naval vessel. As conditions worsened and visibility reduced to almost nothing the hunted down vessel ran aground in the bay of Agios Georgios, which since has been renamed Navagio or Shipwreck Bay. Over the years, the hull of the ship has created a barrier around which the sands swept in on the Ionian have deposited themselves leaving the wreck high and dry.

This abandoned carapace is an effigy that, through its demise, has imbued a spot of immense natural beauty with a tale that has raised its status to one of the most visited on the island. The only practical way to visit the beach is by boat, and short trips can be taken from the tiny bay of Porto Vromi to the south where, legend has it, Mary Magdalene, en route to Rome to petition against the persecution of Christ, stepped ashore to spread the word to the islanders, although there appears to be little hard evidence to substantiate this claim. Unless you are a base jumper or serious climber, the nearest you can get to the bay by land is an observation deck clinging to the cliffs above.

Ithaka

The Night Fishermen

Early stars, eager to stake their place in a darkening sky, made their presence known as the sun eased behind the hills that held Fiskardo in their fingertips. We slipped our mooring as the small diesel engine was cajoled into life by a turning of the crank. The eye of the lighthouse flashed its reassuring glare as we slid over a sea so calm our little caique didn't register the slightest of rolls on leaving the protective arms of the harbour.

Christos sat on his saloon stool by the wheel, smoking and swivelling to chat with the same ease as when we had first met some days ago in a taverna near the quay of the harbour, of which lights were now coming on astern as we headed out into the channel between Kefalonia and Ithaka. I had casually mentioned that I would like to go out on a fishing trip on one of the traditional boats and just as casually he had invited me to join him.

Secluded lights floating on the glassy surface of the sea beneath the hills of Ithaka mirrored the sky above and signalled we were not the first to start our night's work. We headed in their direction edging closely towards the shadow of the cliffs of Ithaka.

Working close in to the shore, Christos moved with the practiced ease of a man who had plied this trade for a lifetime, throwing overboard weighted plastic pots which sank to the seabed at regular intervals marked by a succession of painted plastic bottles serving the purpose of floats to mark the octopus traps.

Feeling our way along the shoreline the fisherman pulled the gear lever into neutral and swung into action in the cockpit casting the end of the piled up yellow net over the roller mounted on the stern. He went forward and eased the throttle back, at the same time engaging forward before moving astern again to guide out the net, the weights on the bottom edge sinking whilst orange floats held the top near the surface.

The June night was still warm as we left the nets and anchored off some several hundred yards away to smoke, and drink some milky ouzo whilst waiting to see what luck would bring us. With only a riding light on the mast, the darkness of the sky provided a perfect backdrop to the constellations, which held me in their thrall as I try to identify the stars in this celestial sphere. Every now and then a shooting star made an arc across the sky and broke that universal blueprint that has remained the same since Odysseus set sail, his flagship leading his fleet from here to fight the Trojan Wars.

The island was the centre of Odysseus' kingdom and the final destination that he sought in Homer's *The Odyssey* after an epic ten year journey following the Aecheans destruction of Troy in the 11th or 12th Century BC. Many scholarly hours have been spent pondering whether this is the Ithaka of legend, but a night spent under the stars here is enough to imagine its credentials are authentic. With every glass of ouzo the geography of this place grows in historical significance and Captain Christos becomes a worthy descendent of his seafaring forebear.

We started the engine again and move in on the net, engaging the gear on the drum mounted to the gunwhale that slowly winches in the fine mesh. Fish glinted in the moonlight and are sorted as they are hauled aboard. Fewer than three plastic crates full were harvested, but Christos seemed content, selecting a couple of gilthead for our dinner. We close in on the shingle beach, throwing the anchor out and manoeuvring towards the beach stern first before lowering the gangplank into the shallow water.

Wading ashore we made fast a stern line around a rock and I was sent off to search the scrubland around the pebble beach for kindling to start our fire. On returning Christos was busying himself gutting the fish beside a well-used fire pit. He lit the dry wood I had scavenged and added coals from the bag he had brought ashore before covering them with stones.

From a blue carrier bag he reveals a loaf of bread, two plates along with some lemons, salt, pepper, olive oil, two roughly tied bouquets garnis of herbs, newspaper and string. We dampen the paper in the sea and lay the two gilthead out stuffing them with herbs and rough slices of lemon before seasoning and dousing in oil and more lemon juice. We tie up the bream in their paper parcels and throw them on the hot stones.

Cutting the string open with his gutting knife, Christos released a wonderful fragrance from the packages before revealing the beautiful steamed fish, its tender white flesh falling apart. We pour wine from a plastic gallon container into tumblers and tear off chunks of bread before demolishing the delicious fish with an appetite engendered by a night in the sea air. We didn't dance a *sirtaki* but the moment was redolent of that famous beach scene from Nikos Kazantzakis' *Zorba the Greek*.

The island had at one time been called *Piccola Kefalonia*, meaning 'little Kefalonia' by the Venetians who wrested it from the Turks in 1499 and it is easy to see why. At only four miles across at its widest point and only 650 yards at the Aetos isthmus, which joins the two halves of the island, it is barely 14 miles long, and is less than a sixth the size of its neighbour lying fewer than two miles across the strait of Ithaka I had just crossed. Kefalonia itself might be the largest of the Ionian isles but it is believed that during Mycenaean times that Ithaka was the capital of the Kefalonian state and later, under Odysseus, incorporated the larger island into its own wider Ionian empire.

Since then the island has usually shared its destiny with Kefalonia, including the tragic earthquake of 1953, which destroyed almost 70 per cent of the buildings and killed hundreds of people. Now a burgeoning tourist trade supplements the island's traditional agrarian economy, mostly serviced by the capital and port of Vathi, which stands on a marvellous natural harbour.

We set out into the strait once more and Christos tried his luck again with the net whilst I dozed on the cockpit bench. Awoken by the creaking of the drum winching aboard the net, the dawn rose as we headed back to Fiskardo, Christos to deliver his meagre catch to the local tavernas, I to sit down to a bacon and egg breakfast at a seafront taverna before returning to my room for a sleep.

Get by in Greek

The following words and phrases are intended to give you a start at getting by in Greek. Use these, and your attempts at speaking the language will always be appreciated. The spellings used below are as close an approximation of words written in the Greek alphabet as I can get, as frequently no exact transliteration is possible. Dive in and have a go, a little Greek can go a long way…

Greetings and Courtesies
Hello *Yasas*

Goodbye *Adio*

Good morning *Kalimera*

Good evening *Kalispera*

Good night *Kalinichta*

Please/You're welcome *Parakalo*

Thank you *Efheristo*

OK *Endaxi*

Sorry *Signomi*

I don't understand Then *katalaveno*

Cheers *Issyia/Yamas*

Questions and Answers

Yes *Ne*

No *Ochi*

Where is? *Poo eene?*

How much is? *Poso kani?*

What is this? *Ti ine afto?*

Do you speak English? *Milate Anglika?*

What's your name? *Pos sas lene?*

What's the time? *Ti ora eene?*

How are you? *Ti kanete?*

Very well *Poli kala*

Not too bad *Etsi ketsi*

Not very well *Ochi ke toso kala*

I'm English/American *Eeme Anglos/Amerikana*

My name is Richard *Me lene Richard*

Weather

It's hot *Ti zesti*

It's cold *Ti krio*

Numbers

One *Ena*

Two *Dio*

Three *Tria*

Four *Tessera*

Five *Pende*

Six *Exi*

Seven *Efta*

Eight *Octo*

Nine *Enya*

Ten *Theka*

Fractions
Half *Miso*
Quarter *Tetrito*

Weights and Measures
Litre *Litro*
Kilo *Kilo*
Gram *Gramaria*

In the Taverna
I'd like *Tha ithela*
Could I have the bill please? *To logorizmo parakalo?*

Drinks
Beer *Bira*
Coffee *Kafe*
Juice *Himos*
Lemonade *Limonada*
Tea *Tsai*
Water *Nero*
Wine *Krasi*

Food
Beef *Vodino kreas*
Bread *Psomi*
Butter *Vootiro*
Cheese *Tiri*
Chicken *Kotopolo*
Eggs *Avga*
Fish *Psari*

Fruit *Froota*

Ham *Zambon*

Lamb *Paidaki*

Meat *Kreas*

Milk *Ghala*

Pork *Hirinio kreas*

Potato *Patata*

Salad *Salada*

Steak *Brizola*

Sugar *Zachari*

Vegetables *Laxanika*

Useful Words

Airport *Airodromio*

Bank *Trapeza*

Bad *Kakos*

Big *Megalo*

Bus stop *Stasi*

Car *Aftokinito*

Church *Eklisia*

Come here/in *Ella*

Doctor *Iatros*

Garage *Garaz*

Hospital *Nosokomio*

Let's go *Parme*

Little *Ligo*

Mobile phone *Kinito*

Petrol *Venzini*

Petrol station *Statio venzinathiko*

Pharmacy *Pharmakio*

Photograph *Photographia*

Postbox *Gramatokivotio*

Postcard *Kart postal*

Room *Thomatio*

School *Skolio*

Shower *Doosh*

Stamps *Gramatosima*

Sun *Ilios*

Ticket *Isitirio*

Today *Simera*

Toilet *Toiletta*

Tomorrow *Avrio*

Tonight *Apopsi*

Rain *Vroxi*

Wait *Perimene*

Well *Kala*

The History of Greece At-a-Glance

Here is a brief synopsis of the major events in Greece's history. For some of the ancient history the dates are approximate, as exact dates in many cases have not been established.

7000 BC Neolithic Period.

2800 BC Early Helladic Bronze Age civilization, Greek mainland.

2700 BC Minoan Bronze Age.

1900 BC Minoan Palaces built on Crete, including Knossos.

1800 BC Proto-Greek speaking tribes, forunners of the Mycenaeans, arrive on Greek mainland.

1700 BC Earthquake destroys Minoan palaces on Crete. New palaces and towns rebuilt.

1600 BC Minoans settle on Rhodes.

1500 BC Myceneans invade Rhodes.

1400 BC Minoan civilisation destroyed by invasion of Myceneans in Crete.

1300 BC First known mention of Kerkyra as an island inhabited by the Phaeacians.

1200 BC The Trojan Wars.

1100 BC Fall of the Mycenaeans displaced by Dorian Greeks.

800 BC Dorians establish ancient settlements of Lindos, Ialyssos and Kamiros on Rhodes.

750 BC Homer writes *The Iliad* followed 20 years later by *The Odyssey*.

730 BC Corinthians settle on Corfu

665 BC An independent Corfu loses the first-ever recorded naval battle in Greek history to the Corinthians.

505 BC Democracy introduced in Athens, making way for the Classical Greek period.

435 BC Corfu allies itself with Athens to gain protection against the Corinthians. Athenians use the island as a base in the Peloponnesian War.

408 BC The Rhodian cities of Lindos, Ialyssos and Kamiros unite to build the new capital of Rhodes Town.

384 BC Birth of Aristotle.

356 BC Birth of Alexander the Great.

340 BC Persians conquer Rhodes.

332 BC Alexander the Great defeats the Persians and Rhodes is assimilated into his empire.

323 BC Alexander the Great dies, Hellenistic period begins. Rhodes forms an alliance with Egypt.

305 BC Macedonian King Demetrius lays siege to Rhodes. Defeated, his abandoned siege engine is sold for scrap and the proceeds used to build the Colossus.

303 BC Corfu occupied by Spartans.

300 BC Corfu becomes part of the Epirotic Alliance as part of a dowry.

280 BC The Colossus of Rhodes is completed.

229 BC Corfu becomes a protectorate under the Roman Empire, gradually all the Ionian Islands follow suit and by 146 BC the Romans control the whole archipelago.

226 BC A massive earthquake destroys the Colossus of Rhodes.

200 BC Second Macedonian War ending in 196 BC with Rhodes remaining independent.

164 BC Rhodes formally becomes part of the Roman Empire.

67 BC Romans conquer Crete.

33 AD Crucifixion of Christ.

40 AD Jason and Sosipater bring Christianity to Corfu.

50 AD St Paul brings Christianity to Rhodes on his Third Mission.

286 AD The Roman Empire divides into East and West creating the Byzantine Empire.

337 AD Byzantine Empire takes over rule of Corfu and other Ionian Islands.

600 AD Rhodian Sea Law instigated throughout the Mediterranean.

654 AD Rhodes occupied by Islamic forces of the Umayyad dynasty, the remains of the Colossus is sold for scrap.

674 AD Rhodes sacked by Arab forces but later abandoned after their fleet was destroyed by Greek attack and sunk in bad weather. Rhodes returns to the Byzantine Empire.

1081 AD Corfu taken by the forces of Norman Knight Robert Guiscard.

1090 AD Rhodes captured by Turkish forces.

1099 AD First Crusade, Rhodes recaptured by the forces of Byzantine emperor Alexios Komnenos.

1204 AD Fourth Crusade left Byzantine Empire in disarray. Crete awarded to the Italian crusader leader Prince Boniface who sold it to the Venetians.

1214 AD Corfu becomes part of the Despotate of Epirus.

1238 AD Kythira becomes a Venetian protectorate.

1248 AD Rhodes occupied by Genoese.

1250 AD Genoese ousted by Nicaean forces, Rhodes becomes part of Nicaean Empire.

1267 AD Corfu conquered by Charles of Anjou.

1309 AD The Knights Hospitaller occupy Rhodes.

1386 AD Corfu again places itself under the protection of Venice.

1401 AD Venice takes sovereignty over Corfu.

1431 AD The first Ottoman siege of Corfu was repulsed, as were those in 1537, 1571, 1573 and 1716.

1444 AD Rhodes besieged by the Sultan of Egypt but his forces are repulsed by the Knights of Rhodes.

1480 AD Knights of Rhodes defeat forces of Sultan Mehemed II.

1482 AD Venice takes sovereignty over Zakynthos, followed by Kefalonia in 1483 and Ithaka the same year. Lefkas taking their example in 1502.

1522 AD Knights of Rhodes defeated by forces of Suleiman the Magnificent.

1523 AD The Knights negotiate a safe passage from Rhodes to Crete before moving on to Malta. Rhodes becomes part of the Ottoman Empire.

1645 AD Ottoman Turks capture Chania on Crete.

1669 AD Candia (Heraklion) on Crete surrenders to the Turks, Venetian presence on the island ends.

1797 AD French occupy Corfu.

1799 AD Russian-Ottoman fleet defeat French and the Ionian Islands form the 'Seven Islands' federation.

1807 AD French regain control of the Ionian Islands under control of Xavier Donzelot.

1809 AD British defeat French fleet and take control of Kefalonia, Kythira, Zakynthos, followed a year later by Lefkas.

1815 AD Ionian Islands become a British protectorate, governed from Corfu.

1821 AD Greek revolution and declaration of independence, although this was not fully achieved for another eight years.

1832 AD Prince Otto installed as King of Greece (at this time The Peloponnese, Athens, The Mani and the islands of the Saronic Gulf, Cyclades and Sporades).

1841 AD Cretan Revolt quashed by Ottoman Turks.

1858 AD Cretan Revolt secures right to carry arms and the equality of worship.

1864 AD The Ionian Islands become part of Greece.

1866 AD The Great Cretan Revolt wins sympathy abroad and some concessions, but is ultimately quashed and by 1869 Crete was back under Ottoman control.

1878 AD Under the Pact of Halepa, Crete becomes a semi-independent state still within the Ottoman Empire.

1889 AD Halepa Pact collapses and Turkey sends troops and re-establishes martial law on Crete, but their violent actions lead to sympathy abroad for the Cretan cause.

1897 AD Creten revolt leads to the 'Great Powers' of Britain, France, Italy and Russia taking over governance of Crete.

1898 AD Independent Cretan state governed by Prince George of Greece founded.

1908 AD Cretan deputies unofficially declare union with Greece.

1912 AD Italy seizes Rhodes from the Ottoman Turks.

1913 AD Following Balkan War Crete becomes part of independent Greece.

1923 AD Greco-Turkish population exchange, West Thrace becomes part of independent Greece.

1923 AD Italian forces occupy Corfu but are forced to withdraw under international pressure.

1939 AD Start of Second World War.

1940 AD Following 'Ochi Day' Greece is invaded by the Axis powers.

1941 AD All of the Ionian Islands except for Kythira put under Italian rule. Crete falls to axis powers.

1943 AD Germans occupy the Ionian islands and following Italian Armistice invade Rhodes.

1944 AD The islands liberated by Allied forces and resistance fighters.

1944 AD Start of Greek Civil War.

1949 AD Greek Civil War ends.

1952 AD Greece joins NATO.

1953 AD Massive earthquake devastates Kefalonia and Zakynthos.

1967 AD Coup of the Colonels.

1974 AD Cyprus crisis, collapse of the military dictatorship.

1975 AD New republican constitution becomes law.

1981 AD Greece joins European Community.

2009 AD Debt crisis plunges Greece into civil unrest.

Greek Food At-a-Glance

The following list is by no means exhaustive, but I hope it gives a flavour of the foods on offer in Greece.

Appetizers, Starters and Mezzes

Dolmades Stuffed vine leaves

Sardeles pastes Salted sardines

Gavros marinates Anchovies in oil, lemon and herbs

Saginaki Deep fried cheese

Saginaki garides Shrimp with cheese and tomato sauce

Revithia keftedes Deep fried chickpea balls

Tsatsiki Yoghurt, cucumber and garlic sauce

Taramasalata Blended fish roe, oil and lemon salad

Kolokythokeftedes Fried courgette balls

Tyrokeftedes Fried cheese balls

Boksades Lamb cubes with feta cheese in pastry

Spanakopita Spinach pie

Tyropita Feta cheese pie

Skordalia Garlic, potato and lemon sauce

Fava Split pea, garlic and lemon sauce

Salads
Horiatiki salata (Greek country salad) Tomatoes, onion, cucumber, feta cheese and olives

Ampelofasoula salata String bean, tomato and olive salad

Patatasalata Potato, onion, parsley and olive salad

Lahanosalata Cabbage, carrot, garlic and lemon juice salad

Garidosalata Shrimp salad

Meat Dishes
Mousaka Aubergines, mince, potatoes and béchamel sauce

Kotopolo me patatas sto forno Roast chicken and potatoes

Arni me patatas sto forno Roast lamb and potatoes

Souvlaki Grilled meat, usually lamb or chicken on skewers with peppers, onions and tomatoes

Gyros pitta Sliced grilled pork, chicken or lamb in pita bread with salad, chips and tsatsiki

Sofrito Veal with wine, garlic and parsley sauce

Kleftiko Slow-cooked lamb with potatoes, garlic, oil and lemon juice

Paidakia Grilled lamb chops

Keftedes Deep fried meatballs

Macaroni me kima Pasta with minced beef, garlic and onion

Beefteaki Seasoned minced beef patty

Sousoukakia Seasoned, grilled minced-beef balls in tomato sauce

Brizole Steak

Pastisada Veal, tomato and onion stew with spaghetti

Tomates gemistes Tomatoes stuffed with minced beef and onions

Moschari stifado Veal stew with tomatoes and onions

Kotopolo me portokali Slow-cooked chicken in orange juice

Gemista Baked peppers and tomatoes stuffed with rice and herbs

Saligaria me ryzi Fried snails with rice

Fish Dishes

Garides Shrimps

Mydia Mussels

Barbounia Red mullet

Ksifias Swordfish

Gavros Anchovy

Kalimari Squid

Astakos Lobster

Kolioi Mackerel

Bakaliaros Cod

Maridaki Whitebait

Sardeles Sardines

Lakerda Tuna

Psarasoupa Fish soup

Psari plaki Baked fish

Puddings and Pastries

Loukoumades Deep-fried dough balls with honey and cinnamon

Pastelli Honey and walnut wafers

Amydalopi Almond cake

Baklava Filo pastry with cinnamon, walnuts and honey

Kataifi Almond and walnut pastry with syrup

Yaourti me meli Yoghurt and honey

Risogalo Rice pudding

About the Author

Richard Clark is a writer, editor and journalist who has worked on an array of national newspapers and magazines in the UK. In 1982, on a whim, he decided to up sticks and go and live on the Greek island of Crete. So began a love affair that has continued to this day, when he still visits the Greek islands on a regular basis. He is married with two grown up children and lives in Kent.

Did you Enjoy this Book?

If you liked reading this book and have time, any review on www.amazon.com or amazon.co.uk would be appreciated, and it would be good to meet you on facebook at www.facebook.com/richardclarkbooks

20633288R00209

Printed in Poland
by Amazon Fulfillment
Poland Sp. z o.o., Wrocław